# SPIRITED

A guide to your innate spiritual
design to transform your life

Danielle Van de Velde

**BALBOA.**PRESS
A DIVISION OF HAY HOUSE

Balboa Press books may be ordered through booksellers or by contacting:

Balboa Press
A Division of Hay House
1663 Liberty Drive
Bloomington, IN 47403
www.balboapress.com.au
AU TFN: 1 800 844 925 (Toll Free inside Australia)
AU Local: (02) 8310 7086 (+61 2 8310 7086 from outside Australia)

Because of the dynamic nature of the Internet, any web addresses or
links contained in this book may have changed since publication and
may no longer be valid. The views expressed in this work are solely those
of the author and do not necessarily reflect the views of the publisher,
and the publisher hereby disclaims any responsibility for them.

The author of this book does not dispense medical advice or prescribe the use
of any technique as a form of treatment for physical, emotional, or medical
problems without the advice of a physician, either directly or indirectly. The
intent of the author is only to offer information of a general nature to help
you in your quest for emotional and spiritual well-being. In the event you use
any of the information in this book for yourself, which is your constitutional
right, the author and the publisher assume no responsibility for your actions.

Any people depicted in stock imagery provided by Getty Images are
models, and such images are being used for illustrative purposes only.
Certain stock imagery © Getty Images.

Print information available on the last page.

ISBN: 978-1-9822-9459-5 (sc)
ISBN: 978-1-9822-9460-1 (e)

Balboa Press rev. date: 05/27/2022

# Contents

## PART 2: SPIRIT DYNAMICS

## PART 3: SPIRIT SKILLS

# Welcome

It is a fascinating time in the human story to be alive and waking up, and it's also increasingly disconcerting. There's a quickening afoot. And unless you have been living under a rock in recent years, you can't deny it. As the world seems to be wobbling with increasing uncertainty, at the same time there appears to be a mass awakening taking place.

More and more of us are starting to really question this state of modern living. The continued focus and relentless mass content around material gain and accumulation, fame and celebrity, body image, time and ageing are soul-numbing. We live alongside the insanity of violence, environmental disdain, and the systematic abuse of children, the gentle and the voiceless. In recent years, the COVID-19 pandemic has amplified this questioning and search for meaning to such a point that many spiritual commentators regard the pandemic as perhaps the best thing that has happened to the human consciousness in the last several centuries. This, of course, is not discounting the immense suffering and loss of lives and livelihoods the pandemic has generated; however, the deprivation of liberties and realisation of the impermanence and fragility of life has shone a spotlight on the question 'What does it all mean?'

The state of our modern world is triggering a deep, unavoidable desire to regain central balance within the hearts of many. Every single day, we are being challenged with the following questions: Who am I within this current world? What is it that I stand for? What is my purpose within it all? More and more of us are seeking to understand our true natures and our purposes, and more and more of us are trying to embody that truth. Perhaps most importantly, there's a growing sense that something is missing, and the search for answers is taking us *within*.

I am one of the people searching for these answers, and I teach thousands of others like me. The people I teach are strong, clever, successful, and very able. Some have a natural leaning towards the spiritual side of things; others don't. All of them have a deep instinct that there's more to themselves and life than they have previously understood there to be. Many have chosen to reject the structured religions of their childhoods yet yearn for spiritual knowledge and expression, and many have returned to the religious structures that they know and are engaging with them in new ways. Nearly all the people in my community, more than anything, yearn for spiritual empowerment.

*Spirited* is written for them. The purpose of *Spirited* is not necessarily to fix something that's broken; nor is it to heal something that's injured, although the perspectives and practices in the following pages will sort out these requirements if that's what is needed. *Spirited* is written for anyone who has the instinct and the desire to make some sense of it all—to find that missing piece. It is written for those who are ready to claim their own natural spirituality. *Spirited* is not a download of another framework or system for inner practice. Instead it offers an upload of different perspectives for modern living—ones that open access to our innate spiritual design and how to work with it. Within this intent, *Spirited* is offered in three parts:

- Spirit Self: an expanded perspective on the visible and invisible aspects of the self
- Spirit Dynamics: an expanded perspective on the nature of life and our engagement within it
- Spirit Skills: an expanded perspective on meditation and working with your energy body

Within each section, I have shared examples of psychic and spiritual experiences from my life and sessions with clients to help explore the ideas. I have altered or deleted names and reference information to honour their anonymity. All meditation practices mentioned in the book are listed in appendix A with links to my guided meditations so you can start your inner practice or deepen the experience of your current practice.

Inner practice is enjoying an unprecedented resurgence. In particular, I refer here to practices that keep the centre of command firmly in the hands of the practitioner and not a third party or agent. We are spiritually stirring in a time when we have open access to wisdom, techniques, knowledge, and experience from other teachers, guides, and traditions from all over the planet and from our ancient past. The learning, revelation, and practices are available all the time now.

Our ability to observe and measure the invisible processes in the body when we engage in inner practice and explorations into quantum mechanics are getting sharper and deeper. In the mind/body arena, science and inner practice are starting to tango in delicious ways, and the mind/body connection is now measurable and largely understood.

However, there's a third aspect to the human being and life that cannot be measured or formulated, and because of this it remains by and large on the fringes of mainstream scientific exploration. It is our core sovereign state, our nucleus. It is our spirit. When we access and embody spirit, we tap the causal aspect that determines what we are experiencing on the outside, out there, in our bodies, our lives, our relationships, our families, our jobs, and our experienced reality. Being spirited takes us to the place where we can find the revelation and energy patterns to consciously operate within our full energetic forms within that causal aspect.

When we operate in this way, we connect our awareness to the fields of intelligence and energy within existence, the motherboard of life, and beautifully come to the realisation that we are, in fact, powerful creators. We are naturally designed for it. It's how we are supposed to be operating.

Throughout human history, and still today, individuals and organisations have tried to capture spirit, package it up and sell it, claim exclusivity to it, commercialise it, and restrict access to it. Over time, these abstractions have brought us along the inner journey, but they have kept many of us outside of spirit's gates, because this aspect of the human being cannot be parcelled up and sold back to us. It is our true nature and can only be mainlined directly, through awareness. Until we reclaim this part of us, we remain in a state of separation, in the paradigm that our life experiences are somehow outside of us or being done *to* us, and that our spirits are separate from our lives and experiences right here, now, in our bodies, on the ground. Entering the gates of spirit requires a new perspective on who and what we really are as human beings and on the nature of life. And we need to put inner practice into an expanded context beyond the simple well-being of mind and body.

Meditation is largely understood to be a way to find the still eye at the centre of the hurricane of modern life, moving us from a reactive to responsive engagement with life, ushering us into mindful living. This, in itself, is a wonderful shift that meditation enables, but it's not the end game. Responsive living continues to respond to ourselves and life as separate, rather than consciously creating it within one unified field of information, intelligence, and energy. A deeper understanding and engagement with true meditation can take us much further than the mind/body arena. It can take us directly into our spiritual centre if we know the way. With expanded perspectives and regular practice, a certain inner metamorphosis is enabled—from *reactive* to *responsive*, continuing into *expansive* and then *creative*. As we move through these stages, we become physically healthier, mentally sharper, and emotionally happier. The experience of life itself becomes synchronistic, fluid, and magical. It's like this anyway; it's just that we change the way we connect with it and start to work with it, intentionally and creatively, as our spiritual senses wake up and guide our thoughts, feelings, and actions.

Inner work is a living art—that is, the magic is realised in the experience. The goal is to embody it, to live it. The invitation to you now is to take the ideas and practices in this book and make them your own. Our design, our minds, our bodies, our hearts, and the living universe around us *are* spirit. Be playful. Be creative. Be spirited. Why? Because it's time.

# PART 1

# Spirit Self

CHAPTER 1

# What Is Spirit?

The big invitation that is being relayed to every single person on the planet currently is an invitation to personally examine where we hold division and judgement within ourselves and, therefore, in our worldviews, life views, and actions.

I believe I'm welcoming many new people into private sessions and course communities as a response to this invitation. There is a deep desire to connect with our spirits and, through that, the spirit of life and others.

To live a spirited life requires a dismantling of our reliance on evidenced, measurable phenomena and control— in other words, our almost total reliance on the intellect and physical reality. It requires learning a new language of meaning beneath words—into the felt, intuitive language of symbols, synchronicities, and sensations—and then finding synergies with the intellect and actions. We are designed to operate within our entire human system, which comprises our physical, mental, emotional, energetic, and spiritual aspects.

Unfortunately, the word 'spiritual' has a pretty bad rap in our modern context. It is often confused with religious dogma or New Age terminology. Or it is associated with the whole 'love and light' meaning, which makes little sense when we are in the throes of hardship, illness, trauma, or, indeed, witnessing a world in chaos.

For centuries, the view of spirit has been associated with a requirement for agency—that is, as individuals, we are unable to connect with this causal power within and around us without the help of a particular structure or spiritual master. Living a spirited life doesn't mean pure continual bliss and butterflies. What it does mean is engaging with life from an entirely different perspective and perceiving the hardship, illness, and chaos as useful and transmutable, and as way finders to personal wholeness.

My purpose and offerings are to enable and empower others to connect deeply with their own innate spiritual cores. To do this takes some deconditioning of paradigms, some tools, and, mostly, new and expanded perspectives on who and what we actually are.

But the essential message in all pathways is that everything we experience in life is happening for us and being generated by us. Our inner beings and our outer experiences are self-organising systems. When we experience dissonance in ourselves or in our experiences, it is this system that messages us that we have separated from our spirits.

A big part of this enablement and empowerment, and this book, is to 'de-woo-woo-ify' what spirit actually is and open up a conversation about spirit—how it feels and what its dynamics are. And it doesn't take much, because as soon as someone makes the choice to connect with his or her innermost nature and core, that intelligent core starts to guide the person through his or her intuitive senses, clear patterns within information and events, dreams, and the drawing in of like-spirited people.

So how do I describe spirit for me? The experience of spirit is so subjective that it's almost impossible to define it in a way that would work for everyone. So I'm going to express my experience of spirit the best way I can, and if you can sense a little voltage in there that puts a light on what it is, then go with that.

Spirit is the vibrational force that holds this whole shebang in place and keeps it spiralling through its manifestations. It is the animating force within every single one of our one hundred trillion cells and the spaces within and in between.

I feel spirit most keenly when I am in the wilderness or around children. I feel it in the energy field of a loving, free person, and I can especially feel it (and work with it) in group practice. It is the energetic current I feel when I meditate and engage in meditative rituals. It is the vibrational power I feel when I fully forgive or choose love and compassion. And it is the activating force that enables me to put those choices into action. It is the palpable vibrating energy that moves through my system when I am healing or seeking revelation for a client. And it is the information that informs my intuition of the presence of a passed loved one and the messages he or she wants me to relay to someone.

It is the movement or flow through my body, mind, heart, and life that carries with it abundance, health, opportunities, true friendships, and protection. It is the force within my creativity, my words, and my teaching. It can be summoned and raised within my physical body and energetic system, and it can be directed to situations and others for healing and change.

But it is more than simply energy. It is sentient, benevolent, living, responsive, and intoxicating. It is the true nature of consciousness, and it is present in everything. *Everything.* It spirals through all manifestations of life, from things to processes to experiences to relationships to rocks, fire, trees, oceans, wind, and the human body and individual consciousness. *It is a living information field* that permeates us and brings us to bear along with all phenomena. And when we live connected and aligned with it, when we embody it, truly knowing that *we are it,* we are steered to our highest possibilities. Lots of people call it lots of things. I simply call it 'spirit.'

Over the years for me, being spirited has come to represent

a state of being rather than any set of actions. It's a way to live 'in spirit'—to have an ongoing interaction with the invisible dynamics that underpin my ordinary reality. What started for me many years ago as a simple daily meditation practice became an incredible journey to living my purpose of teaching, healing, and inspiring others to remember who and what they really are. I live a spirited life.

To achieve this state, there are things that we must do, of course. I see a lot of people getting caught up in doing and not so much translating it into being—or spending a lot of time on social media, presenting themselves as spiritual. I also see a lot of people give their power away to others who present themselves as having exclusive access to spirit.

To be spirited, we need to loosen our identifications with and our attachments or aversions to our outer reality and who we have previously perceived ourselves to be. We have to question it all. I have found that the easiest way to help people do this is to give them knowledge in clear modern terms. It has to make sense to the mind to shift perception and enable a move into the heart and energy realm. With mind, heart, and energy working as a coherent team, the gates to spirit fly open. What we believe to be true about ourselves and the nature of reality determines our experience of reality. Our perspectives and beliefs operate as either key codes or cages. Consciously searching for new perspectives to unlock potential within every experience is key.

As we become spirited, we open our channels to

communicate with spirit itself. To do this effectively, we need to learn how to recognise when spirit is communicating and guiding us and not something else, like our egos or someone else's ego. When we shift from reactive to creative living, our centre of command also shifts from the mundane and the obvious to the true and undeniable signals of our intuitive senses.

Spirit uses the hologram of life experience, all forms, to answer our calls and guide us into alignment. This can occur through teachers, books, courses, dreams, intuitions, gifts, meditation circles, and chance encounters. It uses triggers, discomfort, and illness. It is reliably accessed through the wilderness.

The best way I have learnt to communicate consciously with spirit is to maintain my energetic circuitry through practice, to observe in stillness and keep my awareness firmly pegged in the union of mind, heart, and energy. Spirit talks to me through my coherent system and in patterns of meaning. When I am meant to take notice, I have a distinct feeling in my heart, a knowing in my mind, and a resonance in my cells. When I call to spirit, I do it through spiritual demonstration, meditative ritual, an energy act of the heart, mind, and body, and then the dialogue is on. It is the only way to roll. It is also extremely cool.

You will see that you have a spirited instinct in your life already without realising that you are working with the invisible dynamics that underpin your external, or 'ordinary,' reality. The ways we adorn our homes, our connections with colours, the slightly frenzied spring cleanouts of our spaces, the ways we touch our children when they're sick, and the call to the wilderness are all spiritual expressions. Even the least woo-woo of us do it because spirit is universal and innate within our physical and energetic design and because it corresponds with the true nature of life.

The dialogue is intensely personal, gentle, and often simply an inner whisper or vibration. If we are distracted with the madness of modern life, dissipated thoughts, reactive emotions, and the outer noise of modern living, then we miss it. That soft inner voice needs some space around it to reverberate and be heard, and this is why spiritual practices, especially meditation, are essential.

And it is equally important not to give power away in the process. If your system isn't humming and beating 'yes', then walk away, close the book, switch off the podcast. With the resurgence of inner practices and so many people searching for meaning in a whacked-out world, being on some form of spiritual path or, better still, appearing as some form of spiritual guru has become very trendy. This is not to discount the real thing. Modern-day mystics and amazing spiritual teachers are around, engaged and in service. And believe me, you will know it when you meet one. But also in the fray are many more who aren't the genuine article.

I have the blessing of friendships in the UK, the United States, Europe, Australia and now Asia with active seekers like me. Over many years, I have been to my share of readings, rituals, ceremonies and channellings, churches, ashrams, pilgrimages, and temples, and I have developed an excellent radar for cosmic BS. The underlying theme is, and always is, 'Get to know your Spirit Self, your mind/body/energy system, and listen to that. It's the only way to connect with spirit and live a spirited life!'

CHAPTER 2

# Pings from Peeps of the Past

We know so very little about what and who we really are as human beings, our spirit selves. To 'know thyself' is a constant message, a 'ping from the past' that has been repeated over and over again from the sages of antiquity to our modern spiritual teachers. Why this constant reminder?

'Know Thyself!' was the primary instruction inscribed in the entranceway of the Oracle of Delphi by the Seven Sages of Ancient Greece. It is the foundation of Western philosophy and modern psychological enquiry and is the basis of all Eastern spiritual frameworks. Philosophers and mystics across the ages to modern times have continued the call for us to turn our awareness inwards and to come to know the mystery and dazzling reality of our true nature—and, by doing so, the true nature of life.

There are many beautiful articulations of this nudge from the ancient world's greatest peeps. I couldn't possibly list them all, but following are a few of my favourites. The ancient writings of the Upanishads remind us that 'Enquiry into the truth of self, is the beginning of knowledge.' The sixth-century BC Chinese philosopher Lao Tzu succinctly wrote, 'He who knows others is wise; he who knows himself is enlightened.' Echoing further from Eastern shores, the Indian sage Ramana Maharshi reminds us that 'your own Self-Realization is the greatest service you can render the world.' From the birthplace of modern philosophy, ancient Greece, Aristotle echoed the Hindu writings with 'Knowing yourself is the beginning of all wisdom.' And before him, Pythagoras wrote, 'No one is free who has not obtained the empire of himself. No man is free who cannot command himself.' And again, from Plato, 'The essence of knowledge is self-knowledge.' In the scrolls of ancient Egypt, the same maxim was echoed in the proverb, 'The body is the house of God. Man, know thyself and thou shalt know the gods.' Jesus the Nazarene beautifully stated to his disciples, 'The Kingdom of Heaven is within you.' From the same part of the world, centuries later, the poet and mystic Rumi admonished us, 'Stop acting so small. You are the universe in ecstatic motion!'

From our modern mystics the same steer is repeated

continually: 'The closer you come to knowing that you alone create the world of your experience, the more vital it becomes for you to discover just who is doing the creating'—this from Eric Micha'el Leventhal. From the divine Eckhart Tolle, we read, 'To know yourself as the Being underneath the thinker, the stillness underneath the mental noise, the love and joy underneath the pain, is freedom, salvation, enlightenment.'

It is my belief and experience that this ancient plea to 'know thyself' is more than a call to be clear on our personality and traits. It is a call for a complete paradigm shift in who and what we perceive ourselves and our lives to be. It is quite literal. We are so much more than what the current world narrative dictates, and to be spirited we need to make that shift in our self-perception. To really know ourselves, our spiritual nature, and our power remains the key challenge in modern life. We need to detach from what the collective messaging is telling us about who we are *supposed to* be, what we should look like, how we should be behaving and reacting, whom we should be following, how we should be medicating, what we should be eating and thinking, and so on. These waves upon waves of messages about who and what we are supposed to be are fickle at best, limited and exhausting. They change with trends and are commercially driven. Most of the imagery we absorb is digitally augmented. The Internet is awash with it, and the integrity of even the major media outlets and channels has been seriously brought into question. Aside from all of this, the modern-world lens is almost always materially focussed, which as we'll discover is only one fifth of who we are and even still is presented in a very limited way. It's time to pop on a new set of lenses— some cosmic-coloured glasses if you like—that open up a much more expanded and way cooler view of the Spirit Self!

# CHAPTER 3

# Permission + Perspective = Belief + Possibility

Occasionally my teenage son and I have phases of training together at the gym before school. Whilst he is pounding the treadmill and weights, I make a happy return to yoga asana. The lengthening of body and breath and feeling flow through movement are all delicious, but I have also been strongly drawn to bring back to my middle-aged body the more challenging postures of crow, tree, and headstands. This renewed determination is partly because of the mind discipline they nurture, but they feel and look super cool, and I admit there is an element of showing off with them. I quite like my son seeing that his old hippy mum holds some serious cred in the mind/body department.

Having been off the mat for a most of my years in Singapore, favouring jungle running and cycling instead, I have had to rediscover my centre and overcome the fear of injury, which has been an excellent pursuit to keep my confidence in my body strong and add some laughter and humility to my mind. Let's face it; there is no elegant way to get out of a failed crow pose. It's an unavoidable faceplant.

With the headstand, I noticed that when near a wall, I can execute a beautiful, graceful, and stable rise and long hold, without actually needing the wall at all. Yet when in the centre of the room, I wobble, resort to kicking up the shift in weight, strain my arms and neck to rebalance, and often do not achieve anything. The wall, whilst not physically necessary, allows me to give myself permission to execute well, and with that permission granted, in flows the body memory and central balance automatically.

Permission is powerful, especially when moving into deeper levels of inner practice.

I use the word 'permission' specifically when guiding meditation groups and in healing sessions. Here's why.

The crazy, busy, go-go-go culture of modern life has somehow hoodwinked us into a belief that doing stuff is of ultimate value. Forward! Onward! Upward! Get ahead! Have more! Succeed beyond the pack! Do it! Now! Just a quick scan of online or print advertising will reveal these messages constantly being pushed at us. There are far more verbs like 'do', 'get', and 'have' used than verbs like, say, 'be'. And this subtle and constant emphasis on doing is evident in my classes and courses.

People sign up for meditation classes for lots of reasons, usually because they have read enough or know enough people who do it to understand the benefits and give it a try. Yet initially, to sit still and give the experience fully to themselves feels a bit too much like 'doing nothing.' It's as if their systems have their feet pressed firmly to the accelerator by habit, yet the class has slipped them into neutral, so they sit there revving their engines without movement. I have learnt that expressly inviting them to give themselves permission to be completely present in the class, even just for a few minutes, is enough for them to take their foot off the pedal. I invite them to leave their day's concerns and to-do lists outside the door of the meditation space, and they can pick it all up again when they leave. I invite them to fully arrive. I invite them to gift the session to themselves without any reservation. I invite them to give themselves permission 'to be.' When we start the classes this way, I hear spontaneous sighs and shifts into deeper breathing. I see shoulders relax and bodies sink into mats.

We are entrained into relentless doing, and we realise the extent of this only when we interrupt the pattern with permission to stop. Through the pandemic, I have personally worked a lot more intentionally with permission on several fronts, which has enabled huge expansion in my sense of self, my experience of spirit, and my offerings. I have given myself permission to say no, to switch off my phone, to dance more wildly, to teach more passionately, to walk away from toxic people, to love more fiercely, to express more openly my spiritual path, and to step unabashed and unapologetically into new levels of mastery. I have given myself permission to ask for help when I don't know how to do something, such as creating online courses or engaging in digital marketing and sound production. Therefore, I have gathered an amazingly talented group of people around me, which has amplified my love of my work, the quality of my offerings, and the number of people who are touched by them. Having worked with permission in this way, I have opened the door to a whole new field of possibility, potentials, and relationships.

I can see the power of permission within the healing process of my clients who come for intuitive healing. Their express permission for me to support them and their self-permission to heal are perhaps the most powerful conduits to the healing experience. Permission to connect with the innate lifeward, self-harmonising wills of their systems; permission to let go of the stories and identities they have built upon being unwell; permission to tap healing life force; and permission to simply hold the possibility of vitality, wellness, joy, abundance, and purpose is the key to full healing. Since I have begun working explicitly with the power of permission in this context, I have witnessed radical and liberating healing take place.

Permission has shown me that we hold the ultimate authority over our lives, bodies, minds, hearts, and, especially, our experiences of spirit, yet so many of us don't use it.

My tip is to give yourself permission at the outset of your journey and continually along the path—permission to know yourself deeply, to master the spiritual dimension of your life, to do nothing from time to time and simply *be*; and to experience the mystery right here and right now. And there's no need to worry too much about the how. The permission alone is highly active and will draw the experiences to you. You reading this book is a form of permission to yourself.

Equally as important for living a spirited life are your perspectives on your spiritual self and the spiritual nature of life. We cannot experience what we cannot perceive.

Have you ever had the experience of misplacing something of importance and searching everywhere for it, to no avail? We scamper here and there, mentally retracing our steps, feeling rising sensation and frustration in the conclusion that 'it's lost.' Yet when we let the search go and conclude that 'it will show up'—when we relax into a perspective that 'it has to be somewhere'—then the location of the item bubbles into mind or we see it again, often in a place where we had already frantically searched.

Our perspectives are lenses for our awareness. When the perspective is small or unable to entertain other possibilities, then we remain blind to those possibilities and the experience of them.

The very morning of writing this chapter, I had this exact experience, which was a wonderful intuitive affirmation for me that this is an important point to make. Each May, I hold outdoor meditations at dawn to raise money for my charitable cause for the month—reforestation and endangered animal conservation. It was one of the few group activities allowable under the government restrictions here in Singapore that were implemented during the COVID-19 pandemic. The twice-weekly dawn meditations were a part of this effort, with all proceeds donated, and they were proving very popular. I personally love meditating at dawn. There's something very powerful about participating in the commencement of each day, the energy of rising light, and an awakening jungle or city. And the tropical dawns in Singapore are spectacular.

I'm usually very organised, with audio sets charged and packed the night before so I can greet people at the meeting points around the island, check them in, and allow them to find their space in nature to listen to my guidance and engage with the dawn. This particular morning, I had a full group of twenty dawn-lovers, and to my surprise and frustration, I could not find the transmitter device that beams my guidance to each participant. I searched the bag several time. Two participants searched my bag. It was nowhere to be seen. Whilst I was certain I had put it in the bag, I concluded that I must have accidently left it charging at home. I held the perspective that it wasn't in the bag. Thankfully everyone had a mobile phone (a fixture since the onset of the pandemic), and we pivoted to a group call and were able to practise the meditation with guidance. Yet when I got home, I unpacked the bag to sterilise the ear sets, and lo and behold, there was the transmitter. It had been in the bag all along but had been invisible to my search as I held the perspective that it wasn't there. I messaged the group to share with them that we had experienced an exact example of what I was writing about that day, and I was thrilled to receive several messages back over the following days from others who tried, when having misplaced an item of importance, such as a credit card, Air Pods, keys, and the like, implementing a perspective shift from 'it's lost' to 'it's somewhere' and being able to locate the items within minutes. It was a wonderful lesson for the group. I was reminded of my own medicine, and moreover spirit had given me a real-time example to share in this chapter!

This is just a small, but commonly experienced, example of the power of our perspectives and how they are influencing our experiences and possible experiences, all the time. To heal, we need to hold the perspective that healing is possible. To learn, we need to hold the perspective that we can learn. To negotiate peace with a neighbour or another country, we need to hold the perspective that peace is possible. To experience spirit, we need to hold the perspective that we are possibly spiritual in nature.

Over the years, as I have moved through the beautiful

changes in operating mode from reactive to responsive to expansive and to creative through spiritual enquiry, my perspectives on myself and my true nature, the nature of awareness, and the mind and energy body have changed and expanded, and therefore allowed an experience of a spirited life, reliable intuition, energy healing with myself and others, lucid connection with people who have passed over, and, moreover, conscious creation of my life experiences.

For some, this opening in perspective can be tricky. We may have grown up in an origin culture that denies spirit or has a fear of it. We may have built our identity stories firmly on the paradigms that we are random occurrences in the universe—that life is 'happening to us' and we are at the mercy of fate and luck. And whilst some may hunger for a different experience of life, with meaning and miracles, they can be so firmly pegged in the mundane that an opening of perspective into spirit takes some effort. If this is you, then my tip is to approach the rest of this book like a fun 'spiritual experiment. You don't need to commit to anything. Let your longing for meaning and freedom guide you. Stay playful, and see what makes your heart hum. Perspective is a choice, and a change in perspective can be cultivated. In the following chapters, I will share with you several perspective-shifting and maintenance tricks that I have learnt along the way and now teach. As the wonderful Wayne Dyer said, 'When you change the way you look at things ... the things you look at change.'

When people embark on my shape-shifting course, which is a journey into new paradigms, perspectives, and tools to align the inner and outer worlds and start to consciously create life experiences, one of the biggest shifts initially is into a spiritual reality. That is rather than life 'happening to us' in some random relay of events, with shifted perspectives we reinstate ourselves as the causal aspects of life, and what we experience are the effects. This requires taking full responsibility for our inner ground and what we are emanating in thought, feeling, and action. However, with support and tools, that paradigm flip happens, and then goals start rolling in, much to the disbelief of many at first. It's a delight to witness every single time I run the course. With some evidence of the spiritual mechanism, subsequent shape-shifts become more fluid, easy, and more profound, because the new perspectives become belief.

Belief is felt thought, an embodied perspective that has become part of our subconscious operating systems and governs our outlooks, feelings, choices, and actions—that is, our emanations. We are governed by our beliefs, and we are constantly habituating our subconscious minds with our repeated thoughts and perspectives. And this is why a good part of this book is about the art of meditation. When we master our thoughts, we master the formation of beliefs; we are then able to consciously generate experiences and how we interface with life. And this is spirited living!

What follows are the key perspective shifts that work for

me to open the gates to spirited living. They're not exhaustive; nor are they totally ungraspable. They are different tilts or perspectives on observable aspects of your existence. What we're talking about here is a shift in your operating system, through ever so slightly expanding your perception of yourself. These are my key codes, and from observation, they are enough to shift perspectives and open up new realities and spirited experiences.

CHAPTER 4

# Five Rapid-Fire Key Codes

You are ancient.

The nuclei of all of the atoms in your body were forged billions of years ago in fusion reactions at the cores of now long-dead stars. You are quite literally made of stardust.

These atoms, along with all the others in the world, have been around for eons, shifting, organising, disbanding, and reforming through the processes of creation.

The atoms that currently make up your physical body are universal. They have cycled through mountains, oceans, stratospheric winds, volcanoes, perhaps the heart muscle of a lion, the wing tip of an eagle, the brain cell of an artist, the tail of a comet, and the seed of an apple. You have taken form out of a universal atomic field, and the building blocks of matter that make up the body that you see in the mirror are all ancient parcels of energy. You are ancient, and you have been travelling the universe since the beginning of time—not a bad thing to remember the next time you're looking in the mirror on a crappy day.

You are constantly renewing.

Your entire body totally renews itself in less than two years. The one hundred trillion cells that make up your body are replacing themselves constantly. Every breath, thought, choice, belief, and inner word is influencing this regeneration, because every cell of your body is intelligent (more on that later) and is made up of atomic and subatomic particles, which are organisations of vibrating energy. The perspectives and beliefs you hold about your body influence the natural regeneration impulse of your body, because energy influences energy. Recognise how wondrous you are, constantly creating yourself anew.

You are a continuum.

You are the result of an unbroken line of ancestral survivors and thrivers. Over four thousand ancestors contributed to your existence over the last four hundred years alone. Your existence evidences an unbroken lineage of warriors, lovers, creators, innovators, migrators, adaptors, leaders, and doers. That field of intelligence and mastery of life is within you, in your DNA.

The probability of *every* one of your ancestors reproducing successfully is one in ten. So the DNA coding that you have inherited, which holds your talents, features, strengths, and inherited patterns that serve your evolution, is highly improbable and unique.

You are unique.

The odds of you being born are one in four-hundred trillion. To give you an illustrative example of how unique you are, these are roughly the same odds as flipping a coin thirty thousand times and the coin landing on its edge each time.

Contemplate this for a moment. You are here for a reason. In some unfathomable way, your unique presence together in the collective wave of humanity, at this time, has purpose. How could it not?

You are essential.

The probability of your genetic material combining to generate you in this life is one in four hundred quadrillion. You are highly significant, as the forces of life opened an infinitesimal window for you to be here. You have been brought to bear in the continuum of life against incredible odds. You belong here in this life as you. You belong in this world with your unique design and talents.

You are ancient. You are renewing. You are a continuum. You are unique. You are essential.

CHAPTER 5

# The Visible and Invisible You

Another dazzling truth about your human system is that it is only partially material, physical, and incarnated in form, and the bulk of who you are is invisible and energetic in nature. As wild and crazy as this may sound, we all have daily experiences of this. Our thoughts, beliefs, fantasies, desires, fears, choices, and wills are powerful forces in their own right—invisible to the eye, but undeniably existent and active. The vital life force that animates every cell of your body and maintains its harmonic systems and cycles is a clear vibrational hum that can be accessed through inner practice. For those of you who have experienced energy healing, the palpable energy that moves through the healer to the recipient is undeniable. It can make limbs and heads quiver. It alters brainwave states and facilitates physical, mental, emotional, and spiritual healing. For yoga practitioners, the energy (prana) generated from asana that can then be circulated through the system when lying down at the end of a class has an undeniable effect on mind, heart, and cells. Anyone who has practised meditation to the point of synchronising the nervous system and altering states of consciousness will also know that delicious shift of awareness into the invisible aspects of self.

The visible and invisible aspects of the human being can be viewed as a living vibrational cross. Once we get to know this cross in all its aspects, we are able to operate from our full selves, with all of the abilities within our design.

What I'm going to explain here is, of course, just a construct, because to try to encapsulate the dazzling holographic energetic informational grid that is the human being is impossible to do in words, but the construct I am about to explain is one that I work with and one that allows me to develop and operate from my invisible self.

First of all, let's look at the vertical axis of your cross— your mind. The conscious mind, which is where all decision-making, analysis, and linear and lateral thinking happens, is part of the individuated human being. It is where we form and hold our perspectives, which in turn inform how we feel about ourselves and life and what we believe to be true and possible. It is from here that we consciously interface with life and life experiences. It is also the starting point for altering consciousness and accessing deeper aspects of the mind. It switches off when we sleep. Its language is verbal. It works via logic and thought.

The subconscious mind is where we hold our beliefs and patterns and imprints and our automated processes. It is a deeper aspect of the individuated human mind or being. You could regard it as our 'beneath thought' operating system. It records everything and never switches off. It is built upon habituation—that is, the repeated thought patterns, perspectives, and impressions gained by our conscious minds. It can be reprogrammed through inner practice. It is not linear or logical. Its language is non-verbal, symbolic, and felt. It is a million times more powerful than the conscious mind.

Within these aspects of mind, are blind spots, unconscious patterns, that are observable within our behaviours, inner talk, projections and triggers.

And then deeper, or finer, still is what I refer to as the deep mind, or the unified mind; this is where there are infinite dimensions or realms—archetypal fields and core fields of expertise, such as healing, for example. This quantum informational field is within us. It connects us to the collective and to others, and it exists outside of time and space. We access both the subconscious and deep minds via altered states of consciousness achievable through meditation, various forms of sound, and chemicals (that naturally occur in the body and can be induced), as well as, as I have experienced, through raising the vibrations of our whole systems through energy practices and channelling healing energy. It is from the subconscious and deep minds that everything we experience is influenced and created, and it is through the subconscious and deep minds that we also receive information through our intuitive senses that guides our spirited lives.

This is how my intuitive healing works. Over many years of 'running the reiki' for literally thousands of clients, I have observed that there is a direct correspondence between the higher vibrational and altered states of mind that reiki induces and the clarity and depth of the psychic reading of clients. Within a session, the reiki energy soothes the dissonance felt by the client, whether it be physical pain, mental disquiet, low vitality, or a sense of feeling lost or without purpose, just to name a few. However, the flow of reiki energy through my system opens my awareness to the underlying causes for that dissonance—the perspective, belief or energetic imprint which is signalling for attention. With the client's awareness directed there, a temporary soothing of the 'symptom', and tools or rituals to reprogram the subconscious patterning at play, they heal. Often the healing happens spontaneously, and this usually occurs when the client has already embarked on inner enquiry, is ready, and holds a deep desire for freedom from his or her condition. More recently, over the last few years, my senses have opened up to the presence of past loved ones of clients as well. It has taken practice and some coaching with an established medium; however, this information is exciting and hugely healing. To connect with people in spirit and relay personal and specific information from them to a client evidences a number of wonderful aspects of our human consciousness, the main ones being that our consciousness prevails after the body dies, that we are free and well, and that we continue to love and guide those we leave behind. Knowing these three things with clear, specific evidential validation lifts the heavy pall of grief and opens every single recipient into a deeper spiritual enquiry. Win-win!

Most of us operate from the level of the conscious and subconscious mind. We are governed by our beliefs and patterns, and we are constantly habituating our subconscious minds with our repeated thoughts and perspectives. Occasionally the deep mind will bubble up into our awareness through dreams, hunches, or spontaneous intuitions or synchronicities, but without present awareness, we miss it, and without a developed interpretive language, we don't understand what the symbols and synchronicities and sensations are telling us.

Through mastering our conscious minds and our thought patterns by cultivating mindfulness through meditation, we are able to draw into present awareness and alter our states of consciousness to access the deeper levels of the mind. Mastery of our minds also allows us to witness where our beliefs and perspectives are out of alignment with our true spiritual nature. Our reactive patterns hold the key. When we experience events or phenomena that elicit reactive responses of 'high sensation', our systems are alerting us to a paradigm edge that requires our attention. This can take many forms: a tricky relationship, a perceived hurt or offence, an illness, or an accident, for example. With enough psychic space carved out through regular inner work, we have the pause points established between what we experience and how we choose to respond to it. With that awareness, we are able to choose different perspectives; release paradigms that aren't working for us anymore; heal past imprints from childhood or trauma, for example; and operate from a much more expanded state of being. It is through these deeper aspects of mind that we can also detect and then interpret information that underlies events, interactions, and phenomena. This is intuition.

Now let's look at the horizontal axis of the human 'cross.' The human system operates on several levels: the physical; the pranic, or energetic; the mental and emotional; and the spiritual. For me, the yogic explanation of the koshas makes the most sense in explaining this, and it is what I work with in meditation, teaching and healing with myself and others. Yoga describes our consciousness as existing in five interwoven aspects and realms: the physical body and physical world; the pranic/energetic/astral body and astral realm; the mental body and thought field, or thought realm; the emotional body and emotional field or realm; and the causal/archetypal body and causal field of potential. These are called the koshas. In different schools of yoga and Eastern philosophy, they can be described slightly differently, but it is generally accepted that all these layers or aspects of the self animate and inform the others. They are layers or aspects of one unified system, expressing at different vibrations and operating according to various natural laws. The physical body, for example, operates in the physical world, with all the usual natural laws that it is governed by. The invisible aspects of the human system (the energy body)—the mental, emotional, energetic, and causal aspects—all operate within non-physical dynamics, unbound by time, space, and the material laws of physics.

Our awareness runs like a pole through the entire system, and with practice we can engage consciously with each and every aspect, individually or all at once. The energy body links our physical and energetic forms and capabilities, and we are 'knotted together' at the chakras. We'll jump more deeply into the chakras and the amazing capacities they offer later in this book, but for now, the key perspective to dwell on here is that for many of us, we place 100 per cent of our awareness, concerns, self-doubts, unworthiness, tail-spinning thoughts, and obsessions on 20 per cent to 40 per cent of our beings, our physical and mental bodies—and we have a very limited view of that 20 per cent to 40 per cent to boot. The physical aspect is an incredible aspect of consciousness that senses and communicates spiritual energy and information to our awareness and emanates spiritual energy and information into 'the field.' The mental plane, with its perspectives, refracts energy and potential, which influence all the koshas, the body, our feelings, our auric fields, and our experience of spirit. Our thoughts and our bodies are largely within our field of choice. We can choose how we engage with our bodies, and we can choose our perspectives.

The three levels of consciousness—the conscious mind, the subconscious, and the deep mind, or spirit—exist in all of our horizontal fields as well, and this is important. When we're doing intuitive healing, for example, the information of the person seeking healing can come through in symbols, synchronicity, and sensations through thought, through feelings, within our bodies, or through a gnosis, or a knowing or spiritual understanding.

The gateway between the deep mind or spirit and our own individuated subconscious and conscious minds is the imaginal realm. Rather than regarding the imagination as a function of conjuring up fantasy or memory, in the world of spiritual practice it is regarded as a sacred space. It is in this sacred space that we receive information in the form of vibrating energy from spirit and translate it into conscious mind. But it's also where we imprint spirit to affect change, and this is why the imagination is referred to in various mystery schools as the 'alchemical container of the imagination' or 'the altar of the Most High.' And all of these worlds and dimensions, this hologram, are within every cell, every thought, every touch, and all the spaces in between, which is why the beautiful metaphysical Sufi poet Rumi said, 'You're not a drop in the ocean. You are the ocean in a drop!'

Our intent is one of the highest vibratory forces we can generate consciously. It transcends the gateway into the deep mind, into spirit. Clarity of intent is key.

These next few chapters are intended to vastly expand the more commonly held perspectives of the human system. Given that our focus is constantly being pointed towards our material form by modern messaging, let's start there, and then we will move into our invisible aspects. It's time to really and truly get to 'know ourselves.'

The physical aspect, our biology, is often understood to be in opposition to the spiritual aspect and somehow must be denied or subjugated to access spirit. While a healthy body definitely helps the process of becoming spirited, the idea that the body is somehow separate from the spirit, or simply a container for spirit, is perhaps the ultimate illusion of separation. Our bodies *are* spirit in form, and they are incredible instruments of intelligence, energy, and information, as well as necessary components of the Spirit Self. It's time to reclaim them as such. We are blessed in this current age to have a plethora of material emerging from inspired cellular biologists, neurologists, cardiologists, quantum physicists, modern mystics, and many others who are exploring more and more deeply the energetic nature of reality, the human body, and consciousness, and we have the Internet. If you are drawn to learn more about any of these topics, then go for it. Our physical/non-physical bodies are the conduits for our spiritual circuitry, and they are far more that what we understand them to be. The following offers a wider-angled lens on how we view our form, and in later chapters we will explore the energy body. What I have written here is what I teach people in my courses, and it is enough to create an internal shift that opens the door to the Spirit Self.

# CHAPTER 6

# Your Entire Physical System Is Conscious and Intelligent

*Once we open up to the flow of energy within the body,*
*we can also open up to the flow of energy in the Universe.*
—Wilhelm Reich

We all intuitively know that our bodies 'speak to us.' We feel things. There are lots of names we use for these kinds of messages from the body. Some call it 'gut-feel'; others say they can 'feel it in their waters [or bones].' Our bodies have the ability to communicate to our awareness what is needed to thrive. This 'physical intelligence' and our ability to 'hear' the communication from the body is called 'interoception.' It's a form of intuition that rises through the physical body, but interestingly it also communicates information to us from far outside the body, and this we call 'intuition.'

How many of us have had an experience when we have sensed in the hairs on the backs of our necks a threat or danger before we have seen evidence of it, or sensed through an ache in the heart that someone we love needed help or was unwell? How many of us women feel the lunar cycle within our ovaries or knew that we were pregnant before any testing confirmed it? Many of us have had the experience of someone popping into mind, only to have them contact us shortly afterwards.

Whilst we all have these senses, this 'body-knowing', we simply accept it and know very little about how it works; we do not seek to develop it and work with it. For many of us, we accept it as some uncontrollable fluke phenomenon. Many of these experiences point towards the body being in tune with people and experiences that are not existing in the same space or time. It's as if the body is receiving information from beyond the visible realm. Our awareness is so diverted with the unrelenting stimulus of our external reality that we can become at best passive towards this inner information, at worst dismissive of it altogether.

When we are centred, this information can rise as a strong vibration within the body, especially if we are receiving information of danger, for example. During my corporate days, I was assigned to New York for several months to work on a strategy project. It was a fantastic gig. I was put up in an apartment in midtown and was part of a team of very slick operators. In those days of my late twenties, I had supernatural energy and could work all day and all night and regularly transit to and from my London home when needed. I was in my element, happy and centred. One night I was walking home alone to my apartment after a long session at work and a late dinner. I felt satisfied and very grateful to be having the experience. You could say I was in a high-vibe mode on the short walk home. Within minutes of turning the corner towards Times Square, I felt a strong wash of danger come through me. It was unmistakable. My body was sensing a threat even when my mind had no perception of it.

I turned immediately to look behind me and saw no one and nothing. I stayed for a moment to sense into the situation. There was definitely a threat, but it was outside my boundary of physical senses. I turned and continued to walk, this time at a more determined pace. The feeling of danger was following me. I whipped around again, just quickly enough to catch a silhouetted figure dash into a doorway upon my movement. There was about half a block between us, and I was pretty sure there was enough distance to outrun him if it turned into a full chase, but it was also enough distance for his presence to be unheard, smelled, or initially seen. My body felt his intention.

We continued in this strange manoeuvring of me walking at a serious pace for several metres and my shadowy friend tracking at the same pace. I remembered the advice given to me by a London police officer who came into the office to teach us about self-defence in a workshop I had recently organised for our female employees in the UK. He told us that if there was enough distance to hold one's ground without being in immediate physical threat, then one should continue to maintain that distance, ensuring the follower that he or she has been seen. So I stopped walking, turned, stood tall in the centre of the pavement, put my hands on my hips and waited for him to emerge from his hiding place to continue his hunt. Out he came, and he saw me staring straight at him—not angry, not afraid (although I had the guts to do this only because there was a distance between us), but defiant and centred. I felt the vibration of danger dissipate, and then he turned on his heel and bolted away, perhaps not wanting to be identified.

On occasions when walking along Manly Beach in Sydney, Australia (the best beach in the world by far), I have felt the vibration of a predator in the water, a shark, only to have the feeling confirmed minutes later by the sounding of the shark alarm. I have felt every major change in my life—including career changes and location moves—before evidence of it appeared within ordinary awareness. It feels like a stirring, a building storm, even though the skies are presently still calm and blue. It slowly builds over days and weeks and it is often accompanied by repeated dreams of me standing on a coastline, watching enormous tidal waves approach the shore. Before I found my Spirit Self, these dreams use to scare me a little, but now I welcome them as clear messaging from the field that big change is coming. It's a delight to watch it arrive.

Now I work consciously with this body wisdom. The body doesn't lie or miscommunicate, ever. It holds energetic signatures from childhood (and, as I have learnt, even further back from past lives), and it is constantly signalling to the awareness when we are in harmony and alignment with the Spirit Self and when we are not. What we perceive to be disease is strong messaging from the physical aspect of a disharmony or dissonance in the system that needs our awareness and attention if we are to expand and heal. What we perceive as accidental injuries or temporary illnesses are the same. All energy-healing modalities in some way or another recognise this. The physical body is designed for and constantly reaching for vitality and harmony. When we are not experiencing this physical state, we are out of alignment somewhere in our invisible aspects, and as the human system of spirit and matter is one unified, self-organising system, it will bring this to our awareness, usually through the physical body, for attention and action.

Another way I work consciously with this body wisdom is in private energy sessions with clients. It is very common for me to feel within my own body the vibration being held in my clients' bodies. This inner sense is called clairsentience, and I cover more on this and the other inner 'spirit senses' in chapter 14. This can come through as a physical feeling or an emotion when I place my hands on the relevant part of a client's body. In one interesting case, I felt physical tightness in my heart as I placed my hands on my client's chest. The pain moved down my left arm, and at the same time I 'saw' an image of his father. He confirmed after the session that his father had recently had a heart attack. I suggested he get his own heart health checked as well, and as it turned out, he had inherited his father's heart condition and was advised by his doctor to take immediate action so as not to follow his father's experience.

I feel this body wisdom more keenly when I am maintaining a high level of fitness or engaged in disciplined inner practice. Clients who have undertaken a recent detoxification diet or have an active inner practice also physically resonate at a vastly higher and cleaner rate. Perhaps the most intense and precise cueing of body wisdom I have experienced was when I was pregnant. Well before the pregnancy tests confirmed that I was carrying both my children, I knew. My entire system was vibrating at a different resonance. My senses turned wolverine-esque. In the morning, I could smell the tracks of any animals that had passed through my garden the night before. I could sense when someone was thinking about me, only to have him or her call a day or so later. I knew exactly what food my body was requiring even when my mind didn't realise that the foods I was hankering for were high in iron or magnesium, for example. In my prenatal courses, I hear that this same experience is a common one. Pregnancy has a supercharging effect on a woman's body messaging and physical intuition. It makes sense, as the system is amped with increased life force, intelligence, and energy as a new spirit takes form into matter within her. It's definitely one of the lesser spoken about but dazzling aspects of pregnancy, and one that I love guiding my mums-to-be to lean into and understand fully.

Many people report that the more disconnected they feel from their body and nature, the more dulled their sensitivity to their intuition becomes. And many more come to meditation classes and energy sessions because they can't sense things any more at all.

To reopen the awareness to this subtle messaging from the body, it helps to reacquaint ourselves with the instrument itself and see it in a new way. It was the award-winning work of Dr Bruce Lipton and his book *The Biology of Belief* that totally opened my awareness to the dazzling intelligence of my physical form and its ability to receive useful information from the unified field of consciousness and bring it to the attention of my awareness.

I couldn't possibly relay here everything he writes about, but I can certainly recommend it as a fantastic read. Below is a small summary of some game-changing facts that he illuminates.

We grow up to view our bodies as entirely singular units with the locum of command set firmly within the head, in the brain. When we look in the mirror, we see one body, one unique physical presence, and sadly many of us are particularly critical of various parts of that 'one unit.' But to a cellular biologist like Dr Bruce Lipton, what we really are is a cooperative of approximately seventy-two trillion single-celled intelligent individuals.

Single cells, like the ones that make up our bodies, are the oldest form of life on the planet; they have slowly and steadily learnt to cooperate to ensure their survival. Within us, some cooperate to form a collective that we call the human heart; others, the immune system; others, blood; others, muscle tissue; and so on. Evolution has taught these tiny individuals that their chances for surviving and thriving are much better when they work together in greater and greater specialised communities that form the human body.

Every single cell is an intelligent being that can survive on its own. It is imbued with intent and purpose. Each cell is attracted to environments and substances that support life, and each cell avoids toxic or hostile ones. Cells are highly intelligent, able to analyse all the information contained in the microenvironments they inhabit. They create cellular memories, which they pass on to their offspring. So rather than being one single entity, we are in fact a highly organised co-op of trillions of intelligent cells. You are an intelligent collective, and this collective has organised itself within the human expression through incredible connections and into three very powerful hubs of intelligence: the head, the heart, and the belly. It is through these three centres that information is relayed to our awareness, and we emanate vibrating information into the field around us. These three centres are highly responsive to meditation, and moreover it is through the energy that builds and emanates from these centres, especially when they are in vibrational coherence, that we create our realities.

# CHAPTER 7

# Intelligence Hub One: Your Brain

W e're going to get a little sciencey here for the next couple of chapters simply to help shift perspectives. I am not a scientist, but I do have a long-held fascination with the dazzling design of the body, its constant reach for harmony and balance, and its ability to self-heal. Over the years, as I have shifted my own perspectives, I have developed a kind of a crush on my physical body that goes far beyond skin-deep, and I hope these next few chapters will help you develop one too. The centre that most of us accept as housing our intelligence is the brain. It's pretty much a blob of water and jelly housed in the skull and is largely viewed as a kind of computer with neural networks and electrical power. However, it could well be regarded as an organ of the

Spirit Self, and it is highly responsive to regular meditation practice, both physically and energetically.

The constant sensory stimulation of modern life keeps us in our headspace. The apparatuses for most of our senses—sight, hearing, taste, and smell—are in the head, and they never turn off. Perhaps this is why we perceive our locus of command to be in the head. Our brains are the most powerful data processors ever known and are constantly reshaping themselves with every thought. The more we repeat a thought, the stronger the connections become, and the more that thought or perception gets 'hard-wired' into the brain. When we are not mindful and allow ourselves to slip into habitual looping thinking, we are literally shaping our brains to that reality and fixing it there. Dr Jo Dispenza estimates that of the six hundred thousand thoughts we have a day, when we are unmindful and not present, around 75 per cent of them generate a negative response in our beings. Cultivating mindfulness of our inner worlds and thoughts is critical to shaping how we experience life, and it shifts us out of a pattern of totally bumming out our systems most of the time!

The human brain, like the body's other intelligence systems, is highly responsive, energetically and physically, to meditation, and it reshapes itself with regular practice to enable deeper and further inner practice. Simply entering meditation will create a shift in brainwave activity. As the awareness turns inwards and the system calms, our brainwaves become slightly longer and slower. Initially these waves are alpha waves. Most students can experience this within their first sit. As we become good at meditation, the brainwaves continue to slow and lengthen, enabling altered states of consciousness. It is in the windows of the deeper, slower brainwave states, the theta and gamma states, that we can consciously reprogram old beliefs and, more impressively, access much broader fields of information and energy, which can be outside of the time and space that our bodies occupy. The brain is also physically responsive. With regular meditation, there are five key changes that we currently know of that take place in the brain, and each one of them enables further and deeper meditation. The primary difference is in the posterior cingulate, which is involved in mind wandering and self-relevance. This part of our brain enables us to draw in the dissipated mind and concentrate our awareness. And it gets stronger and physically larger when we meditate regularly.

The left hippocampus, which assists in learning, cognition, memory, and emotional regulation, also rebuilds itself. Prolonged high stress literally erodes the hippocampus. We have all experienced the inability to understand something or to recall what we know when we are stressed. Most mothers I know, when under the pump to keep the family train on the tracks and get everyone out the door on time, will run through the names of all their offspring and pets until they hit the right name of the one yet to put on his or her shoes. The good news is that we naturally rebuild stress-ravaged parts of the body and brain when we give them calm and space to heal.

The temporal parietal junction, which is associated with perspective taking, empathy and compassion, also becomes stronger with regular meditation. This enables our consciousness of connection and interconnectedness. And an area of the brain stem called the pons, where a lot of regulatory neurotransmitters are produced, also strengthens physically. This enables the flow of information throughout the entire system.

The amygdala, the fight-or-flight part of the brain, is important for quick emergency responses and flushes of adrenals. It is responsible for the rise of anger and automatic reactivity. It's the shoot-from-the-hip-and-ask-questions-later part of the brain. This area of the brain shrinks, as seen in the brain measurements of groups that undertake the eight-week Mindfulness-Based Stress Reduction Program. The change in the amygdala correlates to a reduction in stress levels. Meditating lowers stress hormone levels in the blood and engenders a mindful approach to oneself and one's reactions. This then eases rises of anger, which shrinks the part of the brain that enables them. Research confirms that regular meditators are calmer, happier, and more grateful, and the more we meditate on these things, the more we experience them, because our brains change to allow it. How cool is that?

The idea that we are either 'left-brain' or 'right-brain' people is a construct. We use both. However, regular meditators are more able to switch between their left and right brain functions depending on what's required. They are better able to bring together their logical and intuitive minds (or what we might call their masculine and feminine mental aspects).

It is the beliefs that we hold within the subcortical region of the brain that mainly determine our experiences of life and self. The vibrational frequency that emanates from our emotions, feelings, thoughts, and actions correlates creatively, not reactively, to the physical world we perceive and our daily experiences. That is, our vibrational frequency creatively influences the events we experience. Our vibrational frequency is strongest around our beliefs. All beliefs are simply thoughts that have been repeated enough to form a structural pattern in the brain, regardless of whether they are based on truth or not. Repeated thoughts in the brain cause new dendrites to form and new neural pathways to develop. It's the same thing as when we create any habit. The science of neuroplasticity shows us that it takes twenty-one days to create a habit. It takes twenty-one days for those neural pathways to atrophy or stop working when we don't indulge the habit. You could say that reading and contemplating content like this book is generating new neural pathways into a habit of regarding yourself differently and, it is to be hoped, with far more admiration.

The cortex, or the thinking part of the human brain, processes information at forty bits per second. The subcortex, the subcortical region of the brain, can process forty *million* bits per second. This is the region where we hold our beliefs, and they are being held in place by a biological supercomputer. Many of these beliefs were formed in childhood through our adopting them either naturally, tribally, culturally, familiarly, or by force.

By the time we're thirty-five years old, 95 per cent of who we believe we are and how we believe the world works is a set of memorised behaviours, habits, emotional reactions, beliefs, perceptions, and attitudes that function within our subconscious computer programs and govern how we experience life.

So we may decide to consciously employ positive affirmations, or vision boards about our desired bodies, for example, but if our bodies have been memorising the chemical and hormonal effects of our negative feelings and thoughts about our bodies for most of our lives, then our affirmations and vision boards are in opposition to our deeper beliefs, and we need to consciously reprogram before we experience any change. And not only are we able to do this, but we are designed to do it. Different forms of meditation alter brainwave activity into deeper and slower pulses. In these deeper states, with intent, we are able to consciously reprogram our subconscious beliefs, but first we must be able to see them.

As we begin to modify our thoughts, behaviours, and emotional states, we can turn on thousands of different gene expressions that begin to make new proteins and we can switch off unbalanced, unwell gene expressions. The more altered our beliefs and resultant behaviours, the more we change our genetic expressions. We shape-shift our brains, genes, and nervous systems—and with them our engagement with our ordinary reality. So why not consciously shape-shift to vital, happy, spirit-led, love-infused awesomeness?

To consciously create the changes that allow an expanded spiritual experience of life, we first need to be able to hold the possibility of it, and it's our brain's ability *to imagine* that is one of its greatest spiritual capacities. The imagination can be regarded more like a space in the mind—a space that holds possibility—than a function. It is far more than the diverting, unreal, and possibly useless landscape that we are so often told it is as children. I don't know how many times I was told when young, 'Oh that's just your imagination', 'That's just your imaginary friend', or to just 'stop daydreaming.' My parents often joked that it was a lucky thing I was bright, as nearly every school report from kindergarten to high school had a comment reading something to the effect of 'It's a miracle Danielle has achieved these marks given her propensity to stare out the window and daydream. If she actually applied her mind, there's no telling what she could achieve.' And as we grow into adults we are further steered towards that which can be evidenced and measured; that which 'is real.' Our limited view of this incredible capacity of the mind is one of the key reasons why we lose contact with spirit. Redefining our perspective of the imagination and putting it to use spiritually is the first task for anyone seeking to be spirited. It is in the imaginal space that we receive information from far beyond the physical senses and where we envision new realities. When we clear out the dross of dissipated thoughts and learn to enter this space in the mind, it becomes key to being spirited, and the way to do this is through meditation. We will dive deeply into this in coming chapters.

The brain is not the mind. Having just read that sentence, you may find yourself realising that you've just kind of assumed the brain is the mind, but it's not. The brain is but one of our intelligence hubs that facilitates an experience of the mind, or our individuated consciousness. The mind is the intelligence field that permeates the body, and the experience of it is also facilitated by your entire system, especially the heart and the belly, as well as the non-physical energetic aspects of your system. It's this 'mind' and the mastery of it which enables access to spirit.

CHAPTER 8

# Intelligence Hub Two: Your Heart

We know the physical heart; it is a sophisticated pump. It has four chambers and is powered by the autonomic nervous system. The physical heart is responsible for pumping blood and oxygen throughout the body. It's about the size of a fist and weighs around three hundred grams.

The heart actively contracts to force blood out of its chambers and passively relaxes to allow the next quantity of blood to enter. This pulse of relaxation and contraction of the heart muscle, which spirals blood to all parts of our bodies, continues non-stop throughout our lives from the twenty-second day in the womb until our last breath.

It is an incredible organ. It beats 100,800 times a day, and faster in children. It moves 23,850 litres of blood per day through over 154,000 kilometres of blood vessels. Three million red blood cells are created every second to replenish this blood. In the average lifetime, the heart pumps an amount equivalent to one million barrels of blood. This is approximately equivalent to the entire capacity of three supertankers.

Heartbeats are manifestations of the heart's vibrational energy. Our hearts are also the main suppliers of electrical power to our bodies. Every day, the heart generates enough energy to drive a truck thirty-three kilometres. In a lifetime, this is equivalent to driving to the moon and back. So when we say, 'I love you to the moon and back', we are essentially saying 'I love you with all of the power of my heart in this life!' How beautiful is that?

The heart's electricity and movement naturally generate its own electromagnetic field and vibrational frequency, and it is the largest electromagnetic field produced in the body. It can be measured and observed. The brain also produces an energy field and emanates brain waves and thoughts, but the heart field is hundreds of times stronger than that of the brain. This is why it is much easier to sense what someone is feeling rather than what he or she is thinking.

Researchers have analysed the spectrum analysis of the energy field that's produced by the heart, and results have shown that emotional information is encoded into this electromagnetic field and radiates out from the heart centre. So by shifting our emotions, we are changing the information that is encoded into these electromagnetic fields that are radiated by the heart into our bodies and other fields. This impacts those around us. When we are feeling emotions of compassion, love, gratitude, and understanding, our hearts beat out very different messages of beautiful fractal information and vibration, as compared to when we are feeling depressed, angry, or shamed. We have all had an experience of this when in the company of others. We are magnetically drawn to people who are free, open, and joyful, and we can feel the heavy effects of spending time with someone who is depressed, angry, or addicted, for example. Heart fields interact. A heart field that is resonating at a higher, lighter, coherent patterned vibration can lift the heart field of a lower-vibrating, incoherently patterned heart.

Quoting from the Dalai Lama's *The Book of Joy: Lasting Happiness in a Changing World,*

> A scientifically controlled study conducted by German researchers at the University of Kassel has shown that while the chest area of an average person emits only 20 photons of light per second, someone who meditates on their heart center and sends love and light to others emits an amazing 100,000 photons per second. That is 5000 times more than the average human being. Numerous studies have also shown that when these photons are

infused with a loving and healing intent, their frequency and vibration increases to the point where they can literally change matter, heal disease, and transform negative events. Ten minutes of meditating on compassion, on kindness for others, and you will see its effects all day. That's the way to maintain a calm and joyous mind.

The heart is intelligent and has memory. Of the cells that line the heart, 65 per cent are the same nerve cells as the brain's and scientists now conclude that though the brain supplies the heart with perceptions, it is the heart, responding to the reports from the brain, that sends positive or negative instructions back to the emotional centres in the brain and, through hormones released into the bloodstream, to the entire body. In other words, the brain is working for the heart!

There are many documented stories of people receiving a heart transplant and over time experiencing memories, feelings, habits, and preferences of the donor. In one stunning case I read about in Norway, the heart recipient started to perceive the death scene of her donor in her dreams. So clear were the night visions that forensic police were able to sketch the details from her descriptions, which led to the donor's murderer being found and arrested.

Rather than simply being a mechanical pump, the

human heart is a self-renewing intelligent organ that produces electrical currents, has its own electromagnetic field and vibrational frequency, and thinks. And the heart is very responsive to meditative awareness—particularly that achieved through heart-centred meditation. In regular meditators, the cardio-ratio smooths and slows, and blood pressure decreases. Gratitude meditations have been proven to improve physical heart health, speed recovery of damaged heart muscle tissue, and reduce reoccurrence of heart attacks. High resonant states of gratitude, awe and wonder, loving-kindness, compassion, and forgiveness, for example, also trigger the body to release a whole raft of chemicals that bolster immunity.

Moreover, these states connect us back to the field of oneness, the spirit field, because they raise us out of separation and reactive living. They expand our states, and they maintain enough space in the heart to receive and discern guidance and consciously create our life experiences. They also raise the vital life force within and coming through our energy bodies. I learnt this through observing how different emotional states affect the amount of healing energy being drawn through my system by clients in energy sessions. I learnt this valuable lesson as a healer when working with children. Once, when working with a beautiful six-year-old boy who suffered crippling anxiety, I found myself feeling sorry for him during the session. It was a natural response, and well-intended; however, the second I started to entertain pity, which of course has an implied judgement, which separated my state from his, the healing energy dwindled and then stopped. Many different characters come to my healing rooms each week, and some have stories and experiences in their lives or are in such states of self-loathing or desperation that I find it unfathomable. I have had to train myself not to feel anything like pity or sadness for anyone and instead merge with them in a sense, becoming one with them, their desire to heal, and the very real possibility of full healing. This state of compassion and oneness allows for maximum flow of healing energy, and we can cultivate these higher vibrations through choosing different perspectives, different ways to view the situation, and, of course, meditation.

CHAPTER 9

# Intelligence Hub Three: Your Belly

The enteric nervous system of the belly is a rich and complicated network of neurons and neurochemicals that sense and control events in other parts of the body, including the brain. It contains over one hundred million neurons—more than the number of nerve cells in the spinal cord. So when we say we have a 'gut feeling' or can 'sense it in our waters,' this isn't some witchy power pertaining to just a few people; this is the neurons in our belly calling out to our overwrought brain to take heed. There is a greater flow of neural traffic from the belly to the brain than from the brain to the belly. In other words, rather than the brain informing the digestive system what to eat and how to metabolise, the locus of command is stationed in the belly.

When our flight-or-fight response is triggered, our bodies divert energy from the belly to the limbs and prefrontal cortex so we can think and act quickly. The functions of digestion and metabolising become secondary in the face of a sabre-toothed tiger. This is a natural response and one of the dazzling survival tactics of the human body. Out there on the grass savannah, it helped us decide whether to kill and eat a threat or to leg it home to safety. But it's designed to be a flash response, not a prolonged state. When we are in the grips of modern living, we are operating with high vigilance. We are in a prolonged state of high alert because of sensory overload and cultural and worldly anxiety. We lose connection with the intelligent belly and therefore a suite of mood- and energy-raising enablers and intelligence.

The neural network in the belly is largely responsible for our body chemistry. The entire digestive tract is lined with cells that produce and receive a variety of neuropeptides and neurochemicals that were previously thought to be found only in the brain. These include serotonin and dopamine, our mood regulators. Approximately 95 per cent of serotonin is created in the gut. Dopamine is our pleasure chemical and is critical for brain rewiring. The belly and digestive health are essential to maintaining mood, lowering anxiety, and ensuring regular, sound sleep. The entire digestive tract is lined with specialised cells that produce and receive endorphins and enkephalins, chemicals that yield an array of sensations including joy, satisfaction, and pain relief.

The gut also produces an abundance of a class of chemicals known as benzodiazepines. These psychoactive substances are the active ingredients in the prescription drugs Valium and Xanax.

When we nurture a mindful calmer state through regular meditation, we reconnect with a centre of our being that informs the brain of what is needed to be balanced and healthy. That regulates our mood and sleep and triggers the production of the chemicals that help us pull up, feel great, and go for it! The intelligent belly is also highly responsive to meditative attention. It is very common for people to experience gurgling and movement in the belly when they enter meditation. As the system relaxes and aligns, the gates to our incredible natural pharmacy open.

Regular meditation has been proven to vastly improve the health and function of our three hubs of intelligence in the body. Why is that? It is my observation that it's because they are key to spirit. These three hubs enable an experience of our mind, our consciousness, and our ability to work with it. To understand this more deeply, we must look at our non-physical aspects—the invisible you.

# CHAPTER 10

# The Invisible You

In essence, you are a vibration. That's it—a system of vibrating energy and information that is constantly moving and interacting with much larger fields of vibrating energies and information. Not only is this perhaps the most radical view of self you may have considered, but it is also the most important one. To be spirited, to truly understand the dazzling reality of your being, you need to think in terms of vibes!

Let's go back to that atomic material that has been cycling the universe for eons, which makes up our physical forms. If we were to observe the composition of an atom with an atomic microscope, we would see a small, invisible tornado-like vortex with a number of infinitely smaller energy vortices spiralling around it. These are what make up the structure of the atom. As you focus in closer and closer on the structure of the atom, you would see nothing. You would observe a physical void. The atom has no physical structure. *We* have no physical structure. Atoms are made out of invisible vibrating energy, not tangible matter, and so is everything we regard as physical, including your form.

These vortices of energy are constantly spinning and vibrating, each one radiating its own unique energy signature—a signature 'sound', if you like. And that energy signature, that vibration, holds a lot of information, as does the vibration of everything around us that we regard as physical. And the science peeps have been pinging us with this revelation for a long time too. I can't list them all, but here are a few of my favourites who point us towards our vibratory nature:

> If you want to find the secrets of the Universe, think in terms of energy, frequency and vibration. (Nikola Tesla)

> Each celestial body, in fact each and every atom, produces a particular sound on account of its movement, its rhythm or vibration. All these sounds and vibrations form a universal harmony in which each element, while having its own function and character, contributes to the whole. (Pythagoras)

Perhaps my favourite 'vibe ping' from the past is from the Hermetic wisdom offered in *The Kybalion*:

> Nothing rests. Everything moves. Everything vibrates. At the most fundamental level, the Universe and everything which comprises it is pure vibratory energy manifesting itself in different ways. The Universe has no 'solidity' as such. Matter and life experience are merely energy in a state of vibration. (The Third Universal Law—*The Kybalion*)

This vibration within everything is affected by our intent, desire, and will; it is affected most powerfully when these three aspects are vibrating in coherence. This coherence depends largely on what we believe and our self-mastery of our energy body.

A very real example of this may be found within the science of epigenetics. Every one of those one hundred trillion cells that make up the human physical form replicates itself in the body's constant renewal process. Whilst it is gene structures that determine the replication of cell information, the science of epigenetics, which literally means 'control above genetics', profoundly changes our understanding of how life is controlled. Epigenetics research has established that it is environmental influence—including nutrition, of course, but also emotions, intentions, and beliefs—that modifies our genes without changing their basic blueprints, and that those modifications can be passed on to future generations. It was Dr Bruce Lipton's *The Biology of Belief* that opened my mind to this dazzling scientific confirmation of what I knew to be true.

The activity of our genes is controlled by the presence or absence of ensleeving proteins, which are in turn controlled by environmental signals. In other words, DNA is a vast switchboard of genes, but there's something else that's turning those switches on and off, and it appears that the greatest influence on whether genes are activated or not is what we think and feel. The resonance, or vibration, of what we believe and repeatedly pulse into our systems affects us materially and determines whether we experience physical conditions, regardless of whether there appears to be a genetic predisposition for such conditions or not. The health response of the body to the higher vibrations of awe and gratitude is another example of our vibratory nature and how it is affected by what we feel and believe. Experiments in cultivating the feeling of gratitude in cardiac wards, as an example, have shown accelerated healing of heart tissue post–heart attack and a reduced probability for subsequent heart attacks.

It is in honing our awareness of the vibratory nature of things that we are able to sense and know far beyond the physical senses, through our intuition, or 'spirit senses.' We vibe far beyond our skin line; it's a multidirectional flow, and it is self-organising. And we hone that awareness through expanded self-perception and—you guessed it—meditation. This is why our physical system responds so keenly to the practice of meditation, to allow deeper more vibratory experiences, because this is how we are naturally designed to operate—as unique, interactive vibrations. Aren't we dazzling?

One more ping (although there are thousands I could share): 'To enter into the initiation of sound, of vibration and mindfulness, is to take a giant step toward consciously knowing the soul' (Don G Campbell).

We are vibrating energy, and everything that issues from us is also energy in vibration. Every thought, feeling, and action; every word, sound, and non-sound; our intentions; our choices; our hopes; and our dreams are all movements of vibrating informational energy. The same can be said for our world and the entirety of our life experiences. These vibrations are informing, merging with, and affecting others, and they are held within our discreet energy system. In other words, our individual systems are simply part of a greater, ever-expanding system of vibrational energy and information which is constantly vibrating at different frequencies, and the entire vibrational system is constantly seeking harmony and balance.

Our own vibrational fields can now be measured, and they extend far beyond the skin line. Our thoughts are not in our heads. The vibrational information of our thoughts can be measured by magnetoencephalography. It doesn't involve probes in the brain or receptors stuck to the skull. It involves an apparatus held at a distance from the head.

Our feelings are not contained in the chest or belly. Our emotional fields can be measured through spectrum analysis, which can pick up the fractal patterning of high-vibration emotional states like gratitude, or the dysmorphic, ugly patterning of low-vibration states like anger. This field can also be detected far beyond the skin line, and as scientific measurement continues to advance, it will be a delight to see just how far it extends. Many of you will have come across Dr Masaru Emoto's incredible work that recorded how voiced intention, whether positive and happy or angry and sad, literally alters the shape of water molecules. Our human system is made up of around 87 per cent water. If we are in unconscious habits of self-shaming, anger reactions, and judgement, we are pulsing these vibrations into the water molecules of our forms and altering their shape.

Our choices that are put into action generate movement and change, which ripple into the vibrating field of life, changing possibilities, connections, and outcomes. Actions 'activate the field.' The power of *putting a choice into action* is a strong theme in all of my interactions with students. It comes up in healing sessions, in courses, and with private clients. Actioning a choice triggers a very powerful vibration that creates change, even if that action is a small step in the general direction of where you want to go. Action activates!

It's very common for students to report real changes occurring from the moment they book a session or register for a course. They may not have even started their focussed practice yet, but the choice to do so yields results. They can often feel a new sense of calm, increased dreaming, meeting other spirit-led people by 'chance', entering far more meaningful exchanges with others, or new opportunities opening up, just because they have put a choice into action to explore their lives and selves more deeply. When we do this, the experiences of our life fields also deepen; this mirrors the actioned choice. It is also very common for my private clients to start crying within minutes of coming into the healing rooms, before we have started the pre-chat for the energy session. For many, especially new clients, this is quite surprising, as they didn't necessarily feel sadness, yet they start to spontaneously cry (and often laugh at the same time). This is extremely positive. Their systems have already commenced an energy release and healing process, even before the formal energy work begins, simply through their choices to seek healing and to enter the presence of the healing space. And one of the most common ways for the subtle body to release dense, unhelpful vibration is through the emotional body.

We are constantly affecting the vibrational field of life and receiving information from it, whether we are conscious of it or not, because we are part of it. Being spirited is about resonating consciously and in harmony with the field, with spirit. This harmonic unified field, like the energy systems of our bodies and within nature, is constantly striving for harmony, life, and highest possibility. It's a self-regulating system. We experience things with correspondent vibrations like a reflective mirror held up to our awareness, inviting us to shift perspectives and make different choices. When we raise our vibrations into coherence, we raise our experiences of life into flow and coherence too. When we are out of alignment and coherence internally, we experience situations and states that mirror this, such as illness, disquiet, chaos, and blockages to progress. These experiences are not being done to us; they are simply indications from the vibratory field, spirit, that something within us is out of whack. In expanded states of awareness, they can no longer be viewed as 'bad' things, but rather as messages to our awareness that some inner work is required to achieve realignment. Once addressed, the external trigger or symptom disappears. This is the underlying mechanism of all healing and magical practice, and it's why people who are connected with spirit seem to have better luck and success, and less illness. They also don't worry about anything, because they are working with life rather than feeling that they are victims of it.

While our modern world and scientific materialism narrows our focus to the physical senses and what can be physically measured, we are designed to energetically receive and interact with the vibrational universe via our vibrating 'cross.' The dissipated mind may perceive this information only via vivid dreams, occasional hunches, rare moments of still clarity, or, most commonly, experiences of being out of alignment and in a state of separation from the vibratory field of existence. That's when we experience blockages, chaos, illness, and perceived 'negative' experiences. All of these are signalling a requirement to step back into a unified consciousness and into flow. Unless we hone our abilities to master our minds and perceive our energy bodies, information that comes through to awareness from our extraordinary perception tends to be forgotten, not recognise at all, dismissed, or, worse still, fought with as an opposing force.

This vibratory information that comes through our intuitive awareness is far more reliable than what we can perceive with our physical senses. It is estimated that 73 per cent of the matter that makes up the universe is made of dark energy and another 23 per cent is made up of dark matter. Our physical eyes are capable of seeing only 0.0035% of the entire spectrum of electromagnetic radiation. So when you put down this book for a pause to allow the vibration of these words to permeate your system and you look up to the sky to ponder the universe and seek to understand the tremendousness of life, quite literally, 96 per cent of it is invisible to your eyes.

When I hold energy sessions for individuals, it is these vibrational fields of information that I 'read.' Everything has a recognisable vibration—everything. Guilt, shame, procrastination, illnesses, grief, joy, bliss, seduction, worry, uncertainty, property deals, pregnancies, family conflicts, diabetes, cancer, cysts, depression, incoming opportunities, and new loves—everything. Having held energy sessions with thousands of people, I have come to recognise these signatures, and every day I am introduced to others. The intuitive read can be a little freaky for people who are disconnected from the vibrational nature of life, as the information that they are holding within their energy bodies is very specific, and by the time a client has sought help, it can be signalling strongly as his or her system is seeking to rebalance. I do not at all believe this is some exclusive ability. I know that with a daily practise of meditation and connection with my own vibrational frequency, the vibrational frequencies of my clients can be recognised and received by my system and then translated through my mind into useful and communicable information for them. In all of my sessions, I make a point of educating the client into reading this information that he or she is holding for himself or herself. This is true healing. It's not so much resolving the symptom of dissonance; it's more about expanding the awareness of the self and how the vibrational field works through and around us. Very often it can simply be the expansion into this awareness that dissolves the symptoms—especially pain.

My husband is fascinated with this, and it's thanks to his desire to understand it that I am able to articulate it in this book. I was relaying to him a few years ago a beautiful session with a lady who came for an energy session. She was herself a healer and a deeply spiritual woman, yet she had been plagued with health issues that she couldn't alleviate herself. (As an aside, I see many energy healers in my sessions, and I also consult others, because we understand the value in utilising different modalities to expand perspectives). There was a lot of information available from her vibratory body; however, one of the significant indications came from her gut. That her gut translated the issue into my conscious mind is why this story is relevant. When I placed my hands on her tummy, I saw in my inner vision (my imaginal space) a spiralling swirl of what looked like metallic dust. As I moved my awareness into this image, I could see it was free and easily moving. In the session, I swirled it into a fast-moving spiral that moved up and out. When the session ended, we chatted, and I relayed to her what I had sensed. She confirmed that as a child she was exposed to mercury poisoning. The mercury had lodged in the organs of her solar plexus, and she had been working on detoxification methods to cleanse herself. I explained to her that her work had yielded results and the substance was ready to finally be released from her body.

Her body and energy field held this information as a vibration. After years of working together, she is now able to read it herself and work with it. I have huge admiration for her healing journey.

This is how it works. We hold signatures of vibrations within our energetic stories. Low-density vibrations that keep us separated from spirit and keep us small, such as guilt, shame, low self-worth, anger, and jealousy, eventually manifest into physical symptoms. And that is what they are—signals from one aspect of our design that we are out of alignment with our spirit and have reduced our self-perspective into a consciousness of separation by judging ourselves or by judging life with the view that it is happening 'to us.' Once we are able to bring our conscious awareness to it, to understand that we have forgotten that we are spirited, the symptoms dissolve, because our present awareness is in itself a vibration coherent with our highest expression. The difference between me and someone who comes to see me for the first session is that the client has forgotten the language of vibration. He or she is no longer able to sense his or her own unique signature, and the client sees himself or herself as a being that is separate from the whole. With practice we can reconnect with our vibratory natures and therefore detect dissonance or 'messaging.' Through meditation, we open the bridge between receiving these vibrations and allowing them to be translated into our conscious minds. I do this as my life's work. I see around thirty people a week either in person or remotely, so that bridge and my vibrational vocabulary is wide. That's the only difference. We are all designed exactly the same way. It's just a matter of focus and some discipline to master awareness.

In my observation, it doesn't take long for us to tune back into our vibratory natures. I received a beautiful email recently from a young woman who was attending one of my meditation courses. She had attended three sessions and very excitedly informed me that by the third week she realised that she was able to sense when someone in her work team was not being completely honest about his or her work. Untruths and bald-faced lies have very distinct dissonant vibrations. With this new level of information that she could feel, she was able to gently steer conversations towards areas that weren't being addressed and, perhaps more admirably, to examine her own management style for reasons why her employees felt the need to cover up issues in the first place.

Those vibrational fields extend far beyond the physical body, and time and space. One morning I woke early for my daily morning meditation and dawn run. I felt unsettled from the minute I opened my eyes. It was a similar feeling to what I feel when a big storm is building overhead. However, the day was calm and there were no triggers or events within my immediate field that would warrant such a feeling. It was persistent. I meditated on it and felt that there was indeed something coming that was just outside my boundary of immediate awareness. I could feel the vibration of it; a storm was brewing. I went for my run and braced myself. Two hours later, on the way home, I received a call from the mother of one of my daughter's classmates regarding a huge misunderstanding between our daughters. The mother had misinterpreted something her daughter had told her, which had created the assumption that my daughter was in serious error. Of course, my maternal instinct reared! Every cell in my body demonstrated the storm I had felt when I woke earlier that day. My energy body had already sensed what my conscious mind was in no way able to perceive hours earlier. The vibration of this woman's thoughts and assumptions regarding my daughter had travelled beyond time and space. Within three phone calls, the matter was resolved, and the trigger-happy mother had realised (with softness) that her daughter had drummed up events for sympathy and attention. The storm passed.

Every Wednesday I hold remote intuitive healing sessions for clients based outside of Singapore or unable to come to the clinic. They involve flowing reiki energy to the client and intuitively reading information that is relevant to the client's enquiry. I am constantly amazed each week as I connect from the little island of Singapore, in the middle of the planet, with clients based in the UK, India, the United States, Australia, New Zealand, Ukraine, France, Canada, and elsewhere. This vibrating informational energy operates outside physical connections. It suggests that we have a shared spiritual reality. It is the same mechanism that is at play when I can accurately inform a client of a move, a pregnancy, a new love entering his or her life, a potential danger, or the presence of a very jealous person in his or her life, for example, when the client does not have the current perception or even an inkling of such events at the time of the session, yet they are confirmed in the days, weeks, sometimes months that follow.

That is because all possible and probable events also have vibrations. They all exist in this invisible field of creation at once. Those events or phenomena that have the greatest probability of expression vibrate more strongly than other possible events yet to play out. With a honed focus on feeling vibrating informational energy and allowing it to emerge into the conscious mind, the field of 'sensed intelligence' expands considerably, even to the other side of the world or into the future. This is intuition. And moreover, with mastery of our energy bodies, we are able to emanate generative vibrations that influence outcomes. This is spirited living!

Coming to understand our own vibrational frequencies, how they change, how to recognise dissonance, and how to recognise the signature vibrations of elements, people, situations, illnesses, and truth connects us with broader and broader fields of vibrating energy far beyond the physical senses.

One's present awareness is a vibration. When directed through a still, non-dissonant mind, it can be put to use to activate the vibrational body, to emanate coherent vibrations to affect the field of experience, and to receive information and energy from the vibrational universe. Aren't we immense? So how do we activate and work with the vibrational body, the energy body? First, we need to understand its design.

CHAPTER 11

# You're a Living Rainbow

The human energy body can anchor energy, information, and possibilities from the invisible realm into the material plane, and it can also work with energy, information, and experiences from the material plane to affect the invisible plane, because we exist in both. While the physical body is a visible mass, the energy body, or subtle body, is invisible and felt. When the energy body is balanced and its vibration is raised, we can move our awareness into these wider fields of spirit. We can perceive, and bring back to the ground, wisdom and insights in our ordinary lives, and we can seed the energy field of our lives and create different or new life experiences on the ground. We are designed to consciously create.

The energy body links our physical (visible) and energetic (invisible) forms and capabilities, and we are 'knotted together' at the chakras. If perspectives are the keycodes to the mind and beliefs, then the chakras are key codes to the energy body.

The word 'chakra' means 'wheel', and the energy body is said to contain hundreds, if not thousands, of chakras (energetic centres), depending on which ancient framework you are exploring. The chakras are linked by meridians, called the nadis (energy pathways), and there are hundreds, if not thousands, of these too. This intersecting energy grid of the human system feeds through and intersects seven main energy centres located in the cerebral-spinal system, and through three main nadis: Ida, Pingala, and Sushumna. Many frameworks outline other chakras outside of the contained body that extend into the earth below us and upwards into more subtle dimensions. What I have found is that by getting to know, activate, and raise the energy in the seven chakras contained within the physical form, the rest just follow suit. It's easier to work with the main seven because we can sense their activity and resonance physically.

The seven chakras contained within the physical body resonate with lots of different forms of energy and are probably best known for their connection and identification with light energy and, more specifically, the colours of the rainbow. The base corresponds with the colour red. The sacral vibrates orange; the solar plexus, yellow. The heart vibrates in green; the throat, light blue; the third eye, dark blue; and the crown, purple. We are living rainbows of energy. In the natural world, a rainbow is formed when the white light from the sun refracts through water molecules in the atmosphere and diverges into its parts, much like the science experiments most of us did as kids, when we shone white light through prisms to make rainbows on the other side. The way I like to explain the chakras in our own energy bodies is the same. When the unified white light of the spirit refracts through the watery vessel of the physical aspect, it also diverges into its parts—split beams.

The human energy body is a bridge between the visible and invisible realms. The ancient descriptions of the seven chakras contained within the physical system, and the overall energy system that they are a part of, perfectly match our modern anatomical descriptions of the central nervous system and nerve ganglia. The invisible aspects of the chakras and their connection with our thoughts, feelings, and behaviours align with accepted models of Western psychology. My all-time favourite writer on this is Anodea Judith. The signature energy of each chakra corresponds with the vibration of certain colours, sounds, mantras, shapes, planets, foods, and meditations, as well as specific functions and systems of the human body. Working with our chakra system allows us to maintain alignment and, therefore, flow, holistically. When we experience a physical illness, for example, we can choose to treat the physical symptom, which is, in essence, a message for our awareness that an imbalance exists. However, through the energy body, we can also see the mental, emotional, and spiritual causes of the imbalance and address them, which in turn transmutes the requirement for the physical messaging. In other words, we heal. It shows us what beliefs we are holding that have limited our experiences of spirited living, and it is through meditation, ritual, and inner practice that we can unearth and turn over those beliefs.

A beautiful example of this is in an experience I had with a private client, a ten-year-old girl who was on a journey with one of the most aggressive forms of leukaemia. Her mother contacted me about two years into her gruelling treatment because the nature of her chemotherapy was so intense that she was suffering severe anxiety when she knew that the next treatment was coming up. On our initial engagement, I showed her breathing techniques and meditations that she could put to use to calm her system before the treatments. Within a few sessions, she had the tools to deal with the treatments, and our sessions then turned to a focus on energy healing to deal with the side-effects. Her system was incredibly sensitive to energetic healing, and during every session she would slip into a deep sleep as her system set to work to restore itself.

Over the ensuing months, her system started to gain strength. Her hair started to grow back. Her vitality returned, and even though she had another year of treatment in front of her, she was able to return to school after several years of home schooling by her amazing mum. Despite feeling much better, she asked her mum whether I could continue to see her regularly. I was thrilled to do so. Dwelling with such a courageous, authentic soul is a privilege and a pleasure.

I introduced her to sound therapy—that is, bathing her body in tones from crystal sound tubes that corresponded with various chakras. Because her system was so sensitive, she absolutely loved it. Before one session, I could sense she was wobbly. I didn't know the reason why, but when I thought of her, I could feel a wobble. I messaged her mum, as was our routine, to ensure that her daughter was okay for a session. She was. I then asked her mum to check which part of the body her daughter had been most aware of in the last week. The answer was her legs and feet. They had been aching for days and felt weak when climbing stairs and even walking short distances. The legs and feet are correspondent with the solar plexus chakra (called 'Maniupura'). This is the centre of our self-esteem, personal power and volition. Her legs and feet were indicating a hit to her self-esteem. When we chatted, she admitted that she had been comparing herself to the girls at school, and with teary eyes and a quavering voice, she said, 'I just wish none of this ever happened to me.'

Her mum and I reminded her that whilst her experience was intense, it had taught her skills that many people never learn or master in their entire lives. She had learnt to master fear and pain. She had learnt to allow her body to heal. She had learnt an incredible amount of biological science and understood that perhaps, just perhaps, this was all going to be put to use one day. I reminded her in any case that comparison is a futile game—especially comparison of hardships, because they are all unique to the experiencer and we can never know the depths of others' suffering. What we can do, though, is focus on our own games, our strengths, our attitudes, and our abilities to be whole.

A little smile emerged as I explained all this, and she remembered a conversation she had recently had with her counsellor. She was asked what she would like to do with her life in the meeting, and without any hesitation she said she was going to be a children's cancer specialist. She just hadn't made the connection that her own experience would make her perhaps one of the finest, because she had a very deep knowledge and experience of what it's actually like to heal from such a huge disharmony. And with a cheeky glint, she added, 'And I won't need to study for years at medical school … because I know so much already!' With that, the pain in her legs and feet subsided.

Meditating on the chakras and their corresponding colours, forms, and meanings enables us to accept an expanded sense of self. The chakras activate and spin when we connect our meditative awareness to them, and they reveal the invisible causes and roots of our perceived smallness.

The main chakras are common to all streams of yoga (and interestingly are also aspects of many shamanic frameworks), and we benefit today from thousands of years of wisdom and practice which define the chakras and nadis, and the movement and flow of energy, or prana (vital life force). Yoga teaches that the chakras' ebb and flow, can be underactive or overactive, that they appear as spinning discs, and that they are affected by spiritual and intentional chanting and other sounds, specific postures, colours, focused attention, and a knowledge of their nature. Knowledge is best attained through practice. I encourage my students to work with one chakra at a time; to intentionally engage with its correspondent energies, elements, and colours, and to journal what they realise. The chakras are intelligent, and they teach us when we move our awareness into them.

Another beautiful way to learn about our energy bodies is through the wilderness and, especially, trees. Trees hold a beautiful circuitry between the invisible energies (sunlight, atmospheric pheromones, and so forth) and the visible earth. They do for the wild planet what the human energy system is able to do for the human collective. They draw energy down from the sun and atmosphere and convert it into growth and new matter, and they draw up useful material from the earth to sustain growth. They shed material that no longer serves into the earth to be recycled into new growth for themselves and the forest. They offer unconditionally their bounty of shade, beauty, fruits, and seeds to all. They share a very similar central nervous system and intelligence to ours. They communicate to all living creatures around them and through vast distances in the forest via their root systems, fungi networks, pheromones, and other slightly more mysterious means that point to a shared consciousness. Scientists have observed that the energy system of a tree shows signs of stress and awareness when the tree is being felled or when a fire approaches. And studies show that trees of the same species that may be scattered throughout the forest, kilometres from the endangered tree, show signs of stress and awareness of a threat at the same time. In lab tests, some plants respond energetically to simply the intention of a threat, which suggests a connection between the invisible aspects of our energy fields, our thoughts, and the energy systems of plants.

In Native American shamanism, trees are called our one-legged brothers. The energetic signature of a tree can also assist the connection and strength of our own spiritual circuitry. Spending time meditating under trees—base to root, spine to trunk, crown to canopy, with the intention of receiving its medicine—is a potent and enjoyable activity.

There's a reason why the tree is referenced as a common symbol of the human spiritual experience. Buddha achieved enlightenment under his bodhi tree, the prophets of the Torah came from the Jesse tree, the Tree of Knowledge of Good and Evil grew in the centre of Eden, and Christ was crucified on a tree. Odin, too, died on a tree, and Kabbalah's framework for our spiritual circuitry is the Tree of Life. A beautiful student and friend of mine, Tine, is a seasoned midwife. During a session on connection with trees and what they can teach us, she told me that the network of life-sustaining meridians that link the life force of mother to child within the human placenta, when held to the light, reveal an almost perfect Tree of Life symbol. As we spiral into form within the womb for nine months, we gaze at and are sustained by a tree. The trees teach us about the correspondences between our own energy system and the signature vibrations and aspects of the elements in the wilderness. Understanding this gives us a pallet of energies to work with.

A tree takes root in the silent darkness of the Earth, which corresponds with Muladhara, the first chakra. This base chakra is our taproot into the here and now. Its energy corresponds with the felt experience of security, belonging, tribe, and blood memory. It is all about trust, stability, and presence. It is our spiritual soil bed. The root (our consciousness) emerges from the seed and secures our presence in this life by reaching upwards. This movement is enabled by water, the energy of the second chakra, Swathisthana, our centre for flow, movement, relationship, and feelings. Once the movement raises the seedling above the soil and into the light, it receives heat from the sun and determination for growth. This is the energy of Maniupura, our third chakra, the element of fire. Finally the seedling transforms into a magnificent tree and extends its green offering far and wide. Anahata, the powerful heart centre, corresponds with the colour green. As it matures, the system is able to convert greater and greater amounts of light into its offerings of fruits, shade, beauty, and oxygen. The element that corresponds with our heart centres is, of course, air. The heart and higher chakras of the throat (Vishhuddhi), third-eye (Ajna), and Crown (Sahasrara) are our power centres for spiritual expression, interconnectedness, and expansion. The entire system works as one. Once we have connected our primal centres of being and movement with the fire of our will, it culminates in the enormous, expansive capacity of the heart, our connection with spirit, and our creative expression.

And trees have spirits! In finding a favourite tree, admiring its beauty, spending time in its shade and connecting with your own invisible self in its presence, you will discover that a subtle relationship develops and the most incredible revelations start to flow whilst in meditation in its presence. This is facilitated by the correspondences between your system and the that of the tree.

The same can be observed of all wilderness. There is a symbolic, living, and direct dialogue that takes place when we spend time in nature and have a cultivated the capacity to sense and observe. The wild does far more than provide the human species with all of its physical needs. Yes, if you think about it, all of them are derived from the wild, and most from the botanical realm. The wild is a broad and ancient spirit, a harmonious field of energy and information that is responsive to and feeds the human spirit in all forms of vibrating energy and information, including colours and light, sound, medicines that heal and expand consciousness, and the very air we breathe.

# CHAPTER 12

# Raising Your Rainbow

Once you have tuned into your energy (subtle) body, that connection and perception remains. It's a bit like riding a bike or finding the right receiver frequency on a walkie-talkie. Aside from the sheer delight of palpably sensing the flow of life force within your system, the chakras provide a framework to understanding what's rippling through our lives and how to engage with it. The more you practise meditations and inner practices that attune you to this life force, the more refined your senses become for detecting it. Around 80 per cent of people can feel it on their first attempt in my classes, and another 10 per cent on their second. The other ten either can't feel it at all, but many may perceive it in other ways, such as strong perceptions of inner colour and light. With practice you are then able to tune into another's energy body, sense the imbalances, and direct vital life force to the person's system. This is the art of energy healing in all its modalities. Energetic healing is enjoying a revival, and we now have some fascinating current research that captures and proves its efficacy.

One of the pleasures of living in Singapore is the cultural openness to all forms of spiritual expression and expertise. I used to be part of a team of beautiful reiki healers who volunteered their time each fortnight to offer reiki treatments to the residents of the Red Cross Centre for the Disabled. The involvement is by the request of the families, and the staff welcome the group each fortnight, as they have observed the calming, healing effect a team of energy healers creates in the space. The centre's residents are highly responsive to the reiki, which involves the healers placing their hands close to the recipients' bodies, in alignment with certain chakra points. We were not allowed physical touch in these sessions; however, it is not required. I was amazed each time I volunteered at the centre how radical the effect of the energy healing was. I am sure it was because disabilities had enclosed the residents in bound bodies and a very bounded life—often, for the most part, a dormitory bed and room—and they are therefore protected from the frenetic distractions of the modern life outside. Every recipient we saw as a team was clearly able to sense into their invisible side and feel the energy. It was incredible to watch, as the current connected, the immediate easing of muscles and deepening of the breath.

Agitated rocking and wailing gently stopped, and stillness was established, every time.

In my private energy sessions, I work my way down the client's chakra points. With permission, I prefer to touch their bodies, although again it is not necessary; it's more my way of establishing a deeper connection, and we all need more touch generally. Each chakra responds differently and pulls through the healing energy to put it to use, and each chakra holds an incredible amount of information about the client's current patterns and denser energies held through limited beliefs or patterns that are producing the requirement for healing.

There are lots of different ways to engage with our chakras, such as through dance, yoga, and chakra-balancing therapies, for example. Because they are energy centres, they are also activated by other forms of correspondent energy, such as colours and sounds. However, I have found that the easiest and most efficient way to connect with these resonant centres of our energy bodies is through meditative awareness. Just like our physical bodies, our energy bodies are highly responsive to meditative awareness. By entering into meditation and leaning all of our awareness into a particular chakra, we can actually feel it stir, rise in energy, and then send information into the conscious mind.

Aside from feeling fantastic because of the practice itself, our physical bodies heal and become whole the more we do this. It opens access to the game of spirited living and creation. Working with the chakras and correspondent energies is very powerful.

I have included at the end of this book some basic tables that list correspondent colours, mantras, asanas, minerals, herbs, and foods for each of the chakras. They are very basic, but they are enough to give you a pallet to experiment with to get to know your chakras. Working consciously with the energies of your subtle body will then inform all your inner practice.

Each chakra also has an elemental correspondence, and this is how I engage with them the most, through elemental connection and colour. Muladhara, at the base, is correspondent with the colour red and element earth. Swathisthana, at the sacrum, is correspondent with the colour orange and the element of water. Maniupura, at the solar plexus, is correspondent with the colour yellow and the element of fire. Anahata, at the heart, is correspondent with the colour green and the element of air. The higher three chakras are correspondent with finer, non-physical elements: Vishhuddhi, at the throat, is correspondent with light blue and sound; Ajna, at the eyebrow centre, is correspondent with dark blue and thought; and Sahasrara, at the crown, is correspondent with violet and ether.

When, for example, I am seeking presence to stabilise a project and to then gain traction with it, I enter rituals that connect me with the Earth and focus the intent within my base chakra. When I am broadening relationships and networks and desiring greater flow of ideas, clients, and healing energies, I connect my inner practices with water and work through my second chakra. When I am seeking to transmute a lower vibrational pattern—uncertainty based in fear, for example—I use a fire ritual and engage my third chakra, holding the vibration of clearing, transmutation, and purification in this centre. When I am seeking higher vibrational resonances—unconditional love, forgiveness, gratitude, or awe, for example—I will engage with air, breathwork, and heart-centred practices.

Perceiving the energy body is a happy outcome of meditation. It is of course there, vibrating away through our bodies, minds, feelings, and spirits, but we just don't sense it, because we're not aware of it or we're otherwise distracted with the shadow show of our modern lives. Some of the indicators of the energy body rising can be felt after your first good meditation sit. A resonance in the palms and fingertips; a sensation of energy rising up the spine; a deeper, longer, silent breath; a buzzing under the scalp at the crown; perceptions of inner colour and symbols; and a feeling of an ever-expanding heart space are all universal signposts of the energy body coming into your awareness and your ability to affect its resonance.

Resonance is the frequency or vibration emitted by you, the field of your energy body. It is at its strongest when the mind, heart, and body are aligned and present in the current moment. When there is disharmony or imbalance in the mind/body/energy system, our resonance is dulled or otherwise affected. Our fields of resonance are strongest closest to our physical presence, but they expand well beyond this and are not limited by physical space or time. The part of one's resonant field that's closest to the body, the aura, can be captured on biofeedback cameras, and they shift and change depending on what information is dominating the etheric field. I found a place in Singapore with such a camera and started to track my inner practices with aura photos, and the results were both beautiful and very accurate. After certain focused workshops, healing practices, or visioning practices with my teacher, my aura became very bright and wide, rippling with very different colours specific to the practices.

Through mastering meditation, we not only move our physical systems—brain, heart, gut, body chemistry—into balance and vitality, which in turn enables deeper meditation, but we also bring into coherence the 'spiritual dynamics' of visioning (brain), high-resonance emotional states (heart) and choice (belly), and this is when we start to shift into spirited living.

The higher and more coherent the resonance, the wider our awareness can perceive vibrating information and translate it into conscious thought. The higher and more coherent our resonance, the clearer that information signals through our intuitive senses. The higher and more coherent our resonance, the more able we are to emanate organising patterns of energy and consciously create our experienced reality. We are entering the world of spirit dynamics now— juicy, magical, and innate to your dazzling design!

# PART 2
# Spirit Dynamics

# CHAPTER 13

# Mirror, Mirror on the Wall

How you vibrate is what the universe
echoes back to you in every moment.
—Panache

We are creating our life experiences all the time. However, without a deep, felt, and conscious connection with the causal field of our being—our spirit—we are creating life unconsciously. The human energy body is activated and raised through our awareness. When it is raised, we communicate and consciously connect with spirit. The first step in accessing this flow and all the beauty and ease that it brings is to reclaim our awareness from the blinding binds of busy modern life and rotate it inwards to where all the real action is taking place. This doesn't mean we disassociate from our modern lives—quite the contrary. The challenge is to reset how we perceive our lives and how we engage with them.

Our life experience is our teacher and our greatest opportunity to express creatively. It emanates from our inner state, reflecting back to us the beliefs and resonance of our energy bodies. And when we are out of alignment with our truth, when our unconscious beliefs and fears are influencing what we are experiencing, we perceive those experiences as working counter to us as blocks, bad luck, or fate. Moreover, the emotional energy that judging these experiences generates, which we so easily label as 'anger', 'frustration', and 'dislike', is actually a reservoir of energy made available by our system to disrupt the prevailing pattern and emanate a new one. The most efficient way to reclaim your ability to witness what's actually happening, free from unconscious biases, and to direct the energy generated from it is through the art of meditation.

Metaphysics is the study of coherence between our individual vibrational fields and wider and wider vibrational fields of life. When the heart (emotional field), mind (conscious and unconscious), and choices (will in action) are aligned, we send out an harmonic vibration into this field and experience life correspondent to that vibration. In other words, we consciously create.

When we are not aligned, we create a dissonant vibration, which is then experienced as dissonant experiences. We are shown the dissonance 'outside of us'—triggers, obstacles, illness, and so forth—as a means of signalling the dissonance within to our conscious minds, to then take action on our inner ground.

Life is a magic mirror, yet for many of us, we have grown up believing that the reflection in the mirror is reality. We judge that reflection constantly, without the inner understanding that we generate the light show of the reflection. We are constantly waiting for the reflection to smile at us first.

Some of you may be asking at this point, Well, if we are causal to our life experiences, then how and why would a little girl manifest something as intense and challenging as blood cancer, for example? And the same question may be asked of any person who has suffered trauma, chronic illness, serious accidents, and so forth. To be honest, I don't have an exact answer to this question, but I do have some ideas on it from what I have experienced in sessions. Karma, lineage trauma, past lives, and collective energies (like what we are experiencing with the pandemic), influence our reality in very real ways. Yet it still all boils down to what your perspective, belief system, and emanations are doing right now. It is this that heals and positively influences life experience and contributes a very different reality and power into that karmic field, family lineage, and the collective.

Another way to express this idea is to say that we exist in a hologram of potentialities, intricate weaves of information in the form of vibrating energy. We are not separate from anything. All is interconnected—or, rather, all is reflections and refractions of light. Depending on what we are focusing on (either consciously or unconsciously) and feeding with our life forces through thoughts, feelings and actions, these potentialities start to gather into possibilities and then probabilities of phenomenal experience. In my energy sessions, I can psychically perceive this tunnelling within and around a client. A potential move to a new home or country; a very new conception even before the mother is aware she is pregnant; a successful upcoming IVF cycle, months before conception; a new career opportunity arriving unexpectedly; and a potential misunderstanding or conflict are all vibrating and changing potentialities. The greater the application of mind and energy of the client (even if unconsciously) to any of these potentialities, the stronger the probability of the occurrence. Nothing is 'fixed' or 'fated.' At any moment, we can change the trajectory of this tunnelling into our phenomenal experience.

Healing and manifestation happen when we master our awareness and resonance, when we bring to light what we're really buying into and what we're charging with the voltage of our energy bodies, our repeated thoughts, and our patterned behaviours. Being occurs when we start to consciously choose what we are 'giving life to.' With mastered awareness and coherent and raised resonance (feeling), we transform potential into possibility and then into probability, and we're guided into and through the creation dance by our intuition. Because the potentialities are not yet experienceable and are therefore out of reach of our mundane senses, our intuition is tapping the dynamics of our field of potential and is constantly guiding us.

So it's worth jumping into what intuition is. Far from being some witchy, rare skill born into a handful of pure bloodlines on the planet and exclusive to a few, intuition is your birth right. You are born with all eight intuitive senses and an intelligent, vibrating system that signals through all of them. You just need to remember how to use them—consciously, that is!

# CHAPTER 14

# Intuition—Your Fantastic Living, Vibrating Compass

For some, the concept of intuition is a spooky woo-woo idea belonging to the New Age movement; for others it doesn't go far beyond interoception—physical intelligence or body-knowing. Yet for many of us, intuition is our primary guidance system, our operating inner compass. We are naturally trained towards our physical senses mainly for survival. And in our modern lives, the training and wisdom of accessing our inner senses, our intuition, sadly exists only in very few cultures and families. Our addiction to the perception of physical phenomena has many of us disbelieving in the existence of information and communication beneath the more obvious sensory stimulation and resultant thoughts. If only one fifth of our being is visible or physical and four-fifths—our thoughts, feelings, energy fields, and spirits—is invisible, it defies nature to assume that we are equipped with senses that perceive only the physical. We also have senses that perceive the non-physical. All of us have them—eight known ones, in fact (and probably many more subtle senses yet to be defined)—and they are communicating to our awareness all the time.

Intuition is the natural function of sensing and interpreting the vibratory field of energy and information through the human system. Rather than being an 'up and out there' kind of motion of consciousness, intuition is more a 'down and in' kind of motion. In Aboriginal shamanism, it is called the 'strong eye', and what it requires is present awareness, established abilities of witnessing and detachment, and an ability to open one's own gateway between one's conscious awareness and one's 'deep mind', and then to interpret the language this information uses as it rises into awareness. Intuitive information comes through in symbols, synchronicities, and sensations in the energy body, and it takes its reference points from our own personal libraries of references and experiences. More on this soon, but first let's dip into what the intuitive senses are.

The siddhis are the spirit senses that boot up along the journey to becoming spirited. In the West, many of them are called 'the clairs.' They are regarded in yoga and other schools as the inner aspect of the outer senses. So, for example, clairvoyance, or the ability of inner visioning or receiving information visually in pictures and symbols in the mind, is connected to the outer sense of sight—that is, taking photons and patterning and movement in through the optic nerve and having it translated by the brain. And similarly, clairaudience, the faculty by which we hear intuitive guidance spoken in words or in sounds within us, is connected to our outer sense of hearing sounds coming in through the ear canal and through the mechanism of physical hearing. What's important to remember here is that the inner senses and the outer senses are actually one thing. They're just operating on opposite poles of the one sense: inner hearing within, outer hearing without, and so on. There are eight recognised siddhis that relate to the intuitive senses, amongst several others. I'm going to go through each of these and give examples from client sessions to give an idea of how they can be expressed. When perceiving intuitive information, I always pay more attention to the information that is signalling through more than one intuitive sense.

In my observation of my intuitive healing students and working with other psychics, I have determined that we all have one inner sense that is particularly stronger than the others. However, as we consciously move into spirited living, the others senses become more obvious and useful as well.

## Clairvoyance—Psychic Sight

Clairvoyance, psychic sight, or the second sight is probably the most recognised of the intuitive senses. Clairvoyance is my main inner sense. This is the faculty by which intuitive information is displayed within the mind's eye as images, scenes, and symbols. As it is multilayered, every aspect of the inner image holds information either symbolically or literally. Here's a simple example. A beautiful woman came in to see me for guidance. She was feeling the desire to leave her current career and try something new. She didn't tell me what direction she wished to take. All she said was that she felt stuck and she didn't know which way to go. When I put my hands on her crown, I immediately 'saw' an image in my inner vision of her holding a painting, and she was surrounded by members of her family that were all wearing academic cloaks and gowns, as though they were at a graduation ceremony. They all looked very happy, and she was looking down and holding the painting and looking very sad and sort of shameful. Her head was bowed low. There was other information that came through in the session, but when I spoke with her at the end, I told her the image that I saw. She immediately had a release and started crying. She said that she came from a family of very highly educated academics. Both of her parents were academics, and her siblings all ended up following academic fields, but she never finished her degree and always felt a degree of shame about that. Her real passion was in visual arts. The symbolic scene that I saw in my inner vision held a lot of information that was very relevant for her. And once we understood that her confusion and her lack of clarity were based around a vibration of shame, we could then set to work to clear that. This particular session also involved information coming through as clairsentience, or empathic feeling. I 'felt' her shame.

## Clairsentience—Psychic sensation

Clairsentience involves a clear physical feeling. Information is perceived as a physical sensation within the intuitive realm, which doesn't belong to the clairsentient person but which signals relevant information through his or her physical body about an energetic pattern within another person.

Some of the more common examples of clairsentience that I have experienced are as follows: When a client has been keeping silent on an issue or the dynamic of a relationship rather than speaking his or her truth and this is the cause of his or her issue (usually unconscious), I will spontaneously start coughing, which can be a weird experience in a session. Once the energy has cleared from the client's throat chakra, my coughing spontaneously stops. It's as if my body is assisting in the clearance of the dissonant energy held there. If a client has undiagnosed precancerous or cancerous activity in breast tissue, a fizzing, sparking electrical feeling presents in my own.

In one interesting experience, a client came to see me with an ongoing stomach infection due to a bacteria that she had picked up in her travels. She had been suffering chronic diarrhoea for weeks. When I placed my hands on her lower stomach, my own stomach cramped, and then a rush moved through my own body. I had to leg-it to the bathroom mid-session. My body had cleared for her what her system was too weak to clear for itself. I wasn't a fan of that one!

## Claircognizance—Psychic Knowing

Another inner sense is claircognizance, which is a clear knowing. Again, this is a very interesting and beautiful inner sense. They all are! I find that this is usually the inner sense that pairs with other inner senses and that strongly signals in my spiritual coaching. I have the feeling and knowing of the relevance and importance of certain information or guidance to the healing process of my clients. The information 'drops' into my mind as if released from a great height. It has a very different feeling to one of my own thoughts. Once it arrives, it establishes as if it's information that I have always known. Claircognizance has a particular feeling to it. It ignites the energy body too, like a ripple of vibration that knocks out all doubt and fills the mind and heart with a calm certainty.

A woman came in to see me as she was suffering from

several very advanced autoimmune diseases. Her life experience was a litany of different medical practitioners trying various forms of intense Western medications and therapies, yet her body refused to heal. Her whole adult life was defined by being sick. And when she came to the healing rooms and I greeted her with a 'Hi, how are you?' she launched into a well-laid script of specialists' names, medications, pains, symptoms, and body shaming. She identified almost exclusively with what was wrong. There was an immense story built upon her illness. In this session, she was expecting to receive the reiki to dissipate the symptoms of her autoimmune disease. I explained to her that intuitive guidance is about revealing the true underlying causes of illnesses. The illnesses in her body were signalling a deeper energy grid that she was holding. This was quite an intense session. There was a lot of information that came through on each of her chakras, but the causal one had a very high voltage; I could feel it.

When I 'saw' what was going on in her body and the cause for her autoimmune disease, I had, without a doubt, a very clear determination and knowing that this was it. I put my hands on her sacral chakra, Swathisthana, and I immediately had an inner vision of her as a little girl around the age of seven or eight, cowering in the dark in a little girl's bedroom. In my body, I felt the emotion or vibration of sheer terror. Standing at her bedroom door was a man who I knew was her father, and standing just behind his left shoulder was a faceless man I couldn't see. That combination of several different inner senses, the chakra that was communicating to them, and the voltage and the clarity of the information was undeniable. Her autoimmune issues were stemming from childhood sexual trauma.

It was a tricky conversation to have, and I went very gently and started off by asking her if her father had hurt her in any way when she was little. She immediately started to cry, so I knew we were close. She confirmed that around the age of eight, which is what I saw in the vision, her father was finally arrested and placed in jail because he had tried to strangle her to death. She lived with her mother, and both had suffered massive physical abuse and trauma. Her energy body, even as a grown woman, still held the vibration of terror. I then told her that given the information I obtained from her sacrum, there was also sexual trauma, and I gently asked, 'Did your father ever sexually abuse you?'

She immediately stepped back. 'Nope, nope, nope, he never abused me. He beat me up, but he never sexually abused me.' I could see her starting to lock down.

Very gently, I said, 'I saw another man who's connected with your father in some way. I think he's involved in this. Was there an uncle or—'

Again she released a huge amount of held emotion through a great deal of sobbing and tears, and she confirmed that her father's business partner would regularly rape her whenever he visited and drank with her father. Once we uncovered the causal vibration that was creating this massive expression of self-destruction within her body, we were then able to set about working on a healing process. Given that it was such a long-held and well-buried trauma, I also recommended that she see a trauma expert to thoroughly and safely unpack that memory to fully release it from her body.

## Clairaudience—Psychic Hearing

Another very interesting inner sense is clairaudience. This sense has been slower to present for me in healing sessions because I have always tended towards inner sight and inner feeling and knowing. However, interestingly, it is one of the main senses that people in spirit communicate with me. A beautiful example of this is the time when a woman who had low vitality came to see me. She was a health nut herself, so she understood detoxing, and she was going through a very serious process of eliminating heavy metals from her body, which I didn't know at the time. Yet she just couldn't seem to make that final step into healing, into wellness. During the session, when I had my hands on her sacrum, I could feel a voltage there. There was a high flow of energy in the chakra, so I knew that I was on a causal spot, and I leant my awareness into this part of her system. Initially I heard in my inner sense a rhythm, and it sounded a bit like 'dah-dah … dah-dah-dah … dah-dah, dah-dah … dah-dah-dah … dah-dah.' This rhythm became louder and louder within me. I focussed all of my awareness into her sacrum and into this rhythm, and slowly the beat started to form words and became clearer and clearer. Her sacrum was conveying vibratory information that was being translated through my sense of clairaudience. The words formed in my 'inner ear': 'The loss of the life not lived. The loss of the life not lived.' I knew this client was holding some form of dense vibration—guilt, grief, shame, or a combination of these—around being pregnant and losing a baby. It felt to me that she'd been holding it for a long time—so long that it had become a rhythmic pulse of dense vibration throughout her life and throughout her body.

This required a lot of tact and diplomacy in the debrief after the session. My feeling was that she'd had an abortion, but I decided to ask her whether she had experienced a miscarriage in her younger years. She said, 'No, I've never had a miscarriage, but I found it very difficult to fall pregnant and have my son.' She had needed to go through several rounds of IVF to conceive her son, who at the time was thirteen years old. Yet despite the negation on a miscarriage, the messaging from her sacrum was clear. The cause of her continued low vitality was an underlying dense vibration, held for many years, around 'the loss of the life not lived.' I had to raise it with her, so I shared with her the words her sacral chakra was rhythmically pulsing into her body and into my inner senses. The message was immediately confirmed with a big, spontaneous movement of emotion. The tears burst through in big, healing waves. She was astounded. She said that the abortion had been her secret since she was a twenty-year-old woman and she was now close to fifty. Not even her parents knew, and her husband didn't know, but as a younger woman she was not in a position to raise a child; nor was she in a family culture that would have accepted the pregnancy. She said that she held enormous guilt around it and that she thought about that lost baby, that loss of the life not lived, every single day. She was pulsing guilt into her energy body every single day for the last thirty years, and as a result, that vibration was not allowing her system to lift and to heal and to move back into its original design of health.

In a wonderful spirit contact with a client, her mother came through loud and clear. She had an intense love and closeness with her daughter that I could feel (clairempathy), and I was also shown several items belonging to my client (clairvoyance) that validated the mother's presence with the client. But beautifully (and initially confusingly), her mother spoke into my inner hearing the word 'potato.' It was as clear as if the client in the room had spoken it. And with it I had an unwavering knowing (clairgnosis) that this was some kind of a nickname. But when I relayed this to the client, she couldn't recognise it. 'Did she call you something like "my little sweet potato" … or anything like that? I asked, feeling perplexed because the word 'potato' had been so clearly relayed. The client came up with nothing, so we decided to put that piece of information aside and focus on what came through that was personal and evidential. To my delight (and slight relief), two days later I received a message from the client. She had relayed her session to her father over the phone, who confirmed that the mother's nickname for him was Daaloo. The Hindi word for 'potato' is '*Aaloo.*' This clever mum in spirit, who knew that I didn't speak Hindi, gave me the closest-sounding word to the nickname she used for her husband and gave me the 'knowing' that it was a nickname. The father and daughter pieced together the rest, and that very conversation gave great peace and joy to her father as well.

## Clairtangency—Psychic Touch

Another inner sense is the sense of clairtangency, which is clear touching. This is a very subtle inner sense, but once you connect with it and you trust it, it's very revealing. The first experience I had with clairtangency was with a woman who was the mother of a client and was visiting Singapore. Her daughter was keen for her to experience a session with me. Her mother was inclined to flat moods for long periods of time, and she was keen to understand why. There was a lot of information in this woman: connections to the loss of her first husband, whom she was still deeply in love with; guilt around her second marriage; and not having the same degree of love for her current husband, all of which was playing into her sense of vitality and joy. But the clairtangency triggered when I had my hands on her lower stomach. It was at the changeover line between Maniupura, the third chakra, and Swathisthana, the second chakra, so I couldn't clearly determine which chakra was communicating with me. But in any case, when I put my hands there and very lightly touched over her clothes, no pushing or massage or anything like that, I had the very distinct feeling of small, hard balls underneath my hands. They felt like golf balls. They varied in size but were moving. There was an activity present. They felt as if they were growing. I ran the reiki energy to that space, and I was filled with a sense of urgency.

At the end of the session, we spoke about the emotional information that had come through, which she validated, and we talked about ways she could bring all of herself to the present moment and at the same time honour her past. I then asked her whether she felt well in the bottom of her stomach or in her uterus and her womb, and she said, 'I have had a few tummy issues, but you know, I just get on with things and don't let it bother me too much.'

I had a very strong sense of urgency about this, and I said to her, 'I think that when you go home, you need to check in with your doctor and ask them if they'll do an ultrasound of your tummy and your pelvic floor and your uterus and so on.' She promised she would and hopped on the plane home the following day. Four days later, I had a message from her daughter. Her mum did go in for a checkup, and the doctors found a series of aggressively growing tumours in the base of her stomach. They checked her into hospital straightaway, and she underwent surgery to remove them. In usui reiki there's an energy scan practitioners do called the Byosen method. It also engages clairtangency, amplified by the reiki energy. It's a method in which the practitioner slowly and carefully 'scans' the recipient's body from head to toe by moving the hands over each chakra. The felt vibration in the hands tilts and changes when the practitioner is over an important centre for the recipient's healing.

**Clairsalience—Psychic Smelling**

Another really interesting inner sense is clairsalience, which is the faculty of clear smelling. I haven't actually experienced clairsalience in a healing session, but I have experienced it when doing private coaching with a woman who was wanting to conceive a child. She had tried several rounds of IVF, and despite there being no medical reason why she wasn't conceiving, a pregnancy eluded her and her partner. She had a deep longing for a baby and decided on a spiritual approach. She was also putting herself under a time pressure too. She was only thirty-five, but she believed that if it didn't happen soon, it was never going to happen. I had been seeing her for about three weeks for meditation coaching and spiritual mentoring. It was the final session of a course that I offer women who are looking to fall pregnant called I Am Mother, which is about changing perspectives on their body and working with their desire and their longing to bring about the experience that they yearn for—motherhood.

This woman had a beautiful faith and prayed every day. We held our sessions in her prayer room, and her altar was always kept hidden behind a curtain. During the meditation with her this day, I had a very clear image of Sai Baba, the beautiful avatar and spiritual guru for many people of the Hindu faith and many others. After the meditation, I asked her whether she had a devotion to Sai Baba. She started laughing and pulled back the curtain of her altar to reveal a deep and abiding dedication to Sai Baba. She had Sai Baba photos and Sai Baba incense, and she prayed using Sai Baba chants. So I suggested that we go back into another meditation and call in Sai Baba. My plan was to petition him to guide her through the energetic shifts that needed to happen within her body to allow a baby to come through. And so we did this. We went into a very deep, beautiful meditation, and she chanted Sai Baba chants, which I don't know because they're in Sanskrit, but I could feel them. And then, right in the middle of the meditation, the whole room filled with a very distinct smell of wild jasmine. I could smell it as clearly as if there had been a bowl full of fresh jasmine somewhere on the altar. We came out of the meditation, and I asked her, 'Did you smell Jasmine?'

She said, 'Yes, I smelled it.'

I asked, 'What does that mean to you?'

She said, 'That is the signature scent of Sai Baba.'

Jasmine, when smelled psychically, is an affirmation for many of Sai Baba's devotees that he has indeed heard the call; he makes his presence known through the inner sense of clairsalience. That experience of smelling the jasmine was powerful enough for this woman to change her vibration, and a month later, she fell pregnant. She is now a very happy mama of a beautiful little girl.

My most consistent experience of clairsalience occurs when I am travelling. During a relatively recent trip to Scandinavia, my friend Kate and I arrived in Stockholm for a few days before continuing north-west all the way to Iceland. Kate is a very spiritual intuitive, and we love travelling together to ancient places, stone circles, and sacred sites as often as we can. Between us and our different inner senses, we're able to piece together stories and imprints held with the spaces, and we hold beautiful rituals together in these places.

Early one afternoon, we decided to walk through the old quarter, Gamla Stan, find a café, and book into some local walking tours to make the most of the few days we had there. As we stepped into Stortorget, the grand square, I had the feeling that my mouth had filled with blood. It turned my stomach, and I felt immediately nauseated. I could taste blood. I could smell blood. And a dense heaviness came down onto me as though someone had dropped a lead blanket from a great height. I groaned and said to Kate, 'There's a lot of blood in these stones.' The following night, our evening tour took us back through Gamla Stan and into

Stortorget. We learned that in 1520 the square had been the scene of a horrendous massacre of over eighty members of the Swedish nobility by the invading Danish king, Christian II. The story went that the executioner grew weary with the morning's beheadings and asked for lunch and a break. He subsequently got drunk. When he returned for the afternoon beheadings, his axe was blunt, as were his wits. He started to hack at his victims, and he escalated into a murderous rage when he was mocked by the Danish soldiers in the square. By the end of the afternoon, the square was strewn with body parts, blood, and a heavy horror. It started to rain, and the human debris blocked the ancient drains of the square, and it filled into a bloody bath. The incident is referred to in Swedish history as Stockholm's 'Blodbad' (blood bath), and it is believed that this is where the term was first coined. Without any knowledge of this history when I first stepped into the square, nearly five hundred years later, my psychic senses could distinctly smell and taste the blood, and feel the horror.

## Clairgustance—Psychic Taste

Clairgustance, or clear tasting, is certainly surprising and undeniable when it occurs. The first time I experienced it was in a session with a very proud man who came in to see me because his wife had suggested it. He was considering changing his career path, and he had low vitality. He made it very clear that he was very healthy and worked out all the time. I sensed there was a little too much emphasis on this from him. We went into the session, and there was a lot of information that came through at each of his chakras, but one that was very clear and took me quite by surprise was my inner taste. Within seconds of putting my hands on his stomach I had a very clear taste of whiskey in my mouth. The session was at ten o'clock in the morning, and it was as if I'd taken a sip of whiskey. I knew that this man was a drinker, and probably in denial of it, and that was where he was losing his power and his vitality. This was not much because of the alcohol, although we know that it's not great for the energy body and for the system because it overworks the liver and zaps us of energy, but it was more his dependence on it, which was where he was losing his life force. Also in that session, when I put my hands on his sacral area, I had very clear images of pornography. I have come to learn that an addiction to pornography has a very clear energy signature. This is not a judgement call on the use of pornography, but rather an observation of how it interferes with life force and vitality if an addiction to it has been established.

After the session, I asked him about drinking and how much he drank. I was even able to tell him what kind of whiskey he preferred. It was a beautiful, aged malt whiskey. He, of course, was astounded, and he admitted that he had got into the habit of drinking whiskey every night and that if he didn't have it, he missed it. I was able to guide him, to start to put all of his awareness on that and to maybe not give it up straight away, because that would have created a lot of dissonance in his system, but to pick two days in the week on which he would commit not to drink, just to give his body a bit of a break. Once those breaks were established, he could add more, until he could enjoy the whiskey occasionally rather than the whiskey enjoying him.

I also raised the pornography issue, and he denied it categorically. I could feel his whole body stiffen up when I spoke about it. I admit, it's pretty intense to hear from a woman you've met only an hour beforehand that you have an addiction to pornography that is draining your life force and adversely affecting how you are relating to your wife and life.

A day later, I received a beautiful email from him. He admitted that he did watch pornography every day, whilst drinking whisky; that intimacy with his wife had flatlined; and that he felt very ashamed about it. I wrote back to him and affirmed to him that I was not making a moral call of good or bad on pornography. The issue was that the reliance on it was dissipating the life force out of his system. About a month later, I heard back from him in an email. He said he had stopped drinking and had put himself on a 'pornography diet.' As a result, his vitality had returned, he was training more, and he felt alive again. That shift in vibration resulted in a new career path opening up for him.

I also reliably experience clairgustance when clients are low in minerals. When I place my hands on their stomachs in a session, if they are low in iron, potassium, or magnesium, I will have the distinct taste of metal in my mouth. If they are low in a particular vitamin or other substance, I will often 'see' the food type that contains the most of it. For example, if a client is low in vitamin C, I will see a wall of oranges. The intelligence of their systems are communicating through my inner senses as to what they need, but they are dull to their own bodies' messages.

## Clairempathy—Clear Feeling (Feeling What Another Is Feeling)

Clairempathy is the faculty of clear emotional feeling. This will often occur for me when I'm dealing with someone who has been exposed to quite a strong negative vibration from another person in his or her life, such as jealously or bullying. I especially experience clairempathy when I have my hands over my clients' hearts. As an example of this, another client of mine felt very lonely in Singapore and was finding it very difficult to make friends. When I put my hands on her heart, I felt the emotion of jealousy. I felt that she was surrounded by the vibration of jealousy. At the same time, I 'saw' her standing alone in a crowd with a gap around her, and other women were standing in a circle around her and being jealous of her. When I spoke with her about this after the session, she said it was true that ever since she was a little girl, she had had the experience of other women competing with her and feeling jealous. She realised during the coaching that because of this, she had created within herself an aversion to connection, especially with other women, for fear of not being seen for who she really was and for experiencing the very dense, quite nasty and disruptive vibration of jealousy. With this confirmed awareness, and combined with the energy healing, the jealousy started to dissolve, and a new approach to connection and friendships was established.

Interestingly, with clairempathy we are able to feel another's emotions as if they are our own. Many people who come in for sessions are highly empathic—that is, they are strongly affected by the emotional vibrations of others and collectives or groups. Since the COVID-19 pandemic began, I have seen more and more people come in with overwhelm. In their own lives, they are safe and well, yet they are filled with dread, fear, and hopelessness. They are experiencing the collective angst of the pandemic. This can be cleared from their systems, and with the right instruction on energetic cleansing and boundary maintenance, they are set right again. The dense vibrations of fear or anger, for example, can be very intense to experience when they come through the sense of clairempathy. Grief and heartbreak also tend to send me into floods of tears during sessions, and it takes a well-established 'witnessing capability' to remind myself that I am feeling what is in the client's heart, not my own. These emotions are powerful, and yet at the same time I believe it is my system, through empathy and expression, that is helping to ease them from the client's system.

Often I will feel through clairempathy the possibility that is available to a person. It feels like expectation and possibility, even if the client is yet unaware of the change about to happen in his or her life. A beautiful example of this may be seen in a client of mine who is an artist. She booked a session because she found herself questioning her validity as an artist. She was finding it difficult to make ends meet from her art, and this had her feeling confused about her choice to be an artist. She felt that she was being indulgent, even though she was very talented and she couldn't stop painting even if she tried. When I put my hands on her heart, I felt an overwhelming feeling of success and possibility. I saw her standing in front of a large, very beautiful abstract painting with specific colours and forms in it. When I mentioned this to her, she said that she was indeed leaning towards more free-flowing, abstract-style art. She left the session feeling buoyed by the vision and energy.

Not long afterwards, she moved away from Singapore back to her homeland, and she sent me a photograph of her standing in front of a beautiful abstract piece in the colours that I saw. She had just finished exhibiting a new installation of her works, which was very warmly received by the art community, and I believe she sold them all. She was realising the clear emotional feeling that her heart was connected to months before the event happened. This example illuminates a beautiful dynamic of intuition, and that is that intuitive guidance is outside of time and space. Sometimes just relaying that possibility and that feeling to a client opens his or her vibration to the possibility of it and gets things moving, drawing it into his or her reality more readily. I have countless examples of this from clients' feedback. Unexpected pregnancies, job offers, career changes, the finding of dream properties with specific features and views, moves to different countries, new loves, impending turbulence and challenges—all of this information is within our auric field and can be read with our intuitive senses, but it needs to be developed and strengthened for the information to be perceived clearly. And the good news is that it can be!

In my experience, there are three key ways to develop your intuition: through consciously engaging with your outer senses, through consciously engaging with the resonance of your system, and through regular meditation. We will explore the significance of these are methods in part 3, 'Your Spirit Skills.'

CHAPTER 15

# Death

One of the greatest blessings from the current pandemic has been the new level of connection in my family. After months of lockdowns, home-based learning, and working from home, my little tribe has a much deeper and closer appreciation for each other. In our small apartment in Singapore, we have found ways to work much more cohesively and respectfully as a tribe, and we have discovered so many new levels to each other and each other's lives that were obscured by the manic busyness of school, work, and travel. When the busyness was taken away, we were left with each other and up-close and personal insights into our respective worlds. We share more meals together. We check out each other's playlists and have music playing in the house. We run ideas by each other. We help each other with homework and projects. We allow each other space, rest, and occasional hissy fits. We buy each other hot chocolates and coffees and watch movies together. It's all pretty sweet, really. During this pandemic, my family transitioned from two working parents and two school-engulfed teenagers to a smoothly operating commune of caring adults. This pandemic has reminded all of us of the impermanence of life, of liberties once taken for granted, and of an acute realisation of our blessings. I am enormously grateful for this, and especially that the kids have a much greater understanding of my inner practice and the work that I do.

Every Wednesday, I retreat to my bedroom for distance energy sessions with people all around the world. The kids know this and ensure I am not disturbed. They see me meditate and do energy practices every day. And over meals we share our respective days' events, which are, for the most part, experienced in different rooms of the same apartment. These conversations can be hilarious as each of us reports on his or her day.

My husband will tell us about the property deal he's working on—the challenges and solutions found. My son will update us on where in the Russian Revolution his history class is taking him and that he has finally cracked solving polynomials in maths. My daughter will show us her latest artwork, update us on how she solved the dilemma for the character in her latest story that she's writing, and what her girlfriends are up to. And I will talk about the people I connected with around the world and how someone's grandmother who died three years ago arrived in a session to remind her daughter of where a missing diamond ring was in her home. All of this is completely normal. All of us are living and sharing our worlds. It's just that my world also includes the non-physical, the world of spirits. The kids will often ask, 'Did you speak to any dead peeps today, Mum?'

I am a psychic medium, yet I have to say it is only in the last couple of years that I have really started to identify with the term and the role, despite my having had clear connections and messages from people in spirit for many years. Now that I am intentionally developing a much more measured and masterful approach to mediumship under the wonderful guidance and coaching of Christine Morgan, a highly regarded and established medium and teacher, I have experienced an entire paradigm flip on death and how our unspoken fear and limited understanding of death is at the root of most the ills of the modern world. Through my experiences in mediumship, I know, without a shadow of a doubt, that our consciousnesses prevail after the event that we call 'death.' We continue as living minds. We heal. We are vibrant and have purpose. We continue to love and guide our living loved ones, and we're keen for connection with them. Our consciousness prevails.

Early on in my healing work, this contact with people in spirit was happening; however, I engaged with it in a more 'ancestral' framework based on my shamanic practices. Once I commenced a healing session—and usually when my hands were connected with the client's crown, the starting position of a reiki treatment—I would become aware of ancestors present in the session. I came to understand that the lines that ran from the right side of the client usually were connected with the paternal lineage; and those running off from the left, with the maternal lineage. After a time, it became clear which generation they dwelt in. For example, if an ancestor made himself or herself known one or two places back in the line, I knew it was a message from either a maternal or paternal grandparent or great-grandparent. Aunts and uncles would present themselves off to the side of the main line. Close friends, teachers, or significant others who were not in the direct line would often present themselves in my awareness, standing either behind my left shoulder (female) or off the back of my right shoulder (male). I came to understand that if they appeared hooded or veiled, they had a developed spiritual practice in their lives before they passed. The hooded ones would often appear in my inner vision with a spiritual or religious symbol, such as a cross, statue of a Hindu deity, or rosary beads, accompanied with a message for the client to engage in the spiritual practice of their family's origin. Almost always when I relayed these messages to the client, they would confirm that they had only recently found or dusted off said rosary beads or had been feeling the pull to the familiar practices of their upbringing. It was a simple system that proved accurate and very useful for my clients, both in the specific messages given and in the knowing that they were indeed receiving guidance and love from the other side.

Once this experience was normalised in my sessions, I started to engage directly with the people in spirit who were presenting. I would acknowledge that I could perceive them and ask them to show me something that the client would recognise. This made the contact much more specific, recognisable and the information was evidential, even if it had to be validated after the session, with living family members. As my main inner sense is visual, the ancestors would 'show' me things. I have so many treasured memories of these early connections with loved ones in spirit, but following are a couple of examples, to show how amazing this communication can be.

A lovely client booked me for a session to explore why he continued to come up against obstacles in his work endeavours. He was intelligent and had started and sold several successful businesses in his career, yet for the previous couple of years, he had trouble getting even the most robust business idea off the ground. During his session, a line of ancestors appeared off to the left, and a hooded gentleman stepped forward three 'heads' back. I knew from our prechat that his mother was alive, so the figure fell in the position of her grandfather, the client's great-grandfather in his mother's lineage. I acknowledged the spirit's presence and asked him to show me something that the client would recognise. In a flash in my mind's eye, he held out a large bowl of what looked like hand-rolled loaves of bread. The message from the hooded ancestor was clear: for my client to experience flow and abundance in his life, he was to reengage with spiritual practice, especially that of his lineage. This would generate a new movement of energy through his system and his field and generate flow in his business dealings as a result.

When I mentioned the bowl of bread to my client, he sat quiet for a moment, and then a huge grin crossed his face. He remembered that his mother's grandfather ran one of London's largest flour mills and provided flour to most of the London bakers in his heyday. Upon further investigation with his mum, who greatly benefited from the subsequent conversations with her son about it all, he learnt that his great-grandfather, her grandfather, was indeed a deeply spiritual man and had written a book on his meditations and practices. Both mother and son found a copy and started to practice the spiritual practices of their lineage. Within a couple of months, he started to receive orders for his business and to grow his endeavours.

In these early days of spirit contact, I had not formulated a full understanding around what the psychic phenomenon actually was. It didn't occur in every session, and I had no determination over whether it would or not; but I was open, accepted it as part of certain healing sessions, and delighted alongside the client in the revelations and healing that the messages brought. I wondered whether I was psychically 'reading' memories perhaps, although for many clients it was only upon asking other relatives that they were able to validate the specific information. They themselves did not hold all the direct memories. I didn't know whether I was tapping useful information held within the clients' own energy bodies or actually connecting with living minds on the other side. I just bundled these experiences into a general phenomenon I called 'contacting the ancestors.'

When COVID-19 reared its head into the world in 2020 and we were all, in no small way, reminded of the fragility and impermanence of life, two significant things changed within me and my experiences. Firstly, the sheer number of spirit contacts increased significantly. Whilst I was still remaining responsive to them rather than initiating them, in a typical healing day, more than half of these sessions involved contact from people in spirit. I allocate three days a week exclusively to healing work, and contact would occur in at least ten of the twenty or so sessions each week. This was a big shift from perceiving the occasional 'ancestor.' I don't know exactly why it picked up so dramatically in the last few years, but I have some theories. I believe it's a combination of a few things: the entire world much more actively contemplating death and searching for meaning, my own personal meditation and energy practices developing, and, perhaps, much greater activity on the other side with so many COVID-19 deaths occurring in such a relatively short period of time.

Whatever the reason, I also started to feel an undeniable and powerful draw to reframe my ideas about death and dying, and, moreover, to intentionally develop the art of mediumship. I figured that it was happening anyway, so I might as well do it well. What was absolutely undeniable was the healing that this contact was enabling.

As life's nature is amazingly synchronous when a spirited choice is made, I was very quickly recommended by a friend to my current mediumship coach. I reintroduced more complex meditations and energy work into my daily practice, I started documenting each experience and how I might improve upon it, and I commenced weekly circles under my coach's guidance with a group of developing mediums around the world.

I am learning something new every single day. I have realised that the world of spirit is unconquerable. You can never learn it all, which fills me with an intense feeling of glee! I have expanded my understanding as to how to engage with each person in spirit as he or she is—a living unique mind who is as keen for contact as I and my clients are. This has vastly changed my approach and vibration when engaging, which in turn has sharpened the clarity and quality of the messages coming through.

In another enchanting encounter, a client's grandmother appeared. To identify herself, she showed me a very pretty old-fashioned china teapot. It was in the dark at the back of a cupboard. She then showed me pouring a cup of hot tea from it. She seemed very insistent about this, and the message was loud and felt. My client was to make tea with the beautiful pieces, to use them and love them, to live every moment now. There was indeed a pretty inherited china teapot that was carefully stored away for safe keeping, which the client took out and now includes in her daily tea rituals. The message was even more significant for her approach to life. Her beautiful grandmother, through the aid of her cherished teapot, gently woke her granddaughter up to the beauty of every moment and living each moment fully.

In a subsequent session with the same client, her father appeared. He showed me his love for her two young boys and then showed me a vision of one of them on the side of a busy road, ready to run across it. I couldn't tell at this stage of my development whether this was a warning or a memory of a recent event. The vision didn't have a sense of urgency. The client confirmed that only days prior, one of her little sons started to chase a ball that had rolled onto the busy road. He was outside of her reach, and she called urgently to him to stop. He kept running, but then, as if halted by an invisible force, he stopped before leaving the pavement and waited for his mum to catch up to him. She's a very intuitive woman and had the thought at the time that the event seemed like some kind of intervention, and now she knew that her father was close, loving and protecting her little family. This was hugely reassuring and healing for her.

In another beautiful session, a woman came to see me about a pattern she kept repeating in her life within romantic relationships. As soon as she started to feel herself falling in love, she would end the relationship, afraid. During the session, a lovely man presented himself. He felt very close to her, and I wrote in my session book 'father?' I asked for something that she would recognise, and he told me the name 'Jake', and my heart filled with the deepest and sweetest love. He also gave me a thumbs up on her current lover. And that was it. Then he left. When I relayed this to the client, she started to cry. After years of psychotherapy and inner work, she had identified that her fear in relationships stemmed from a fear of abandonment, established when she was a much younger woman and her father had committed suicide. The principal male of her younger years had left her, and the fear that all other men that she may open her heart to might do the same and cause the same kind of pain was affecting her ability to open into and be vulnerable to love. I had enormous admiration for her self-enquiry and determination to heal. I asked her whether her father's name was Jake. With wide eyes, she nodded. I told her that he was here, that he loved her, and that he had given the thumbs up to her lover. In one beautiful session, the entire foundation of abandonment dissolved in the knowing that despite her father's story and obvious issues in his own life, he continued to love her, was involved in her life, and never left.

In a more recent contact in my mediumship circle, I

learnt another interesting feature of the afterlife, and that is that we consciously create it!

I was sitting in a new weekly circle. It was a new circle for me, as the change in daylight saving time meant the time difference to Singapore wasn't easy. So I switched to the afternoon circle, which in some ways was excellent, as I didn't know anyone in the circle—no backstories, no personality types, and no risk of retrofitting previously known information into the reads. During the sit, a very flamboyant man came through. He wore a colourful patterned shirt and arty thick-rimmed glasses, and he had a rotund belly. He was a very fun spirit indeed. He showed me all his wonderful collections of objects, appliances, and books. He was successful and loved finely made items. A man in my circle recognised that this man was someone related to him. The spirit showed me validating information to evidence this—a golf ball, an exotic bird, and a fat ginger cat—all hobbies of his brother still alive and in the circle. There was a lot more information shared between these two brothers, but what is relevant to this chapter is that his brother came out at sixty-five years of age after living a life disguising his true nature. He passed shortly afterwards. Yet in spirit he has woven his afterlife, in all its glorious, fun campiness. My coach told us that this is a common phenomenon in mediumship. When we pass, we weave the elements of our afterlives. Our living mind, which prevails after the body is gone, continues to generate realities. This is another incredible reason to start to master the mind-and-energy system whilst we have the tool of our physical bodies. We weave our realities not only in life but after death too.

These burgeoning forays into death and the afterlife have really got me thinking, and I am coming to the conclusion that it is our fear of death which is perhaps the greatest illness of the modern world. Mental well-being, prolonged stress states, and the resultant anxiety and depressive states are attributed to the mad pace of modern life, the pressure to succeed, the pressure to survive, and the pressure to win some kind of race—a race against time, a race against ageing, a race against death. And the enormous polarisation of wealth on our planet and our propensity to hoard, save, and consume beyond our requirements seems to be driven by the compulsion for physical survival and security. It also shows the modern world's attachment to the material and physical aspects of life. I wonder, how would our attitudes and choices change if we all held the realisation that we are, in fact, on a continuum of experience and expansion—that our consciousness prevails and that this game of life is like a school, a place of learning, and an invitation to mastery, and it is not the end game.

The study of death and experience of mediumship has vastly changed my experience of life. My awareness has stepped more deeply into the uniqueness of each moment and each aspect of my life, the blessing of it all, and the mystery of the immense universe that we dwell in and that dwells within us. It has been a game changer and has affirmed my choice to lead a spirited life and to make this my paradigm for living and relationship. It strikes me that to fully embrace life, we need to also embrace death, which means radically expanding our understanding of what this event really is as we also radically expand our understanding of who and what we really are.

I could fill the rest of this book with recounted sessions during which loved ones have reached through the veil to deliver a message that, in its simplicity, or even just by validating their continued existence, heals. And while each experience in mediumship is unique and wonderful, there do seem to be very similar messages that come through in their own specific and validated ways:

We prevail after death as a living, feeling, loving mind or consciousness. Our love prevails beyond death.

We continue to be close to our loved ones, guiding and protecting them after we pass.

It is so important to live with presence and celebration of every moment in life, even the tough ones. This is not a dress rehearsal. Use the good teapot every single day!

It is important to have an active spiritual practice, however that practice may be expressed. In life, we can master our awareness and become more fully conscious, which serves us not only in life but also when we pass. We determine through our awareness the kind of afterlife we experience, just as we determine through awareness the kind of life we are living now.

CHAPTER 16

# The Spirit in All

Along with writing this book during the pandemic, I also got busy on several other projects that have been sitting, gathering dust in the boxes of my mind as I was 'too busy' to get them up and running. When all my in-person group gatherings came to an abrupt halt during lockdowns, I finally decided to embrace the world of digital content, and I am so happy I did. Amongst developing online meditation courses, guided meditation tracks, and instrumental albums and online circles, I got out and dusted off one project that I had been wanting to do for years. I started a podcast called *The Modern Crone*.

The first season of the podcast is a collection of conversations with shamanic teachers and friends I have met along my own journey from very different traditions and backgrounds. These friends share their views of the world, self, and spirit. I called it 'The 21ˢᵗ Century Shaman.' Producing the series was a delight. With my usual annual spiritual pilgrimages suspended, I had the opportunity to get deep and personal with some of the greatest minds I know on what it is to live a spirited life, which somewhat assuaged my frustration at being grounded.

Similar truths emerged with every conversation: the necessity to cultivate our spiritual dimension, the essentiality of relationship with the wilderness and its sentient nature, the living presence of our ancestors, the very real and active states of trance and dreaming, and, especially, the Spirit in All.

What is common in all of the shamanic world views that I have come to know is that every phenomenon, everything, has an organising field of energy and information that brings it to bear. A tree, the forest it lives in, the weather, the mountains, the creatures, the sacred sites of Java, the yidaki (didgeridoo) of Arnhem Land and the sounds it makes, the plant medicines of Peru and the icaro of the shamans that brew them, and the sacred pipe of the Lakota, its holy tobacco, the fire that burns it, and the smoke it produces. Everything—inanimate objects and animate living beings, even our potentiality and possibilities—has what my friend and Bolivian shaman Miguel Kalvin calls 'a principal idea', even, and especially, each one of us, along with our desires, dreams, fears, illnesses, and triumphs. In nearly all the shamanic traditions that I have studied and experienced, including QueChuan, KeJawan, Lakota and Aboriginal shamanism as well as a strong and ever present Celtic Pagan bloodlines and Druidic Shamanism, this principle idea is simply referred to as 'a spirit.'

Our consciousness receives from, translates, and emanates information into this field through both our physical and energy bodies, through the vibratory resonance of our awareness. This sounds very woo-woo, yet we experience this every single day in every moment; we just don't stop to consider it. How information moves through us is not the linear process we perhaps assume it to be; thoughts move through linear connections in the brain, an emotional response ensues, and then a resultant action occurs. Researchers have found that information can be transferred in electrical waves throughout the neural tissue without following the traditional synaptic pathways, and our bodies are full of neurological tissue. The electrical field is a low-amplitude one, but the wave of energy will activate and excite nearby structures in the body which will then become excited and spread to other nearby structures. Just visualise something that you are deeply grateful for or someone that you adore, and the warm, fuzzy feeling spreads around your body. This slow-moving but effective method of informational transfer spreads throughout your entire system. There are more senses in the human body than the traditional five, and there are more energetic fields of information that these senses are interacting with than those that are known to science or that can be measured currently. Scientists are beginning to discover a whole set of electric senses that may explain why some people can feel the flow of energy in other living things, sense information outside of time and space, or know when someone is about to contact them.

By opening our awareness to our true designs, we can access the true design of existence, or the Spirit in All, and we realise that rather than the physical body simply being a sophisticated lump of matter, flesh and bone, it is in fact a vehicle for consciousness that is capable of interacting with the unified conscious field of life and spirit. And perhaps more spectacularly, we realise that our life experiences are more than just a random set of occurrences that we are constantly reacting to, but rather an extension and refraction of that same field of consciousness. One's life field, what one experiences, and one's human system are one thing! There is a cosmic dialogue that's taking place all the time between expanding planes of life and our human system. When you adopt this perception, every experience in your outer reality, your life, becomes animated and meaningful, because you are fully engaged with it as an expression of yourself and the movement of spirit. Every encounter, conversation, touch, exchange, mouthful, breath, sound, and colour—everything—is part of it, even (and perhaps most importantly) the challenges.

The most beautiful field of information, or spirit, in my

experience, that has the most reliable and dazzling guidance and platforms to create, is the wild field. Shamans and those that live in land-based spiritual communities who are in a love affair with and have deep admiration for the wild earth know this. They also know that there are ancient, interconnecting correspondences between all living things, past, present, and future. They know the power of the ley lines and celestial alignments. They communicate on the wind and heal with water. They know that the information of spirit travels through these correspondences and, moreover, that we are designed to work with them. This is because our entire makeup and design is also a correspondence and field of vibrating energy. When we connect with the correspondences and vibrations of our own systems, we can move our awareness through the correspondences and vibrations of wider and wider fields of life.

This is what I experience when receiving psychic information for a client about an event yet to play out or an event in the past that is affecting a client's present situation.

I love playing with these ideas and have done so for years. A great experiment in connecting with the Spirit in All is conducted through connecting with the spirit of a species. In the Blue Mountains in New South Wales, Australia, in the early spring, the lyre birds get busy building their nest mounds and calling for potential mates to come by and check out their architectural skills in the hope they might be chosen. For those of you who may not know, a lyre bird is a very shy, very clever ground-dwelling bird native to Australia. It is so named because of the shape of its beautiful tail feathers, which look like a musical lyre (harp) when on display. They are notoriously mysterious and difficult to spot. They scratch their way through the undergrowth, hunting bugs, and they build lovely big mounds that they stand atop and sing loudly to attract a mate. An image of a lyre bird adorns the Australian ten-cent piece. But it's the lyre bird's song that is so breathtaking. You see, they are mimics. They are able to replicate to digital precision any sound they come across in their environment—every bird call, every animal call, and even the footsteps of bushwalkers as they pass across a creaky bridge. They don't just pick one sound to sing; they string them together in a unique medley of all the sounds they love, a sort of signature song for their life.

One holiday the kids and I were staying in my cottage in the Blue Mountains with one of my closest friends, Abi, and her children. We were keen to walk one of our favourite tracks nearby with the specific intention of spotting a lyre bird. We had been talking about it with the kids, and on previous walks, we had sadly come back disappointed each time. As everyone was preparing to head out one morning, I sat on the back step of the cottage overlooking the garden. It was a crisp, beautiful day; there was a clear blue sky, and the early spring bulbs were beginning to blossom underneath the trees. Daffodils, freesias, and bluebells were all reaching up towards the growing warmth and light of the season. I so wanted the kids to see a lyre bird that I found my spirit calling out into the morning air in a plea to the wilderness for an encounter. In my mind's eye, I saw a magnificent lyre bird, and then the revelation came: I was sensing the spirit of the species. I acknowledged its presence and relayed in my heart how beautiful we all thought it was and how desperately we would love to hear its song. In my mind's eye, I presented the children, four beautiful little beings still with a wild love of nature at the ages of five to seven.

It's difficult to explain, but I felt without any doubt that this was a communication that was both received and acknowledged. I just knew that despite there not having been a sighting by us days prior, nor by our local mountain friends who know the bush and its cycles so well, we would have an encounter. We set off, took the scenic railway (an old repurposed mining train that was used to haul coal from the mines in the cliff faces and forest floor back up to the town in the 1800s), and alighted at the valley floor. Within minutes of starting our walk, the lyre birds appeared. They were at a distance, but the excitement of both kids, Abi, and me was contagious. Around every bend, someone spotted another. The count was on, and we sighted twenty lyre birds in a one-hour walk. And then, as if to totally delight us beyond what our senses could take, we heard rustling in the undergrowth near where we had stopped for a drink and rest. A very young, very beautiful lyre bird emerged from his hiding place, stood on his mound just beyond the track, in full view, and sang.

He gave it all he had, and we were transfixed. We heard Magpie, Kookaburra, Robin, Willy Wagtail, Parrot, and Owl. We heard animal calls from unknown places; we even heard the twang of the wire on the wooden bridge—echoes of other walkers that had passed by this little guy's territory. He had woven together all the threads of sound in his life, sounds of the forest, in his own unique and amazing song. The spirit in his song, feathers, and spring mating drive, was the same spirit I had connected with on the back step of my cottage. It was a dazzling dialogue that was based in love and respect, which transformed the remote potential of a siting into a possible siting, then into a probable siting, and finally into twenty-one incredible experiences.

I have a particular connection with the Spirit of the Dawn. I have always been an early riser and absolutely love greeting the new day. In February 2020, I committed to connecting with the Spirit of the Dawn every day. Sometimes I connect with this spirit in the botanic gardens before my qigong class. Sometimes I do so in sharing a ride with my friends, sometimes through a wild tropical storm, and sometimes at my altar, in meditation. In the main, most days, I wake early, excited and expectant for what the dawn holds for me, and ride the thirty-seven-kilometre round trip across Singapore island to the east coast and back. Coming from the east coast of Australia, the sights, sounds, and scents of the sun rising over the ocean make me hum. The atmosphere is charged with all the elements, and this allows an incredible full-body somatic immersion into my dawn meditation and energy practices. Dawn on the sea is a double 'dragon point.'

Junctures where different powerful signature energies meet are described in the Taoist tradition as dragon points. They are the points at which one form of qi (vital life force) meets another. In nature, for example, it is where two rivers merge into one or the mountain peaks scrape the sky. It is where the ocean meets land or when the light emerges in the darkness at dawn. When dwelling on a dragon point, one can easily enter a light trance state where intuitive guidance and revelation abound, and where, especially, one can connect with the Spirit in All.

These areas and moments in nature are considered to be extremely powerful, and if you can recall those moments in the wilderness when you have been truly moved, and your consciousness spontaneously altered, when you have had a glimpse of the majesty and the mystery, I am willing to wager that you were dwelling in dragon points at those moments. In most ancient cultures, the most sacred sites are either on or near natural dragon points; this includes most ancient world temples, the pyramids, and stone circles. In shamanism, these 'in-betweens' are where the shaman accesses the spirit of things, the principal idea, which also includes the day that is yet to unfold. Dragon points can be found not only in spaces but also in times—for example, midday and midnight, dawn and dusk, equinoxes and solstices. Have you ever wondered why witches and shamans get busy at these times?

How I greet each dawn when I am on my own varies. I usually engage in breathwork, some qigong, Kabbalist energy practices, meditation, stillness, and mantra. I find it good to have a selection of tried and true practices in my 'medicine bag' and to be responsive to what dawn and my system are calling for. And I'm not alone! There are other dawn lovers out there, and whilst we all engage in different ways, the one thing we have in common is a recognition of the moment and a mutual respect that the Spirit of Dawn has drawn us all there together.

Beneath and beyond words and thoughts is a state of being-ness that the dawn slips me into, and I can locate and connect with the highest potential of the day. The day is yet to play out, but within that potentiality, at the dawn, it can be found, sensed, and drawn in. On the days that seem impossible to pull off, that have me feeling tight and contracted—like, for example, days on which I have overbooked healing sessions or on which I am launching a new course (with new tech involved)—I have been able to sense into the highest path within, before the day has started, and stay pegged to that potential. This yields results every single time.

In certain seasons in Singapore, traipsing around natural places before the sun rises can make you breakfast for myriad tropical biting insects. After enduring many itchy, burning bites, largely because of my aversion to spraying my body with pesticides, I decided to connect with what I call the 'Spirit of the Bitey Things' at my meditation sites. The ritual is simple and heart-felt. I park my bike, ask for permission to cross the threshold of the space, and directly address the Spirit of the Bitey Things. I honour the spirit's home, recognise the spirit's amazing fierce nature, give a water offering to the earth, and respectfully ask that the spirit hold off until I have finished my practice, adding that the spirit is very welcome to partake in the energy I generate through it. The Spirit of the Bitey Things and I now have a well-developed mutual respect. I am left alone for my practices, and when my energy peaks during the practices, I intentionally offer it to the environment that is hosting me. I have learnt, though, not to dwell too long afterwards. After the hour or so during which I'm walking back to my bike, the pests will often close in!

My ability to consciously connect with the spirit of inanimate objects is developing. It's easier for me to consciously connect with certain spaces, such as sacred sites, stone circles, or temples, because of the layered energetic imprints of so many who have dwelt there before me and because of the energetic 'technology' within their designs, orientations, and positions over ley lines and within hotspots in the wilderness—a technology that the ancients knew so well. For modern objects, such as a mobile phone or car, for example—this takes more work. Yet all things have a principal idea, and it was with the aid of plant medicine in Bolivia on the shores of Lake Titicaca that I witnessed and communicated with the spirit of a traditional ceremonial musical instrument.

The human system is not an anomaly within creation. The way we are designed is correspondent to the design of the universe, its vibratory nature, and its intelligence. Aside from direct teachings from shamanic teachers, the best explanation I have found on the law of correspondence and vibration is in the seven Hermetic principles, captured in writings such as *The Emerald Tablet* and the *Kybalion*.

The Kybalion lays out the seven Hermetic principles for existence: the principles of mentalism, correspondence, vibration, polarity, rhythm, cause and effect, and gender. Whilst authored by the mysterious 'Three Initiates', the book remains a staple in the bulging libraries of spiritual seekers. It is said to be one of the clearest explanations of ancient plain-speak cosmology that we have. I devoured it when I first came across it twenty years ago, and I continue to do so. My intuitive healing and transformational courses use the Hermetic principles as axioms for magic and healing. Once this ancient framework caught my attention, I started to see it everywhere. Every ritual-based spiritual framework, every organised religion in the world today, and the nature-based shamanic practices of the world have an awareness of these archetypal laws and patterns and intentionally work with the laws of correspondence and vibration.

The principle of correspondences is often expressed as 'As above, So Below. As within so without', and the principle of vibration as 'Nothing rests. Everything moves. Everything vibrates.'

These principles illuminate that there is a harmony, agreement, and correspondence between the planes of manifestation, the visible and the invisible, or our consciousness and the Spirit in All. Different traditions define these planes differently. I like the yogic understanding of the koshas because they acknowledge that the human being exists well beyond the skin line and that each invisible layer of us operates in its own realm of energy. The visible physical body is the slowest and most dense vibration, and the highest self, the spirit self, is the quickest and lightest vibration of us. The higher our vibrations, the more deeply we can consciously connect with spirit.

In our individualised states, putting it simply, we attract and experience in 'ordinary reality' people, experiences, and incidents that are vibrating at the same rate. When we lift our vibrations, we lift our experiences of life. Vibrate internally as a well, vital, happy, creative lover, and this will be your experience—your reality. As simple as the principle sounds, the reality of it takes dedication and work. But rather than viewing the life experiences that we don't like or don't desire as life happening 'to us,' I have learnt that the better perspective to work with is that these experiences are illuminating to us that somewhere in our beings, we are out of alignment with our desires and truths, and that rather than ninja-fighting the mirror, we should rotate our awareness inwards to our unconscious belief systems and fears that are manifesting the situation. Until we do, similar experiences will continue to manifest. Life is always working in our favour, even—and especially—when it's uncomfortable and challenging.

To live a spirited life is to operate with the laws of correspondence and vibration intentionally, to generate the frequency of the change we are seeking, to incarnate spiritual energy, to create. Our modern state is constantly luring our awareness and belief systems to the outer occurrences alone, triggering us into a state of reactivity and diverting our awareness away from our inner lives and work. When we lean our attention back into our inner realities, our invisible selves, we find balance, and our bodies receive and perceive the movement and engagement of spirit. When we align our perspectives and beliefs to an expanded view of the self and life, we create a coherent vibration from the intelligence centres of the body. Our spiritual engines gets started, and the human energy body rises. We move into flow. We start to directly experience spirit in everyday life. We realise unreservedly that we are far bigger, more interconnected, and more divine than we have allowed ourselves to accept. We wake up. As Thích Nhất Hạnh so beautifully says, 'Enlightenment is when the wave realises it is the ocean.'

The fields of energy and information available to us are infinite. When we consciously engage in our own expansion, we are able to access wisdom and guidance from within our own DNA codex, from ancestral fields, from the field of nature, and from the fields of teachers and healers and draw it directly through our own energy bodies. This is the basis of the healing I offer others. When moving energy through their physical bodies, with their permission, I perceive information held within their energy fields that is useful for their healing, which they can be too distracted to perceive consciously themselves. This is possible when sharing the same space and time in a healing session or through a remote read. The information available is very specific and practical.

We bind ourselves into loops of experience and illness through energetic patterns that we hold, yet with cultivated awareness and expanded perspectives, we are also able to perceive those patterns and choose to change them to allow alignment and flow to reestablish within us and therefore within our lives. All of this information is held within our energy bodies. The secret guilt-inducing abortion from years ago; the shame-inducing porn addiction; the unresolved relationship with a parent, held since childhood; the nutrient-deprived diet; the habit of comparison and jealousy—these are but a few examples of the binding energetic patterns that have held healing at bay from my clients. With awareness and energy management, we can start to work consciously with our incredible design. This is also how I perceive the directions held within each new day and each new year. I start every day by connecting with my inner aspect through meditation and sense the vibration of the possibilities within the day that's breaking. I start every year on a vision quest, where I go away on my own, sometimes for a few days and sometimes for longer if I can swing it with my family. I always enter the wilderness and deep meditation practice, and then I can read what's coming my way in the year to come and how to engage with it and seed what I desire to experience. When I am writing a new transformative meditation course, I connect with the information field or spirit of my teacher and lineage of teachers for guidance. When I become aware of a sticky limiting pattern that I am holding in my unconscious, which is being highlighted to me by repeated triggering external experiences, I access the field of all the people who have overcome the same blockage and more readily transmute it. We are all able to do this for ourselves and, if we are called to, for others.

In part 3 of this book, we will explore different methods for consciously accessing various fields of information for various purposes. The methods I use and explain in this book are those that I have learnt and mastered over the years, but the reality is that our ability to engage with spirit in this way, to live a spirited life, to heal, and to rise into our true purposes is within our design. We don't need to have studied all the world's great spiritual methodologies or call ourselves shamans or witches or gurus. We don't need to be certified in a hundred different energy modalities. With an expanded awareness of our spirited design and an ability to stay present and raise the vibrations of our energy bodies, then it simply requires our desire, intent, and action to unlock.

# PART 3

# Spirit Skills

# CHAPTER 17

# A New Take on Meditation

The human energy body is activated and raised through our awareness. When it is raised, we consciously connect and communicate with spirit—within us and within all. The first step in accessing this flow and all the beauty and ease that it brings is to reclaim our awareness from the blinding binds of busy modern life and to rotate it inwards, to where all the real action is taking place. This doesn't mean we dissociate from our modern lives—quite the contrary. The challenge is to reset how we perceive it and how we engage with it. Our life experiences are our teachers and our greatest opportunities to express ourselves creatively. They emanate from our inner state, reflecting back to us the beliefs and resonances of our energy bodies. The most efficient, beautiful, natural, and proven way to reclaim awareness is through the art of meditation.

In reality, I don't think it matters what the reasons that get us started with meditation are. What matters is staying with it until the required push towards the practice flips to the practice drawing us towards it, and this occurs quite quickly when we hold the intention for it and commit to practice. When push turns to draw, and we can sense the intrinsic benefit and power of meditation, then we're cooking with gas!

There are four commonly held misconceptions around meditation that I have encountered through teaching it for over twenty years. Sadly, they appear to be the main reasons why many try meditation once or twice and then let it go. To dispel them, I find it useful to start with listing what meditation *is not*.

## Meditation Is Not about Clearing the Mind of All Thought

If you try to clear the mind of thought, you soon realise that you're on a hiding to nothing. Sometimes, just for fun, I will settle a new group in for their first practice and invite them to do just this. I guide them into stillness and then invite then to simply empty their minds of all thoughts. It's a little cheeky, I suppose, but I do love watching the little twitches and frowns that appear, usually around the three-minute mark, when new students start to realise that thinking about not thinking is actually a thought. And yes, some people really do twitch with it. The mind is thought. I find that a better way to view it is that meditation combines the use of the breath, the posture, and a single point of focus to *draw in* a *dissipated mind*. When we do this, we experience the revelation that there's a difference between our awareness and our thought-fields. They're not the same thing.

By regularly practising meditation techniques, we are able to lengthen and smooth the brainwave patterning, which in turn calms the frenetic thought activity of the mind and weakens the tugging action that our thoughts have on our awareness. This shift in brainwave activity and resultant calming of thought correlates with a coherence in the central nervous system. This state does not equate to simple relaxation. In fact, the hallmark of the meditative state is that you are very alert, calm, and present within your inner environment. Nor does this state equate to no thought, necessarily, although in very deep meditative states this is experienced. What does happen is that our centre of awareness separates from the thought field and our emotions. We realise that we are not our thoughts or our feelings, but rather we are the intelligence that is observing them. Thoughts may still pass through the mind while meditating, feelings may still arise, but they lose their 'pull' on our awareness, and moreover, we are able to observe them clearly.

The single point of focus used in any meditation can

be anything: the senses, the breath, a symbol, a mantra, a candle flame, or a count, for example. The game is to peg the attention to that point of focus and gently hold it there. Whenever we observe our attention chasing after a thought, we just need to catch it and gently bring it back. In a relatively short period of regular practice, this strengthens one's ability to concentrate the mind, and over time we can dispense with an obvious point of focus because we have trained our minds to settle and draw into presence when we will them to. This alert, calm presence, our awareness, is, by its nature, energy. Awareness at the centre of a calm, present mind has a voltage or a current. Once we are able to detect and build it, we can learn to direct it and to bring it into coherence with the other energy centres of the mind/body system and the energy of life.

Thích Nhất Hạnh, the much-loved Vietnamese Buddhist and prolific teacher and writer, describes the energy of consciousness in the mind beautifully. He uses the analogy of sending a current through a light globe. Trying to direct our awareness through a dissipated mind is like sending electricity through a soft-glow light bulb. Yes, it lights up and glows, but the intensity of the light is dim, and the range short. However, when we direct our awareness through a calm, concentrated mind, it is like sending electricity through a diamond, producing a laser beam of intense light and long range. Meditation is a way to gather the mind into presence, the here and now, the only living reality. Our past has happened, and our future is yet to be. Our only reality is the here and now, this moment. When our minds are gathered into the deep now and our systems align and calm into stillness, the light of our awareness grows and can be directed. When we direct it towards the vibrational energy in our systems, our spiritual engines start!

## Meditation Is Not about Denying Your Body

Another thing I see quite a bit in meditation circles are keen practitioners forcing their legs and hips into stiff, unsustainable lotus poses or holding their arms and hands aloft in some sort of flashy mudra, and often both. There is a very common misconception that we must hold the posture of an ancient yogi and then muscle our way through numbed limbs into stillness. It's pretty hard to achieve inner calm when circulation to your lower body has ground to a halt. The idea that we have to somehow deny our physical aspect as a trade-off for higher awareness is both erroneous and damaging. The concept that spirit and body are diametrically opposed couldn't be further from reality. The body is integral to the process of meditation and being spirited. The body and spirit are inextricably linked. In fact, they are one total system, with aspects simply vibrating at different rates. And when I say 'the body', I mean all physical aspects: the physical form, the brain, the central nervous system, the heart, the enteric nervous system, every cell and the space that holds it, the breath and the senses, and the energy body that permeates and radiates from the physical form. It is true that certain meditation techniques allow a temporary loosening of our association with the physical matter of the body, but to enter those deep states, we must work with the body and its energy systems.

Our bodies are already present. They occupy a physical space, and they are in the moment. Our bodies are here and now. The body is the perfect anchor to draw in the mind. Simply by placing attention on parts of the body, the feet's connection with the earth, the contact points to a mat or chair, the subtle movement of air on skin, or the curves and contours of the form, we can very effectively settle the mind and connect the awareness with the energy fields of the body.

And the physical body is highly responsive to meditative attention because it is intelligent. As we shift the awareness inwards, the brainwave patterning becomes slower and longer, the breath becomes deeper and smoother, the sympathetic and parasympathetic arms of the nervous system come into synchronicity, the electromagnetic fields emanate from the brain, and the heart and the solar plexus become coherent, and this enables a shift in the state of consciousness, deep into the centre of our beings and deeply into 'the now.' Needless to say, this wholesale settling and arrival into presence feels absolutely divine, and just hanging here at the point of the initial shift can be a perfectly worthy practice on its own. We now know that regular meditation is enormously restorative for the physical body. Overall levels of cortisol drop, the brain rebuilds itself, the physical heart becomes stronger; it even slows the ageing process and boosts immune function. It is the ultimate in preventative medicine. And the fact that our physical bodies respond so readily and in such lifeward ways to regular meditation is powerful evidence that we are designed to engage with it.

If you watch very closely an adept meditator in action, the Dalai Lama for example, you will notice that he is far from 'outside' of his body. Nor is he sitting totally still. On close observation, you will find that he is constantly adjusting his posture, the length of the neck, and the space and alignment in the spine, mainly through very tiny microadjustments. Rather than denying his body, he is acutely aware of it and working with it to ensure the best alignment to maximise the flow of life force through the system.

## Posture

The most important postural considerations for effective meditation are a stable, even base and a long, stable spine, with the shoulders down and back to open the chest and the chin very slightly tilted towards the collarbone to lengthen the back of the neck. This can be achieved on a meditation stool or sitting cross-legged with a cushion or yoga block tucked under the tailbone to lengthen the lower and middle back, or in a chair with upright back support. The central nervous system and main energy centres of the energy body are located along the spine. When we sit upright and long, we are better able to detect the nervous system coming into synchronicity and, with practice, the pulses of energy moving through our central energy columns.

Some meditations, like yoga nidra, are practised lying down in shivasana (also spelt savasana). Shivasana is a Sanskrit word that translates to 'dead man's pose' or 'corpse pose.' While that sounds a little grim, it is so named as it is a passive asana. When shivasana is assumed correctly, there's a lot happening despite you lying still. When lying in shivasana, the back of the head, spine, and tailbone should be aligned. You should feel an even symmetry between the limbs. Legs should be hip width apart, the feet gently falling outwards, the arms slightly away from the sides, palms facing up. No pillow should be used. Shivasana provides a beautiful feeling of receptivity with belly and palms exposed. The curve of the back of the head naturally lengthens the back of the neck. The contact of the spine to mat brings the awareness to the central column of the spine and energy system, and the overall posture allows a surrender of the mind—a wholesale letting go, which is required to ease the mind and any tension we might be holding as we enter meditation. The settling towards the floor of the brain, soft tissues, and fluids within the body creates space for the airways to open. Within a minute of lying in shivasana, the breath lengthens and deepens, and this is critical to changing brainwave activity.

If the body is tired, however, meditation in shivasana will make you sleepy. My guidance is to only practise meditations in shivasana in the morning or when well rested—unless, of course, you want to fall asleep more readily. In that case, whip out your pillow, follow my recording of yoga nidra, and slip off into the deep blue of dreaming. It's not meditating, but it's perhaps what your system needs if you're tired and run-down.

## The Senses

Shortly after I started regularly meditating as part of my formal studies, my neighbours started a renovation next door. It involved jackhammering through rock and large vehicles that emitted high-pitched beeps whenever they reversed. They seemed to be driving backwards all day, and the jackhammers always, without fail, started up when I sat on my meditation stool. The noise became a huge distraction, and I fought it internally. It became my excuse for not meditating until my teacher simply said one day, 'Use it. Don't fight it!' Hooley dooley. These four words flipped my thinking and opened me to a beautiful journey of not only appreciating but also honouring my body and removing all resistance to what my senses were delivering into my awareness, especially as I moved into meditation. I started drawing the mind in by putting my awareness on the weave of sounds I could detect outside my home. These became the point of focus: the neighbourhood sounds, the birds and insects in the garden, the beeping of the construction lorries, the rock-cracking thuds of the jackhammers, the faint thrum of a busy city beyond. Then I would draw my awareness into my home and place it on the internal sounds: the whir of a ceiling fan, the subtle creaks and groans of the house itself warming up in the sun. Then I would draw in further to the sounds of my body: the gentle stream of the breath, a deep gurgle in the gut. And then, finally, I would put my awareness into the silence in between. I used the sounds instead of fought them, and I very quickly learnt how to draw in my mind quickly and effectively, regardless of the external environment. I then went through a slightly nutty phase of strengthening this practice by meditating alongside construction sites, noisy playgrounds, and shopping malls. I can attest that this method works at all noise levels. And not only that, it also opens you to the miracle of hearing and how sound moves through the mind/body system.

Using the soundtrack that the day provides is a wonderful shortcut to acceptance and gratitude. Each time we sit to meditate, the sounds around us, the light, the time, the season, the temperature, how our systems are in that moment, the colours, the breath, the scents, and the intention will never be repeated again in that same combination. This is true of every single moment. Every moment is woven in a unique and unrepeated combination of elements. Honouring this and working with it, rather than resisting it, helps us draw into the deep now. Trust the soundtrack you have been given each time you enter your inner world. It can carry you in if you let it. Sound as a tool for meditation is one of my favourite mediums. I have a slight obsession with metal and crystal singing bowls, drums, and rattles. I love using them in my classes and personal practice, and I chant every day. Since the pandemic began, I have stepped into the world of music production and guided meditation recordings too. We are, after all, made of sound—vibrating energy.

All of the physical senses provide beautiful points of focus to draw in the mind for meditation. There are some sublime meditation practices that focus the awareness on the senses: taste, smell, sounds, touch, and sight. Many come from the yogic tradition that maintains that our physical senses that enable us to interact with ordinary reality and the physical universe are not only connected to, but are aspects of, our inner senses that enable us to interact with our energetic and spiritual reality. Our senses work on a pole between inner and outer realities. Some beautiful examples of these are the practices of trataka (soft gazing, usually at a candle flame), sound bathing, and the raisin contemplation meditation. Trataka has some incredible restorative effects on the physical eyes, optic nerve, and pineal gland, and by practicing trataka, we also sharpen our inner sight. Our inner sight is enabled by the mysterious pineal gland and is the area of clear and reliable clairvoyance, dreaming, lucid dreaming, sensing spirit, and perception of energy body through colours, symbols, and visions in meditation. Gong sound bathing, kirtan, mantra, nature sounds, and the use of singing bowls are divine vibratory experiences that also sharpen the inner hearing, the ear we hold to the heart, where we perceive guidance and whispers from spirit. The infamous Buddhist raisin contemplation meditation opens our awareness through the sense of taste to the energetic nature of our foods and the worlds and information that are contained within.

These beautiful practices are not only very effective at bringing the awareness inwards and sharpening our inner and outer senses; they remind us of the miracle of our senses. The sheer pleasure of a sweet mango, the sound of birdcall, breeze on the skin, dawn sunlight on the face, and the perfumes of the earth and forest are pure medicine for the spirit. When the senses and heart are opened to the wonder of these forces, the awareness is also opened to the intelligence, healing, and guidance they offer.

**Body Awareness**

One of my favourite practices to explore with new students, and especially children, is the ancient and potent practice of yoga nidra. Yoga nidra allows a direct experience of the old adage 'Energy flows where attention goes.' It is a guided form of meditation that directs the attention through parts of the body. It is often referred to as a body scan. There are lots of different versions of yoga nidra, and it's one of the few meditations that needs to be guided. I learnt yoga nidra from my favourite yogini, Radha, in the Satyananda tradition. It's this version that is regarded as the truest and best, as the sequence of body parts and systems that you are guided through in this practice follow the natural flow and symmetry of the body. With new students, I guide them into meditation and then into scanning half of their bodies through the Satyananda sequence. I then ask them to expand their awareness to take in the whole of the body and observe how both sides feel.

To date I haven't had a student who couldn't sense a palpable difference between the scanned and unscanned sides of his or her body. The students perceive the sensation differently, but they all feel it. For some the scanned side feels heavy, soft, and almost melted. For others the scanned side feels light and vibrant. Some describe the difference as a change in sound scale; and others, as a shift in vibration or a heightened buzzing sensation on the scanned side. All of them have a very real experience of the voltage of their awareness. I then guide them through scanning the other side so they can even up the system and not feel lopsided when leaving the class. So responsive are our cells to meditative attention that yoga nidra is used with great success in trauma recovery wards. Studies show that patients who incorporate yoga nidra or body scanning into their recovery therapy heal more quickly and holistically, and their damaged connective tissue reconnects more thoroughly. Directing our meditative awareness to the physical body is the basis of myriad energetic healing techniques, including body talk, quantum healing, and reiki.

Another interesting body response to meditation is 'release phenomenon.' It is a very common experience; however, I have only found it written about in Joel Levey's book *Luminous Minds*. I haven't found a physiological reason why it occurs. It is a natural physical response to calming the system. Very often, but not always, when people enter meditation and start to draw their awareness into presence and stillness, the body will release held energy. This can be felt by a sudden pang of pain in the neck or back, a little coughing fit, yawning, sneezing, or, as nearly always occurs with me, gurgling in the tummy. I always explain release phenomenon to new students before we start to meditate, because the twangs can be quite sudden and the new student can easily think something is wrong. But it passes quickly, and I advise them to acknowledge it as an affirmation that they are successfully bringing the mind and body into alignment and that pent-up energy held in the physical aspect is naturally releasing itself.

**Diet**

Many spiritual traditions advocate a pure, light diet—that is, no meat, alcohol, or other toxins—as necessary for meditation and spiritual progression. There is an enormous amount of energy diverted by the body to digesting, metabolising, and cleansing, especially if it is slightly overworked by heavy, dense meals and a little overindulgence on all fronts. In my own practice, I can feel the difference. I grew up in a family of foodies. Meat was eaten every day, and Dad always kept an exquisite wine cellar. It wasn't until much later in my spiritual journey that I started to realise the effect it was having on my practice. If I ate a meat meal or drank wine the night before, my morning practice was sluggish and required a lot more effort to move into a meditative state. Moreover, it was harder to maintain a link between my awareness and spirit throughout the day, because the resonance of my energy body was dulled.

But despite being a vegetarian now and still enjoying wine, I do believe that beautiful food, shared meals, and red wine are part of the sumptuous bounty of life and absolutely should be enjoyed if that's what you sense you are needing. The keys are balance, coming to know yourself, and taking action when your energy system is low and sluggish and signalling a need for change and lightness.

There are times when I fast, usually when I am exploring a new meditation technique or working on a specific personal theme with spirit and always when preparing for pilgrimage. And there are times when I overindulge, don't touch my meditation stool for a few days, and feel energetically dull and bleary. Teaching every day tends to keep me far more sensible than the days of my youth, and I am grateful to my students for that. I also prioritise moving my body every day, as soon as I wake. This movement has changed over the years as my body has changed. My yoga practice for many years changed to daily running, and now, since the pandemic began, to daily early-morning bike rides. This balance works for me and earths me and my inner life in this world. No one but you can know your energetic system and how you connect with spirit. Your only responsibility is to work with it, experiment, and find the balance that allows healthy connections, playfulness, and a rich inner life to match. What appears to be common is that as we move more deeply into spirited living and connection with life and the earth, we naturally tend towards a diet that is plant-based. The desire for meat and stimulants naturally diminishes, and we crave the feeling of lightness and higher vibration. This transition seems to happen of its own accord with many and vastly raises the resonance of the energy body. Despite what we have been led to believe, the body does not need meat for protein, and commercial meat farming and fishing is one of the greatest threats to our environment.

A wonderful effect of regular practice is that we become increasingly aware of what foods, minerals, vitamins, and hydration our bodies require, and we are prompted as to the best sources to find them. Many of us eat out of habit and, often, laziness, but our guts know what they need, and as stated in chapter 9, there is actually more neural traffic running from the gut to the brain than the other way around. The gut is telling the brain what to put in the mouth, but we need to cultivate some inner quiet to be able to hear it.

After I had my first child, when I was starting out with breastfeeding, I was starving all the time for—wait for it— fruit cake and eggs. I would munch my way through a family slab of fruitcake nearly every day and down several soft-boiled eggs. It was only later that I learnt that eggs and the dried fruit in fruitcake are very rich in iron. My body knew what my brain didn't at that time—that my iron reserves where low and my gut knew exactly where to find what was needed. And because I was delirious with new-mum fatigue and baby love, I just did what my body told me to do. Meditation helps us tap into that dialogue all the time, from a vital state of consciousness and choice. By following our bodies' natural prompts, we come into a far more beautiful relationship with food and with the earth, and in the meantime, we drop any guilt. Guilt is far more toxic and resonance-depleting than enjoying a glass of Shiraz.

## Meditation Is Not a Religion

I come across this misconception enough to address it here. Sometimes when I am commissioned for corporate workshops and talks, the HR team will make the point that they have several employees of various faiths in the office, and they ask me whether I can please keep God or religious references out of it. Meditation is not a religion, even though nearly all major world religions and spiritual frameworks acknowledge meditation as a vehicle for prayer, ritual and ceremony, and spiritual evolution. And while the frontrunners in meditation techniques are the Eastern traditions, they are not exclusively the source of the practice. Meditation is a human practice, and very beautiful meditation practices are offered by all world religions and cultures.

The changes in brain activity when we meditate enable feelings of deep connection, slipping out of time, acute awareness, and bliss. For example, in deep states of meditation, sections of the prefrontal cortex go into what's called 'temporary hypofrontality', which is a super impressive term that I throw around occasionally to appear, well, super impressive. It just means they temporarily deactivate. In particular, the part of the brain that clocks past, present, and future and places self-awareness somewhere in that context, shuts down. When this happens, you have the sensation that you have deeply penetrated the present moment. It brings an acute sense of awareness and self, and many equate this with a religious experience. I would define this experience as connecting with spirit, but it's not the doing of some strange god that might or might not agree with other gods or, worse still, the effects of the devil. (Yes, I do get that sometimes as well.) This is an inner neurological effect of changing brainwave patterning into deeper and longer waves, and it's very, very, good for you to experience it on many levels, and regularly. Another part of the brain that deactivates is the self-critical section. That naysaying, slightly whinging inner voice that can be pretty consistent and loud for some of us is silenced temporarily. We all know this voice—the one that says, 'You'll never master meditation; you don't stick with anything long enough', 'You're doing it wrong', 'You're not worthy of that love', or 'Don't say a word; your idea is silly.' That gnarly voice is a function of our risk assessment centre, but in modern life, without the presence of a sabre-toothed tiger to assess and advise upon, it turns its attention to any perceived threat, even if it's that job opportunity you have been wanting to apply for. This inner critic also temporarily deactivates in deep states of meditation, and for many of us this creates a rare experience of inner quiet, and with it a feeling of self-worth, possibility, and creativity, which some people equate to a religious experience. In my experience, the more I dwelt in that inner quiet, the more the self-critic lost her voice in general, and eventually she just packed her bags and left completely.

In regular meditators, the frontal parietal junctures are also much more active than in those who don't meditate. This is the part of the brain responsible for feeling empathy and connectedness. And this is a very gorgeous effect of meditation. Sense of connectedness with family, friends, community, and all of life, as well as a growing intolerance for inequality, are also the goals of many religions. Our brains literally shape-shift to increase these feelings. Researchers believe this is why meditation in nursing homes is so effective at stemming the onset of Parkinson's disease and dementia, which have been seen to develop quickly in people who feel isolated and alone.

The techniques of meditation are not religious. That association is up to you. Meditation is about finding your innate ability to connect with spirit, via your energetic aspect. If you do follow a religious framework, then developing your meditation skills can vastly deepen and activate your connection within it.

I believe it is part of the deliciousness of meditation to remain flexible and responsive with the actual practices. Once you access the field of spirit, spirit will guide you. In my opinion, it's the strict prescriptions and rules of religions that insist upon an intermediary to spirit which have disempowered many seekers in finding their own connection and spirited selves.

**You Don't Need to Escape into a Himalayan Cave for Years to Establish a Meditation Practice**

It surprises lots of people to learn how mainstream meditation has been for quite some time in the Western world. And it surprises me that some still hold the view that meditation is a hippy woo-woo activity practised exclusively by New Age drop-outs and the holy men of India. I am thankful that, owing to meditation's renewed trendiness, this misconception is slowly fading, but I find I do need to address it in my talks and courses.

Meditation and mindfulness practices are used extensively in the medical and psychological arenas for treatment of chronic pain, depression, and addiction, and they have been for decades. More recently, they have been used in trauma and cardiac wards with amazing results. They are also used effectively in palliative care and support of the elderly.

Meditation is a critical enabler in underprivileged schools and for troubled students around the world and is now accepted as a key practice in building resilience in children and teens. It is common practice in law enforcement in some progressive countries, such as Canada, and in the sports psychology practices of the professional sports arena. A sport and fitness clinic that I used to collaborate with here in Singapore in several wonderful wellness programmes, hosted the Singapore Rugby Sevens players, and we were thrilled to see the South African Rugby team meditate together before training and games. I have to admit that I find this enormously attractive! I also offer prenatal meditation guidance, and it is a beautiful and natural way to enhance body chemistry during pregnancy and conscious connection with the baby as it forms and during the birth process.

There is a plethora of empirical evidence, studies, and research now that has followed the various applications of meditation and the effects regular practice yields in all sorts of settings for all sorts of people living busy modern lives.

Meditation doesn't require a specific space or method; it just requires the intent, choice, and action. It is with regular practice that the benefits start to become evident. There are a couple of very useful things you can do to help establish a regular practice easily by working with your meditation space, starting ritual, and regularity.

The actual space where you meditate is ultimately inconsequential, but I do believe choosing a quiet, beautiful space and honouring the practice with a cloth, candle, oils, and flowers makes a huge difference to the experience. Meditation is, in many respects, a sacred art. We honour our true nature and ourselves when we engage with it. Making the time to set a sacred space acknowledges this and can also be very helpful in the initial stage of establishing a practice. I suggest to my students that they obtain a dedicated cushion or stool, cloth, and scent. I encourage them to establish a space at home for the practice and to also try to meditate at the same time each day, at least initially. And most importantly, I suggest they use the same kit and follow the same preparatory steps each time. The reason for this is that the mind, with repetition, will create an association between the smell of the incense, the turning out of the cloth, the settling into the favourite corner, the light of the dawn, and the act of meditation. Your simple preparatory ritual and entering meditation become linked in your system, and this can greatly serve you in settling your system efficiently and turning your awareness inwards. I always meditate and teach while burning Nag Champa incense and have done so for decades. I love the stuff. I have a very strong association between the scent of the incense sticks and deep states of meditation. Now when I open my wooden chest with all my teaching kit inside and get a gentle whiff of the perfume, I can feel my whole system start to 'draw in', even when I am rushing out the door. Making the meditation experience beautiful, with simple ritual, makes it sacred and helps establish it as an important part of a busy life. When you start to meditate, follow your instincts to make the act sacred through simple, heartfelt ritual. It's an art, and we come to know its importance and power by engaging in it.

In my courses, I don't prescribe any particular method for meditation. I try to teach from a wide enough pallet so each student can find his or her groove with his or her inner aspect. For the beginners, I do advise that they meditate for at least ten minutes a day and that they intuit the meditation technique themselves from that pallet. Ten minutes a day for around twenty-one days will establish a neural pathway for meditation. The habit of meditation will be formed within the brain, and this makes each meditation sit much easier. The ability to concentrate the mind and bring it into presence can be strengthened with practice and habit, fortunately. The psyche and the body cleverly respond to this habit. After a short time, just planning your meditation sit for the day will trigger a subtle 'drawing in' of the body and mind, even before you start your practice. With regular practice and neurological pathways established, an expanded awareness becomes the operating mode day to day, and the many physiological benefits become the physical norm. It is in this state that we are able to move through the transformative steps from reactive, to responsive, to expansive, and into creative living. We become spirited.

A beautiful friend and fellow meditator, Bonnie, once described this path-laying process as she felt it. She said that when you start to meditate, it's a bit like trekking into a field of wild golden barley. It is exciting, but it requires a bit of effort to fell a pathway. But after repeatedly walking the same route in, the barley stems bow, the path to the interior of the field is defined, and the effort provides a cushioned path. And once you enter and feel and know you are living in a spirited way, you find that you are creating profound and intricate crop circles in that barley field of the soul.

# CHAPTER 18

# From Reactive Living to Responsive Living

Being spirited requires intent, desire, energy, and actioned choice, and at the outset it's always best to start with building your ability to concentrate the mind and bring it into present awareness. This is key, as it allows us to contain and amplify our resonance—the vibration of our energy body.

The good news is, that by engaging in concentration meditations, we actually strengthen the brain's ability to concentrate, amongst several other mind-blowing cognitive improvements, like restored memory, greater lateral thinking and problem-solving, increased ability to learn new things, heightened creativity, to name a few. These wonderful upgrades start to happen relatively quickly. Current research tells us that within eight weeks of regular meditation practise, the brain picks up its act considerably and starts to structurally change to keep doing it. To improve your ability to concentrate your awareness, initially can take a bit of effort, because most of us have lived our adult lives holding on to the back of a seriously out of control, highly dissipated monkey mind by our fingernails!

The most readily available way to directly change brainwave patterns, and therefore dissipate frenetic thought activity, is to master the breath. And what I have found to be most helpful to all my students to enable them to do this quickly is to teach them the connection between the act of breathing and their physiology. When you understand what's actually happening in your system when you employ different breathing techniques, you are better able to work with those natural connections and detect the shifts.

This is what the Holy Men of India and the shamans figured out thousands of years ago through applied practice, observation, and access to higher fields of information, well before medical science existed as it does in modern times, and certainly before there was any means to measure it.

There is a direct connection between how we breathe and the activity of the mind. A favourite analogy I use when teaching new students how to prepare the system to meditate is, 'If the mind is a kite, then the breath is the string.' I don't know who coined this phrase, but it's old, and I discovered it in a yogic text, I think. I wish I could credit the originator, because this is a spot-on beautiful metaphor for this connection. When we wield the breath, we can draw in the mind. And the breath deepens and lengthens of its own accord when we place our attention on it.

There are five key connections between breath and the brain/body/energy system that can be worked with through specific meditation practice. When students have a cognitive understanding of what these connections are, they are more able to sense them and their effects and therefore deepen their meditative experience. In all of my courses, I teach a range of breathing techniques that vastly impact the experience of meditation. Mindful breathing is one of them, but there are many others, mainly from the yogic tradition called pranayama ('*Prana*' meaning 'life force', and '*Yama*' meaning 'breath'). Meditative breathing, or pranayama (energy breath) draws in the kite-mind from the windy heights of modern life, changes brainwave patterns, and synchronises the nervous system. When the physical system eases into presence and calm coherence, the energy body rises. And as it does all of this, it also regulates itself to allow deeper and more nourishing breaths as you go. How cool is that?

When you understand these connections and have correctly adopted the breathing techniques, you're up and running. The online resources in appendix A contain several very accessible and effective guided breathing techniques to prepare the system for meditation.

## Detoxification, Oxygenation, and Prana

The breath is the only function of the autonomic nervous system that we can control. When we are stressed or not mindful, our breathing becomes shallow and quick. This is sometimes referred to as 'stress breathing.' Placing our fully concentrated awareness onto the act of breathing is called mindful breathing. Mindful breathing naturally produces deeper inhalations and longer exhalations. Breathing is one of the physical body's most important detoxification systems, and mindful breathing is our subtle body's most important clearing and energy-raising system. When we breathe in long, smooth, even movements, we also oxygenate the brain, allowing sharper attention and focus on the inner state.

After several minutes of simply noticing the feeling of the breath in the body, you will find that the character of the breath changes. It becomes softer, deeper, and longer.

This shift in the breath indicates deeper shifts in the brain and nervous system. It's one to look for. When you sense it, you can introduce a simple mantra to keep you moving more deeply into the practice. For example, as you breathe in, mentally say, 'Receive', and as you breathe out, 'Release.' By leaning your attention into the sensation of the breath, you connect your awareness with the renewal process and energy of your breath.

**Providing a Resonant Point of Focus for the Mind and Body**

The breath is our most portable and accessible point of focus in meditation. The breath makes us feel good, especially when we allow it to deepen. It also has a resonant quality, creating a vibration through the body and a gentle sound. All of these factors help to engage the attention. Some pranayama techniques, such as ocean breath (ujjayi breathing) and black bee breath (brahmara breathing) ramp up the vibratory action a little further with soft snoring and humming techniques, with amazing results on concentration and brainwave patterning.

There is also a mystery to the breath. We can never really know the breath. The closest we can get to it is to observe the feelings that it creates as it courses through the body and mind. A lovely contemplative thought to include in any mindful breathing meditation is 'Am I breathing? Or am I being breathed?'

**The Connection Between the Diaphragm and the Brain**

In general, the modern state is a state of perpetual high alert, at least from the body's perspective. Sensory and data overload, world anxiety, and competitive social and professional environments all take their toll on our physiology. Our brainwave patterning becomes short and quick (beta waves) when we are hypervigilant or stressed.

The sympathetic arm of our nervous system becomes

overstimulated, and this triggers the release of adrenals and other stress hormones, along with a series of physiological reactions, including tummy lockdown, interrupted sleep patterns, and low libido, to name a few. This state is characterised by shallow thoracic breathing. Most of us during the day breathe from only the top 20 per cent of our lungs, and many of us unknowingly hold the breath regularly during the day.

With the intention to calm the system and the attention on the breath, our breathing automatically settles and deepens to diaphragmatic breathing. This changes the air pressure in the abdominal cavity, which in turn triggers a neural sensor in the abdomen that tells the brain to calm down. Diaphragmatic breathing enables a shift into an alpha brainwave state initially and then into deeper brainwave states, such as theta wave and gamma wave states, which are associated with very deep states of meditation and expanded awareness. Thích Nhất Hạnh's beautiful quote speaks to this wisdom: 'Breath is the bridge, which connects life to consciousness, which unites your body to your thoughts.'

**The Breath, the Brain, the Energy Body Connection**

Breathing through the nose is important for calming the mind/body system unless your body is working through a cold or other virus and your nose is blocked. My suggestion to my students is to always breathe through the nose when meditating.

With every breath, the airflow in the nostrils stimulates our microscopic hairlike nerve endings, the cilia, which line the nasal passages. When the cilia are stimulated, they send waves of nerve impulses to the left and right hemispheres of the brain. These messages bring the brain and central nervous system into balance and coherence, and create a lovely still environment for meditation.

Nadi shodhana, or alternate nostril breathing, is a popular breathing method, particularly before practising yoga asana, and is a very effective starting practice for meditation because it expressly works with the connection between nasal flow and the brain. By gently blocking alternate nostrils for the inhalation and exhalation, we can work with the nerve communication between the nose and brain, and bring the system into coherence. The practice of alternate nostril breathing induces a shift to longer, slower brain waves in a relatively short space of time and brings balance to the sympathetic and parasympathetic arms of the nervous system. It also brings balance to the energetic nadis, or circuitry, which allows them to activate, cleanse, and vibrate. You just need to practise it to feel its immediate result.

This, of course, is a very brief overview. There is a rich and ancient tradition that underlies the practices of pranayama and, especially, alternate nostril breathing, and the benefits observed over thousands of years attest to their benefits and fit with our natural design. At minimum you can try nadi shodhana or any of the other techniques listed in the appendices and see for yourself, or simply stop yourself through the day and take some deep abdominal breaths, knowing that the inflow of air through the nostrils is bathing your brain and synchronising your central nervous system.

## Balance in the Blood and Breath

Our bodies naturally seek harmony and balance. Doing so is the nature of the life force that ripples through every cell and every breath. When we give ourselves the stillness and space required, the natural processes for establishing balance will occur. I find this both very reassuring and very cool.

Perhaps one of the best ways to experience this reach for harmony is with the breath. When $CO_2$ levels rise in the blood, the body will naturally open the airways by easing the erectile tissues in the nostrils, throat, and oesophagus to allow a greater intake of oxygen

This delicate balance to ensure highest functioning of all the bodily systems is happening all the time. One of the aims of meditative or mindful breathing is to allow a shift into deep, smooth, and almost silent diaphragmatic breathing. For this to happen, the airways need to be soft and open.

This natural connection can also be mindfully engaged. The Buketyo breathing method and activating the yogic bandhas are two practices I use to open the airways and deepen the breath naturally. Buketyo involves taking a deep, deliberate breath; holding the breath; gently nodding the head for thirty seconds or so; and then releasing the breath in a complete exhalation through the nose. This is repeated for five to six rounds. Within two to three attempts, you can feel the breath penetrating deeper and deeper into your core. The currently popular Wim Hof breathing method engages the same mechanism, with increasingly longer holds after the exhalation.

Activating the bandhas involves retracting the major circulatory locks within the body. There are three main bandhas, which lie at the throat, navel, and pelvic floor. The bandhas serve to slow and even halt blood circulation momentarily and to slow the flow of energy through the system. During the lock, a gentle pressure builds at these natural gateways, and when the bandha is released, blood flow and energy swoosh through the physical and energetic body, knocking out blockages and toxins.

The activation of bandhas is synced with the breath— either the held breath or exhaled breath (empty lungs), depending on which combination of bandhas you use. Either way will cause the levels of $CO_2$ to gently rise and therefore to trigger the body to open the airways and allow deeper, smoother, longer breathing, naturally. A simple use of bandhas is easy and requires a little consistent practice to feel the effects. The neck bandha (Jalandhara bandha) can be activated after the in breath or the out breath. This involves maintaining an upright posture and dropping the chin to the collarbone in a firm hold for several seconds. Then you release the bandha by raising the head and either exhaling or inhaling, depending on the sequence you are following. The base bandha (Mula bandha) can also be engaged after the inhalation or exhalation. This involves pulling up the muscles of the pelvic floor, rectum, and perineum in a firm hold and then releasing the lock before exhaling or inhaling. The naval bandha (Uddiyana bandha) should be engaged only after the exhalation. This involves pulling the navel muscles back towards the spine and then lifting them. You can feel the lock engage with practice. After a few seconds, you can release the bandha and then inhale. The bandhas can be used in combination, on their own, or all three at once after the exhalation. This three-lock move is called maha bandha. Another very accessible way to open the airways is to lie in shivasana when meditating. As previously described, this posture requires the back of head, spine, and tailbone to be aligned without the use of pillows or headrests. The legs are positioned at hip width apart, the feet falling softly outwards. The arms are positioned by the sides, with the palms facing upwards.

Whilst this is a passive posture for meditation, the release into the back of the body has the unique effect of opening the airways and allowing a deeper, smoother breath. But be warned: if your body is tired, you will drift into a supercharged nana nap rather than meditating. But if you are tired, this probably serves you better anyway.

Another fabulous easy practice to train the mind into presence is called Counting Breath Meditation. This comes from the Zen Buddhist tradition and in theory seems pretty simple. All you need to do is settle your system and then start to internally count your breaths. A full inhalation and exhalation is one count. You do this up to ten breaths, and then you start again at one. Counting ten breaths for ten minutes sounds easy, huh? Well, here's the kicker: if at any time you catch your mind dulling to the task or, better still, you wake up to yourself and discover you are well off-piste and deep into the details of your overdue tax return or how to design the kids' book week costumes for school, then you simply start again at one. To be honest, I really disliked this practice when I first started with it. My teacher, Louise, made it a regular feature of my earlier lessons with her. It annoyed me. I thought I could meditate after years of self-instruction; reading many, many books; and having a highly experimental nature. I had wild feelings of bliss. I 'saw' colours and inner light. I knew what I was doing. And then came Louise and the counting of breaths. It quickly made me realise I had very little control over my mind. Even if I was forcing myself onto the count, I realised that I was thinking about keeping the count and not simply being with the count. It challenged everything I 'thought' about my mind and certainly exposed my weak concentration abilities. However, with perseverance and a healthy ego refusing to admit defeat, I made counting breaths my dedicated private practice for months. And slowly but surely, it revealed its secrets.

This beautiful, simple, ancient practice showed me the nature of my thoughts and how my inner attention gets pulled and lulled into non-presence. It showed me the inane things that I dwell on. It showed me the thought patterns that I repeatedly loop through. And most importantly, it showed me that my ability to 'pull in' my awareness can be strengthened. Thank goodness. Each time I caught my mind wandering and I brought it back to the task, it was like doing a little rep for the brain. It is a concentration workout. What's cool about this simple practice is that the count itself provides a benchmark. You can see how far you have come from 'one ... one, two, three ... one ...' to higher numbers and even repeat cycles of ten on a good day. Counting breaths taught me to go gently with myself. A far more productive sit occurs when you catch your mind wandering a hundred times and you gently bring it back, happy that you have caught it. This is far more useful than forcing the mind into stillness, which doesn't work, or, even worse, kidding yourself that you actually are in stillness. Every time your mind wanders and you gently catch it and bring it back to centre, you are strengthening your mind and learning how to control your awareness. You are converting your softly glowing light bulb into a diamond.

So there we have it—the breath–brain connection! Our

awareness settles the breath. Our breath settles the system and mind and gently brings us into presence. This is perfectly captured in another gorgeous quote from Thích Nhất Hạnh: 'To meditate with mindful breathing, is to bring body and mind back to the present moment so that you do not miss your appointment with life.'

# CHAPTER 19

# From Responsive Living to Expansive Living

Meditation occurs when posture, breath, and mental point of focus are combined effectively and brainwave activity and the central nervous system become coherent and synchronised. This in turn alters the state of consciousness so that we can witness our internal environment. The practitioner moves into the viewpoint of the still, steady observer behind the breath and the body, the thoughts and the feelings.

When we dwell in this state regularly, some amazing things start to happen in our mind/body system. We regenerate physically. We have a greater sense of well-being, greater empathy, and greater connectedness. We connect with our energy body and awareness, and through that with spirit. With regular practice and arrival into this still aware centre, it starts to become our new default centre, even off the meditation mat and this, is called 'mindfulness.'

Mindfulness is the ability to experience day-to-day life from this viewpoint of the witness. Living mindfully means engaging in life with choice and discernment rather than reactive patterned behaviours. It doesn't mean we don't feel things or get pissed off or feel anger. These are natural movements of energy that need to be expressed, but how we express them starts to change. Perhaps more importantly, we have the inner space to really see why we are triggered by certain situations or personalities. We start to realise that the edge is within us and not the external experience or other person, and then we can choose what we do about it. We become curious, open, and more accepting. We stop worrying about so much stuff. We start to live in the now and participate more fully in each moment, and this slows the illusion of flying time. It takes us out of the modern world's incessant race against time. Past hurts, regrets, and self-limiting beliefs become evident, and we realise how much inner space and energy they take up, sometimes for many years, like gnarled old roots within our inner ground. When we dig them up and out, we heal them, to allow movement to new perspectives, rather than reactivate them with looped victim patterns, attack, and defence. It's a far more elegant way to roll, and it gives the spiral of transformation some room to move us from *reactive* living to *responsive* living. Once we are moving, it's a natural spiral into *expansive* living. Within this state, we start to contain our spiritual energy and raise our vibration into a lighter and faster resonance, therefore opening our awareness to more subtle, faster, and lighter forms of energies and information.

There are many forms of meditation categorised as 'mindfulness meditations', and this type of practice derives mainly from the Buddhist tradition, but all of the thousands of meditation techniques and practices all eventually lead to living mindfully and from the intuitive heart.

In theory, it sounds so wonderful, and possibly even easy. However, nurturing mindfulness is a choice, and it requires some commitment to reprogram our behaviours, especially reactive triggers that we have held for many years and that we hold as part of our personalities and our life stories. It's an area of inner practice that fascinates me, and it's one that I teach.

One afternoon, I was pondering this very thing in preparation for an upcoming talk about 'Raising Resonance' that I was to give at a women's brunch series titled Meditation for the Modern Woman, in Singapore. I took my notebook down to the garden and set up camp poolside to muse and doodle. I was pondering mindfulness as a tool for transformation, and I was chewing on the obvious question, If we are able to witness ourselves, identify where we need to keep moving, and dissolve the blocks and heal ourselves along the great spiral, then why don't we? We all have had experiences of letting go of something that we know no longer serves us, and the energy and relief that such experiences generate. We may not explain this phenomenon as I do here, but from experience we all know that it's possible. So why don't we do it all the time? Why don't we create as much movement as possible within our hearts and energy fields? What prevents us from expanding our inner space?

It was a beautiful butterfly with fire-coloured wings of red, orange, and yellow (which I later learnt is aptly called the 'painted Jezebel') that arrived on the scene that sunny warm afternoon and demonstrated some key principles of meditation and mindfulness. It was a perfectly timed wild spirit, and it delivered into my mind and notebook the talk for the brunch series.

Right at the point when I was considering the top behaviours that drain our vital energy, or resonance fields, and why we continue to do them, this little being fluttered its way over the pool and dived from a great height into the water. My daughter, who amongst many other things is a passionate animal conservationist, swam to its rescue. Its wings were firmly stuck to the water surface, its legs flailing. She extended her finger, and with its tiny legs, the butterfly grabbed it. She was able to lift it out of the water without touching its wings. We popped it on a plant away from the pool and went back to our morning. As soon as the wings had dried, it fluttered out over the pool again and, as if drawn by a magnetic field, flopped straight back into the water. This happened over and over again. After many rescue attempts, we began to wonder whether indeed the sweet little Jezebel was trying to end it all. But it fought so hard to free itself from the water surface once it was caught that it seemed clear it wanted to live. On several occasions, it managed to flap itself free and gain some altitude, showing enormous strength for such a fragile tiny creature, only to stop flapping and dive back down to certain peril.

It seemed so deliberate that I couldn't help wondering whether there was a principle at hand being demonstrated through these antics. The death-plunges were repeated over and over again right in front of me. It had caught my attention. But it was the resonance in my heart space and body that made me take notice. I felt spirit. I decided to look at the butterfly scene with 'symbolic sight.' If this was indeed a spiritual metaphor, then I would open all my senses and simply witness it thematically. And indeed, this gorgeous fire-coloured butterfly demonstrated five key truths about mindfulness and inner movement from responsiveness to expansiveness, for which I am very grateful. And here they are:

**Butterfly Truth 1: Old Patterns and the Un-Present Mind**

Despite knowing that it doesn't serve any purpose to rehash old hurts, pick the scabs off old injuries, relive in our minds the best retorts to the ones who so smartly hurt us, and, perhaps most commonly, reproach ourselves for not being or doing enough, there is a stickiness to repeated negative thoughts and emotional patterns. Perhaps this is because of the familiarity of the long-held pattern. Perhaps much of our identities and who we think we are is stacked atop it. Perhaps we're unsure of what would fill the space or silence if we turned off that looped tape inside us. But unmindfully and repeatedly returning to old negative thought patterns is very destructive and is one of the quickest ways to deplete our resonance. Why? As Dr Joe Dispenza, author of *Breaking the Habit of Being Yourself*, puts it, 'Because the body is the unconscious mind. It does not know the difference between an actual experience in life that creates an emotion or when an emotion is created by thought alone. As a result, the body can get knocked out of homeostasis just by thinking.'

Harvard Medical School research estimates that for a massive 45 per cent of the waking day, we are not present. That's nearly half the waking day. While driving the car, spending time with loved ones, working, and daydreaming, we are not actually here. Which begs the question, If we have checked out of our present realities, then where are we?

The research suggests that we are not necessarily in

a happy place. When our minds wander about anywhere except the present moment, they usually wander off in a thought direction that induces either a stress response or negative emotions. We're either dwelling on experiences in the past, especially the ones perceived as not so good; or we're off into the future, stressing about the things yet to come. By not being mindful and present, we are flooding our systems with stress responses by way of our negatively biased thought loops.

Moreover, our sense of well-being and happiness has very little to do with *what* we are actually doing and everything to do with the degree of presence that we bring to it. That's right! The clinical research is telling us that we feel unhappy because our minds are wandering, when most of us perhaps think that our minds are wandering because we feel unhappy.

Our systems react to the repeated thought loops and emotional response patterns as if the perceived perpetrator were right there in the room with us. By rehashing negative thought patterns, we are only hurting ourselves on many unseen levels through heightened anxiety, stress, tension, limited sense of self, and a non-presence that takes us away from the potential and delight of the present moment and our spirit selves.

## Butterfly Truth 2: Meditation Creates Space and Light to Illuminate Old Repeated Patterns

We set the butterfly on a sunny part of a tree, and the wings fully dried. It seemed to gather energy while remaining completely still in the light.

Meditation creates a shift in our points of view to a still, detached centre from where we can see the patterns and loops occurring through our minds and systems. Like letting in the sunshine, we are able to become aware not only of them and what triggers them but also of how they make us feel. Regular meditation creates the space to choose to jettison them and enact a different response, and it creates the energy for us to do so.

## Butterfly Truth 3: The Power of Clarity of Intent, a Choice, and Regular Effort.

It took no less than eight rescues of this butterfly before it chose life and could fly over the water without succumbing to its mesmerising draw. It also takes conscious work and repeated application to dig up and remove from our psyches old habitual thoughts and emotional patterns. They have an addictive quality to the un-present mind. The beautiful meditation practice of brahmavihara cultivation is one of several powerful frameworks to use when releasing past hurts. Many students, myself included, find they need to repeat the exercise until they can fully feel the unconditional forgiveness and release the blessing brings, especially when they are forgiving themselves. With intention and choosing to practise brahmavihara regularly, many also report a release from old patterns that they realised they had been carrying on their backs for many years. More on this beautiful Buddhist meditation later in this chapter.

## Butterfly Truth 4: Gratitude Cauterises Old Habitual Negativity

The butterfly took flight once again, to much applause from a crew of neighbourhood kids who had gathered in the pool and were ready to catch it again if it fell. It did a loop over the pool and seemed to swoop dangerously low. But with the sun's energy in its wings, it changed tack and avoided its usual death plummet into the water. It had the strength to choose a different flight path. It flew back around the garden, and then, just for a moment, it landed on my outstretched hand. Now, I know I'm an old hippy, but I had the distinct impression that it was appreciative of its rescues and stopped for a moment to say/flap 'Thanks.' And I, in turn, was overwhelmed with gratitude for the succinct demonstration of mindfulness and awareness this little being had delivered for my talk.

What I have observed in my own practice and in my courses is that just thinking you're grateful doesn't do much. It's the feeling of unconditional heartfelt gratitude that does everything. It heals old wounds. It creates a magnetic field that attracts more of what you're grateful for. It opens up miraculous worlds hidden in the everyday. It makes you strong. Heart-centred gratitude meditations allow gratitude to fill the heart-space and radiate out into life, and gratitude can be cultivated. There are many beautiful psychological writings on the power of gratitude, along with many different ways to cultivate it. Pondering your blessings within a meditative state is one of them. This allows not only the recounting of blessings in life but also the observation of the wonderful energy released into the heart space with it. When engaging in gratitude cultivation as a meditation, you come to feel and know the distinct signature energy of gratitude, and you can direct it into every cell and into your life field. And this attracts more of those blessings, because we create what we are giving our life force to.

## Butterfly Truth 5: Seeking a Higher Perspective Weakens the Draw Below

To a riotous cheer from the neighbourhood kids, the butterfly flew up to a high branch of a tree in the garden, safe and clear from danger, and shortly afterwards was met by another (very pretty-looking) butterfly!

So often when we voice our negative thought patterns and perceived hurts, they find the willing ears of well-meaning friends and family. So often some relationships are based on the rehashing of negative patterns or the roles of victim and saviour. So often we seek out dialogue and content that validates old patterns, allowing it to take deeper root in our mind/body systems. Meditation also throws light on these dynamics within our relationships and content. This can be challenging sometimes, especially when it involves family or long-held friendships. Seeking higher ground in what you read, the company you keep, and the lifestyle choices you make makes the draw to the old contracting patterns weaken and quickly fade. Seek higher ground and find your strength, and maybe another like-minded butterfly! When we resonate with positivity, we attract positive people into our fields. Our vibes attracts our tribes.

The shift to an *expansive* consciousness, in my experience, happens naturally once inner space is established within the heart and feelings, the mind and awareness. It comes more swiftly when we are engaged in regular inner practice and we are starting to trust the process of living from the inside out. The choice to be spirited creates a strong desire in us to make inner space and allow for transformation and growth.

Especially in these current times, we are all being challenged to explore and choose: What is it that I stand for? And more and more of us are seeking ways to change the ways in which we engage with life, and to therefore experience it differently. And here's the thing: to make these choices, we need to take full responsibility for ourselves and what we are experiencing in life. New age pop spirituality has many of us beguiled into thinking that feeling comfortable, safe, or constantly blissful is the goal—that it's all about rainbows and unicorns. But authentic spiritual practice generates a shakedown. We have to claim the discomfort and move into the unknown if we are to ever really transform into fullness. In Lakota shamanism, this archetypal shift is called 'sitting in the fire.' With an expanded spiritual perspective—that 'the fire' is both the message that we are out of alignment with our spirited natures and the raw energy to do something about it—the self-judgement and false belief in bad luck, bad gods, and life being done 'to us' give way to total self-acceptance and self-agency, as well as a deep knowing that life is working for us.

'Cognitive dissonance' is a term used in modern psychology to describe the feeling of discomfort when holding two or more conflicting ideas, beliefs, or values. It suggests that we have an inner drive to hold on to our beliefs and attitudes even if they feel uncomfortable and unstable because they are familiar and we perhaps can't 'see' what an alternative self or life might look like or be like when we release the old. Remember our beautiful painted Jezebel? It can be easier to blame life than to do the work. However, it's in owning and loving the dark, murky corners that we find the treasure. As my teacher once told me, 'The deeper you move into your darkness, the closer to spirit you draw.'

This requires, above all else, a courageous fling off the precipice of comfort, a complete surrender to the process and a deep trust in our divine design and soul journey. It takes presence, intent, and action to stop reacting to life and instead to love it. Or, in the words of my Druid friend Mark, '... to be happy to sit with the murky depths of change. Hold it. Bathe in it.'

Shadow dancing (or murky-depth bathing, if you like that earthy Druid talk) is how we make space in the heart. And for me the three most important supports for this are to find my spirit tribe and have authentic, honest conversations about my inner work; to maintain continued commitment to pause, witness, and intentionally choose responses based in love, thereby rewiring well-laid habitual behaviours; and to practise my inner dance moves.

Your spirit tribe is the circle of people you can talk with about your inner moves. They are people who are also spiritually active and are also learning and refracting wisdom. In sharing our inner journeys, we enable the embodiment of them, and others can help us identify our blind spots along the way.

Continued commitment to transformation almost always involves cycling back over past themes and experiences to ensure they are fully released. This can be disillusioning for many. It is very common in my spiritual guidance sessions for students to lament that similar themes have emerged into their lives after they have done so much inner work on them. The fact that they can 'see' the patterns is already indicating a shift in inner perspective. This circling back over similar ground also creates the opportunity to again choose freedom and space, which releases more energy into our fields, expanding the space and vibration to allow perception of the lessons and facilitate transmutation of the patterns once and for all.

Our murky depths contain our beliefs and other karmic threads from our lineages and past lives. It's not always clear where the root is, and we can tie ourselves into knots trying to intellectualise and 'treat' it. A soul choice repeated over and over to clear our heart space is enough to release the inner binds. The other must for shadow dancing is to make time to practise our inner dance moves and to learn new ones if we keep stepping on our shadow's toes. If the pattern or bind is too sticky to release alone or with the tools you have, then seek help or a new move. When I am in the process of accepting and expanding into a new part of myself, I try new spiritual practices. I'll engage in some reading, attend a workshop or ritual as a participant rather than a guide, or seek out a healer. Transformation is rigorous, but without a doubt, it is the best dance of life. Once you have engaged, you will find that the perfect tribe and dance moves start to draw to you. The reaching eases, and all that is required is responsiveness to what is presented for you to do. Every single day, we are presented with a series of choices. Dr Joe Dispenza estimates that we make ten thousand choices a day. Some such choices are regarding what to eat for breakfast, what to wear, and the best traffic route to work, and some of these will relate to how we respond to others and life events: choices like 'Shall I continue to be hurt by that silly comment, or shall I let it go?' and 'As much as I am being annoyed by that waiter today, shall I smile and tip, or shall I roll my eyes and make him feel bad?' All ten thousand choices each day boil down to a fear response or love response. And we always have the choice—always. All of them are invitations to live more consciously, to honour the other, to be more playful, curious, creative. You will experience ten thousand invitations to freedom just in this day alone. To heal the world of its bond to helplessness and fear, we have to choose love first within ourselves, honestly, all the time. The world is won one heart at a time. It's not a fun one-day project; it's a lifetime commitment.

With mindfulness, we can do this, as we start to see the old conditioned patterns of defence and attack and we then choose to let them go. It's all about living in *direct* mode rather than *narrative* mode. Jon Kabat Zinn puts it so eloquently: 'It involves cultivating the ability to direct the attention to experience as it unfolds, with open-minded curiosity and acceptance.' Someone told me once (and I have no real idea whether this is true but am just using it to illustrate the point) that a goldfish has the memory retention of around three seconds. So by the time it swims around its little bowl and back to the blue rock and plant at the front, it sees them anew every time. 'Heh, look! There's a cool blue rock and plant … Heh, look! There's a cool blue rock and plant.' And around it merrily goes in its little goldfish way. In many ways, it's a guru of mindfulness! But seriously, how can we cultivate this open-minded curiosity and acceptance? How can we learn to bring our presence into whatever it is we are doing so that the mind is drawn and engaged and we are 100 per cent on? How do we release the memories, perceptions, judgements, and fantasies that pull at our attention and energy relentlessly?

Our heart space is the seat of spirit. It is in this sacred central inner temple that we sense our intuition and inner guidance, and experience the flow of the spirit and life. This flow is often described as a spiralling river of living water that rises in the heart, finds its channels, heals, inspires, and lifts our entire beings, and with them, the ways in which we engage with life. But this flow needs space to move through the heart, and we carry so much hardened crap in our hearts—many of us for years. So how do we lighten our heart loads? How do we create the inner space to allow the *spiral* of spirit and all its gifts of vitality, purpose, love, guidance, and abundance to stream through us and out into all that we experience?

The answer is intention and practice.

Firstly, *intend for* space and freedom. Our intent is the powerhouse of all that we experience. When we bring this intent for heart space and connection with spirit to everything we do, we activate it. With inner intent, even the most menial of activities become a powerful spiritual practice. The annual cupboard clear-out becomes a potent ritual for clearing our attachment to objects and fear of not having enough. The detoxes, fasts, and lighter diets become incredible experiences of releasing energy into our higher centres and amplifying our sensitivity to *flow*, rather than the heart-hardening shame-based processes they often are. Even washing dishes and taking a shower, with intent, can generate space-creating energy in our lives.

We cultivate mindfulness by practice. Learning to draw in the dissipated mind is a bit like going to a mah-jong group. The more regularly you go, the more you start to win! It is also similar to working out at the gym; the more regularly you go, the stronger you get and the easier the training gets. We know that with regular meditation our brains and systems start to change. We know that the more regularly we draw into our still, calm, witnessing centres, the better at it we get and the more we tend to hang out there when we're off our meditation stools and going about our days. A bit of cross-training is good too. The next time you are doing something that you once thought made you unhappy, such as ironing someone else's shirts, washing up, or preparing your tax returns, for example, try using your concentration to specifically get present with the task. When you are breathing, eating, walking, taking a shower, or making love, catch yourself and your mind wandering about and come right back to what you are doing and whom you are with. Practise being present for the rest of the time it takes you to read this book, and see what happens.

There is infinite space in the deep now when we go gently and stay present. We can create space every day, every moment. By slowing down and taking in the moment, we can create space in our pace. By nurturing ourselves, we create space within our senses of beauty and well-being. By moving slowly and mindfully, we create space in our kinetics and energy fields. By nurturing compassion with everyone we contact, and by always looking for the good in others—and especially ourselves—we create space in our relationships. Grudges, guilt, perceived hurts, and the need to be right are some of the most heavily loaded, heart-hardening habits to hold.

We build and reinforce hardened walls in the heart with repeated reactive thoughts and the emotions they trigger. With regular meditation, we create the pause point internally to recognise these repeated patterns and all the physical heart-hardening stress responses they elicit. If you are able to engage deeply with inner practice, Spirit will draw to the space you free up in your heart, just as nature rushes to fill a void.

Sometimes when it's a well-worn old mental or emotional track, we can be strongly attached to it, like our fiery butterfly's draw to the water. In these situations, much more intentional pattern-interrupters are needed to create an energetic shift, a softening of the hardened banks of the heart, which makes it much easier to expand our inner spaces and allow spirit to flow. Sometimes the heart-contracting pattern can be a sticky one, especially if it's a perceived hurt that we tend to rerun over and over again, energising a victim position and needing to prove we are right. This is even more so if the channel for the experience is in our lives and is also engaged with us in defence and attack. Usually when we are engaged in this contracting dance, the trigger for the hurt returns, either through the same channel or through different situations but carrying the same theme. When we can see we are in a themed loop of triggers, it's worth ramping up the effort to disrupt the reactive patterns with some quick and powerful pattern interrupters. Following are a few that have proven very effective for me and my clients over the years.

## Brahmavihara Cultivation

For many years, I have included brahmavihara cultivation (more commonly known as metta) in my courses to cultivate my clients' capacity to forgive and love unconditionally. Heart-centred meditations are altruistic in nature. Brahmavihara works with an expanded resonance in the heart to affect the whole, and this can work brilliantly to de-personalise events we are experiencing and introduce a far more noble approach.

Brahmavihara, or metta, is just one of several ancient practices that are powerful, energetic heart-expanders. It is beautifully explained in Joel and Michelle Levey's book *Luminous Minds*: 'The essence of this reflective prayer and meditation for the cultivation of loving kindness is the wish that we, and all beings, enjoy happiness and well-being.'

Brahmavihara is powerful in its simplicity. Many practitioners choose to start and end each day with the practice. The key to its effectiveness is in the realisation that we are all interconnected in spirit and that at the heart of all of us is an eternal purity that seeks expression and unconditional love for ourselves and for all. It is a meditation performed from the heart whilst using images and ideas in the mind to open the heart and shift the consciousness.

Brahmavihara cultivation requires a clear and deeply felt intent to heal and release, both for yourself and those in your life. The traditional steps are to hold this intent and wish for well-being in your heart and mind and repeat phrases of freedom and highest desires for yourself first and then to expand the radius of your loving-kindness successively out to wider and wider circles of relationships. The gentle expanding focus from the self to the fourth and final step, which relates to our enemies, steps us through a process of opening the heart and allowing love to flow through it and into the life field.

True freedom requires us to release all past hurts and patterns that bind the heart, and to shift to a state of loving-kindness; yep, we are to live every single day above the turmoil of taking things personally, and to be loving and kind to everyone and everything. Not only is living this way possible, but we hit peak spirited experience when we do so. To do it, we need to forgive and rise. We need to start seeing things as they are, with everything and everyone being an action of spirit. We often kid ourselves that we have forgiven a past hurt, but we can still hold such hurts in our unconscious minds for a lifetime, and this quietly affects how we perceive life and treat others. We repeat these hurts in our stories, imbedding them into our identities. We use them as excuses and justifications. I taught a woman once who admitted that whenever she was hurt by someone, she would write his or her name on a piece of paper and place it in the back of her deep freeze. 'They are frozen out of my life!' she exclaimed triumphantly during one lesson when we were about to embark on metta for the first time. This highly intelligent senior executive, wife, and mother of two had developed an interesting way to deal with her past hurts. But the reality was that she had frozen them into her heart space. I joked with her that every time she went for the frozen peas, there those past hurts would be, growling behind the ice-cream tub. She agreed and took to brahmavihara with gusto. After mastering the practice, she admitted that for the first time in her life, she was able to let the hurts go, and she experienced a palpable easing and expansion in her heart, not to mention a lot of freed-up space in her freezer!

The only way to fully forgive anyone and release the energetic bind you're holding to him or her is to intend, desire, and choose the very best for him or her—to bless him or her. This is brahmavihara. To tap the immense power of this meditation, we have to get really real with ourselves. We have to establish ourselves on a stable base of truly seeing everyone as equal, and we need to be free enough with ourselves that we can celebrate their freedom and joy. We need to see our enemies free and happy, and we need to want it above all else. What's wonderful about practising brahmavihara is that even if you're not yet centred on that stable base but you want to be, just by trying it, the flow it generates moves you to your stable base. Loving-kindness enables loving-kindness, forgiveness enables forgiveness, and metta enables metta.

Brahmavihara can be practised to heal past hurts even if the person in question has since moved out of your life or has passed on. The important thing is to create the possibility of release. Some experience the release instantly; for others, it may come later. And interestingly, very often, students report some form of affirmation that the release has occurred, beyond sensing it internally. I have received many reports of old school friends making contact out of the blue after they were unknowingly blessed through metta, family rifts miraculously dissolving, and even slow-growing rifts in marriages reconnecting. Metta, when practised with unconditional intent and desire for freedom for all involved, changes people's hearts and changes reality; it heals.

In one beautiful example, a woman I was working with experienced a huge release and shift regarding her mother when working with brahmavihara meditation. They had been estranged for years. One evening after the practice, she received a call from her mum. Her mother had also, at some level, experienced the release and wanted to call her daughter that evening to explain that for years, including throughout my student's childhood, she had been hiding her chronic depression and alcoholism from her family. It was a raw and deeply healing step onto a stable base for both of them.

If you find yourself forcing words and intentions towards the person you are trying to forgive, stop and go back to settling yourself into the heart space, into the part of you which is eternal—the observer, the unconditional. Brahmavihara can only be truly experienced from our highest aspect, the part of our awareness that is above hurts and grievances, jealousies and fear. It comes through us, not from us, so the focus is on allowance and space, not forced heights. People often visualise the sun as shining impartially on all, just as the Brahmavihara blessings rush to all.

Remember to smile when experiencing brahmavihara. It's amazing how powerful a smile can be in taking you to a compassionate place internally. It can also be used for groups of people: for example, a workplace team, a group of friends, or a community.

Whether we choose a known ancient practice like brahmavihara/metta (links in appendix A) or we develop our own practice for the same purpose, the most potent agent in the process of expansion is our intent for freedom.

## Move Your Body

A very effective way to dissipate sticky reactive patterning is to introduce kinetic energy into your practice and imbue it with intent. Using the body's kinetic energy in this way is nothing new. The spiralling whirling dervishes of Sufism, the walking pulsing spirals of mecca pilgrimages, the trance dancing of shamans, and even the more subtle but potent mudras of the East and yoga asana, just to name a few, all engage the bioenergetic field of the body for spiritual expansion and 'spinning off' denser vibrations.

Meditative walking is a beautiful way to gently raise and balance the energy body and connect with spirit, especially if done in a wild setting. Pilgrimages and labyrinths have featured in spiritual practice since the early shamanic vision quests. There is nothing more powerful than walking step by step with body, mind, emotion, energy, and intent aligned and charging up the grid. There's a circular track around a beautiful central pagoda and flanked by old trees in Singapore's UNESCO World Heritage site, the Singapore Botanic Gardens. It's a sacred space where I take either aspects that I seek to grow within myself and life, or aspects that I wish to wind down and dissolve out of myself and life. I intentionally run the spiral. A clockwise motion generates a building, multiplying, generative energy within my system. Anticlockwise motion generates a minimising and weakening degenerative energy within my system. I run the spiral and intentionally dedicate the physical effort to the energy movement I am engaging with. I literally spiral up patience, acceptance and compassion, and I spiral down and out fears, worries and obsessions. It is hugely effective and creates enough of a shift in the stickiness of the pattern for me to start to behave differently and access guidance.

If you don't have access to a beautiful track to run or walk, putting on your favourite dance track—one that has aspirational uplifting vibes—and freely dancing the stickiness away is nearly always a winning move. My kids know to leave me be if they can smell the incense on my altar burning and my electro-flow tracks blaring in my room.

## Welcome High Sensation and Ditch the Labels

Sometimes when I undertake the inner work to lift a reactive pattern, I can find it tricky to engage with the intense emotion that plays out when I am triggered in my day-to-day reality. Even if I have chosen internally to let it go, if the circumstances or person that is involved with highlighting the edge within me are really hitting on 'that nerve', my well-laid instinct to defend, attack, and 'be right' can be strong. The contrast between the inner choice for freedom from the pattern, and the programmed emotional reactions, can defy logic. This is where a shift in perspective can help. Rather than identifying with the intense sensations as 'emotions' and giving them names like 'anger', 'frustration', and 'indignation', for example, I welcome the sensations through my system as nameless forms of vibration. I notice where they are perceivable in my body and how they ripple through my organs, breath, and fingertips. In these situations, witnessing mode is essential—that pause point before the reaction. At their essence, all emotions are vibratory states, and strong vibratory states move through us when there is a spiritual messaging taking place, telling us that we are in a state which is separate from our spiritual nature. As soon as we label the sensation that the event or situation triggers, we conceptualise it and separate ourselves from it. We halt the progression of the high sensation that is working in our favour; we judge it, defend or attack, and effectively weave the old pattern back into our operating systems. As nuts as this sounds, talking to yourself in these situations can be enormously effective. 'Ooooooo, this is an intense vibration I'm feeling … Yes, I can feel it rippling through my tummy, throat, and fingertips … If I were to give it a colour, I'd say it was a burning fire orange and blood red … In feeling it, I know I am on the precipice of transformation …' In thirty seconds of self-observation and vocalising that observation, the old pattern will be interrupted.

Intensity doesn't mean 'bad'! New Age pop spirituality usually labels something as 'wrong' if it feels uncomfortable. However, when something intense arrives, you can regard it as a strong flag for your awareness and as a reservoir of energy to be used to make a different choice.

The mundane or 'muggle' view of intensity will separate and judge the experience. However, the spirited view can hold it all and doesn't judge it; it works with the experience for expansion.

## Journaling

It's no secret that I hold journaling as one of my most loved and powerful spiritual activities. It is an integral aspect of all my courses and mentoring work. For those who are new to the art of journaling, the idea of meditating and writing what bubbles up from the deep mind can seem a little foreign. Many of us hardly put pen to paper these days, as touchscreens, keyboards, voice, and video have overtaken our communication styles. Also, the paces of our lives can exclude time for deeper contemplation and self-inquiry.

There is something highly evocative to the entire system when we make time to dialogue with our spirits, to find our deep truth, and to allow it to stream from heart, through mind, through hand, to page. A flow is created which washes over the critical mind and its judgements and reservations and allows a true, revealing, and transmuting experience to take place. We experience all of life through a subjective lens. Everything we experience—all relationships, events, and even how we see ourselves—is filtered through an interpretive lens that is unique to each of us. This lens is formed through beliefs, perspectives, and paradigms that are part of our unconscious operating systems, formed from childhood via the familial cultures in which we grew up, our life experiences, the influences of significant others, and our memories of events. Navigating our subjective terrain through our subjective lens requires tools to make the subjective objective so we can truly see it and work with it. This is the power of journaling.

Journaling brings the insights gained through introspective processes out onto the page in front of us, creating a means to examine them. The act of carving time with the self; the private safety of the pages; the process of making the space for journaling sacred with silence, candles, and scents; and the use of well-crafted prompts for self-enquiry into the areas you are exploring allows a gentle move into deep honesty and vulnerability with the self. It can be hugely healing and generate profound release. With journaling, we are able to identify and track the events and situations that trigger high-sensation responses, and we are better able to see objectively what edges we are holding that trip the trigger. With compassionate acknowledgment, we can reframe these edges and, through journaling, start to rewrite new scripts for our lives.

Everything we experience starts with a thought form—everything. Sometimes those thought forms are unconscious, created through fears or certain beliefs about lack or inevitability, and charged with reactive emotion. Yet we have the capacity to consciously generate our experiences through creating and positively charging thought forms with the certainty that is born when will, desire, and intent are aligned. This is where a personal practice of journaling takes on a whole new dimension. The creative journaling of possibilities, in enough detail to invoke an emotional vibration of excitement and a felt sense of those possibilities, is highly magical. It's a way to generate strongly charged thought forms that start to influence our experienced realities. This beautiful form of journaling draws our awareness from looping doubt or disappointment and opens up worlds of potential. Journaling the stories of our desired realities is a form of spellcasting. Have you ever wondered about the origin of the verb 'to spell'? Another reason, among many other wonderful reasons, why journaling is a spiritual power move is quite simple but also very useful. Journaling naturally records our spiritual journeys. Retrospect is an incredible gift. When we have generated a wholesale shift in our realities, our memories of the paradigms that we have expanded from fade. Yet to have a record of our spiritual approach—our old triggers, our new scripts, and our dreams from the past, which are now a lived reality—we hone our spiritual skills and confidence. Our journeys reveal just how far we have come, what is possible, and how powerful we really are as creators of our lives. This discovery and this realisation are perhaps the greatest gifts we can give ourselves, all from the humble pages of our spirit journals.

When spirit journaling, it's helpful to focus on the

themes that are presenting in our lives rather than people, the actual words said, or the specifics of the experiences. Expand your spiritual view and look for corresponding meanings elsewhere, such as in your dreams, your feelings, your insights, your body, and your ponderings. Spiritual patterns are interconnected and will always arrive through many different experiences and perceptions.

## Mantra

Further to the tool of vocalising the description of the high sensations of a reaction, as explained above, employing different mantras can also be hugely helpful in interrupting old sticky patterns. Hearing your own voice, imbued with your intent for freedom and an attitude of self-command, is massively evocative to the subconscious mind.

For interrupting the 'victim reaction', and allowing myself full ownership of my life and the events I am experiencing, I just love Esther Hicks's mantra-hack: 'I did this.' By stating this out loud at the outset of an event that triggers sensations, it interrupts the 'oh, poor me' reaction. Whether it's an event that you may perceive as 'bad' or one you may perceive as 'good', getting into the habit of greeting it into your awareness with the mantra 'I did this' creates a pause point and reminds you that you are the sovereign of all of your realms.

In usui reiki energy healing, there is a particular sequence of mantras and energy practices that the practitioner engages to 'run the reiki'—that is, to generate a flow of felt healing energy through the energy body and out through the hands. Part of this sequence is stating three times the five reiki principles. I have learnt that these are a fantastic meditation in their own right. They have the effect of 'parting the veil' on our dominant reactive emotions, allowing a step onto higher ground not by denying or suppressing anything felt but simply by giving yourself permission to suspend your emotions and thereby experience freedom. They are better stated out loud and repeated as many times as needed until a felt shift is experienced.

> Just for today I am free from anger.
> Just for today I am free from worry.
> I am grateful for everything.
> I work hard on myself for the better.
> I am kind to all beings.

> These five mantras of Usui Reiki principles, were distilled from the father of Usui Reiki, Master Mikao Usui's writings on the keys to a healthy happy life.

## Ho'oponopono Mantra

Ho'oponopono has gained popularity in recent times, even with certificates being issued for its use. I don't believe you need to be certified in this beautiful simple mantra to benefit from its power. '*Ho'oponopono*' is a Hawaiian greeting. In a multi-island country that traditionally relied on intertribal relations to survive, the ancient culture recognised that held grievances were destructive to the whole. It recognised the importance of forgiveness and taking responsibility for one's own actions, choices, and thoughts. In its modern context, this beautiful mantra has an immediate freeing effect. It recognises that if you are involved in any sort of altercation, sticky relationship dynamic, hurt, defence, or attack, at some level of your being, you have called that event to you, and you are ultimately responsible for your part in it. The second we recognise our energetic interconnectedness within any phenomenon, we interrupt any typical reaction we may have, and we own it fully and release it. The traditional Hawaiian greeting simply translates to:

> I'm sorry.
> Please forgive me.
> Thank you.
> I love you.

So simple and so very powerful. I know some practitioners of Ho'oponopono who will engage the mantra whenever they witness anger or unkindness, even if it is not personal to them. These beautiful people have a wider understanding of interconnectedness and regard even witnessing a fight across the street or in traffic between others as if they have a role to play in its dissolution, simply because it has entered their awareness. I have used Ho'oponopono to release past hurts that I may not even be aware of inflicting through unconsciously acting. I use the mantra to release past karma generated from my actions and to release family hurts even if between other family members. It generates a soft, gentle healing energy that is a lot like the way a Hawaiian dawn feels.

## Mudra

The hand mudra, Abhayamudra, or fearless mudra is a powerful pattern interrupter that can be employed when those old familiar reactions start to rise. It is a symbol of fearlessness and protection and is associated with fire. It is a Buddhist mudra related to fierce compassion, which opens the heart with confidence yet sets a clear boundary within that the old pattern is no longer relevant or welcome within a person. The Abhayamudra is engaged either in meditation or when one is in the midst of a reaction rise. In performing the Abhayamudra, the left hand is held in the lap, palm facing upwards, connecting you with your spiritual power, and the right arm is extended with the palm facing out and fingers raised, just like a traffic warden's stop sign. Even though it is an ancient Eastern mudra, the Western association with the gesture of a firm 'Stop; you shall not pass' makes it very effective. Sometimes I will address an old pattern as if it's a slightly annoying and persistent unwanted being, which they can feel a bit like. I will add with the mudra, 'Not today, old friend; I will not entertain you today!' Pattern interrupted!

The Ksepana mudra is also a wonderful mudra to deal with old, stagnant energy associated with a situation, memory, or person and to invite in new lighter energy. The Ksepana mudra is engaged to drain from the system perceived negative, dense, unhelpful vibrations, thereby easing the resultant experiences caused by them, including physical pain, mental fogginess, restless sleep, or emotional looping over a situation or event. In my version (see links in appendix A) I guide you in simple breathwork to start and then to assume the mudra and work with the exhalation for release. We then slightly tilt the mudra and work with the in breath to draw in positivity, life force, and light.

## Gratitude Cultivation

Gratitude is a countervibration to reactive patterns. There are many studies and tools now that advocate the intentional cultivation of gratitude. We know that gratitude improves heart health, mental and emotional resilience, and immune function. Countries that have thankfulness imbedded in their cultures—Ireland, for example—rank the highest in the World Happiness Index, regardless of socioeconomic circumstances. Gratitude is a spiritual superpower. It maintains a felt sense of connection with spirit and the

Spirit in All, and it helps us understand that we are in an amazing ongoing process of expansion. When we stop and look at the intense experience and give great thanks for the experience and the sensations it creates, we interrupt reactive patterning. Greeting the experience gratefully knowing it is teaching you and giving you a real, live drill to make a different choice is what being spirited is all about. Everything is working in your favour—everything.

Gratitude can be cultivated. Keeping a gratitude journal is a popular method whereby you end each day noting down three blessings from the day. These can be as small as the sensation of that first slurp of tea, a random act of kindness from a stranger, an impromptu kiss from your child, or a moment when you stopped and felt the breeze on your skin. It's not so much about thinking you're grateful; rather, it is about using the recollections of the day to generate a vibration in your heart and body. It is this higher, finer, lighter vibration of gratitude that counters dense, low, tight contracted vibrations that accompany reactive unconscious behaviours and thought loops. There's a lovely paradox with working with the vibration of gratitude. When we intentionally cultivate it as an inner practice, we change the lens through which we view life. And rather than waiting for blessings to help us feel grateful, we become grateful as a state of being and therefore start to see blessings all around us all the time, even in the more challenging situations. And this radically changes our perceptions of self and life and our abilities to be spirited. You can find a link to my version in appendix A.

## Depersonalisation and Tonglen

Both of my children were born with congenital heart issues. My son's was picked up the day after he was born. My daughter's revealed itself after she had a heart attack on a netball court when she was thirteen years old. Both required heart surgery—my son at four years old, and my daughter at fourteen years old, exactly ten years apart from each other. I am thrilled to write that both are well, vital, intelligent, and happy teenagers, and I am enormously grateful for the courageous and talented paediatric cardiologists and their teams that have blessed our path in both Australia and Singapore.

Needless to say, these were hugely challenging experiences. The parental instinct to protect can possess beyond sense those parents who have experienced illness and surgery with their children. It requires a massive conscious and continual effort to hold everything together to maintain the most stable and positive atmosphere for the children. As they have their own personal experiences of the events, they learn how to deal with life's twists and turns, largely via observation of the significant adults around them. It was through the first experience with my son that I learnt the power of depersonalising the experience. When my son was first diagnosed, I spiralled into a very dense place of self-blame. I asked myself questions like 'What did I do or not do during the pregnancy that caused this?', 'Was it my wilder youth that caused this?', and 'Was this some form of karma that I generated from my unconscious actions?' Round and round the guilt-tripping went until I was so immersed in my own story and suffering that I became unwell. I was crying a lot. My vitality dived, and thank goodness for my rock-solid husband, as he really had to hold us all together during that time. I wasn't able to meditate. In fact, I rejected meditation. The rebel in me rose, and I slipped firmly into a belief that life was against us, and I questioned the point of it all.

And then one night something shifted. It was days before his open-heart surgery, and I was holding his little body in my arms in the armchair in his room, singing him to sleep, overwhelmed with guilt that in coming days his little body would be cut open, his heart stopped, and his blood diverted through a bypass machine whilst the hole in his heart was sewn shut. This sweet little innocent boy was about to experience a life-changing horrendous event, all because of me. In ways that logically were not understood, I had nonetheless convinced myself it was all because of me. As his breathing slowed and his body slipped into sleep in my arms and syrupy tears streamed down my face, I instinctively started to hum. Out of the pit of my heart, a vibration rose, and I gave it voice. It took form and turned into a melody, which then held words. It was coming straight from a place far below my thoughts and looping guilt-ridden emotions. Out of my broken heart, my spirit stirred. As I sang the song, a simple song about harmony and perfect health returning to us, I started to feel inexplicable gratitude. My mind was so very tired and parched, and the feeling was like a cool flow of water. I allowed it. As my heart opened more and more and my body started to soften and ease, I 'heard' the words 'All will be well.' I knew all would be well. In that moment, I knew. And then I saw it. In my mind's eye, I saw the web of suffering, guilt, and shame of all other parents in the same situation as us. It was like an infinite sticky black cobweb. In an instant, the realisation burst into my awareness that I was participating in a collective field of parental suffering, and what quickly followed was the thought that perhaps I was perceiving this because I had some sort of a role to play in it all. Perhaps it wasn't just about us. That song that bubbled up from my spirit took on a whole new meaning and role. I sang it along the lines of that web. I breathed in the darkness, and I sang out light. I kept going that night as my little one slept deeply in my arms, until I saw the whole web dissolve. I came to learn later that I was instinctively doing a form of a very old Tibetan Buddhist energy practice called tonglen.

'Tonglen' means 'transmutation of energy', and it is an altruistic meditation—that is, a meditation done for the collective, to transmute fear, anger, disillusionment, or any obscuration to our spirited selves.

Fast forward ten years later, when, whilst holding my

daughter's hand as she slipped into deep sleep from the anaesthetic for her heart surgery, I realised a few things. Firstly, how different this second heart surgery experience was from a spirited viewpoint ten years on. We categorically experienced no fear. We both knew that in some obvious ways and in other ways that we may never understand, the experience was essential to her life journey. And once again, I welcomed the natural adrenalin and deep motherly desire for her wellness and healing as sacred sensations to be put to use for that healing, rather than weapons to beat myself into a pulp with. My heart extended to all the other parents in hospital ward, and for the duration of my daughter's operation I practised tonglen, until I 'saw' light completely infuse the space and hearts of those sharing the same field of experience. I realised that the experience with my children taught me an incredible way to transmute dense energy and put it to use. My underlying and long-held practice and curiosity in spirit meant that even in this situation, I was firmly within a spiritual process. I used my meditation, breathwork practices, and ritual to alter my state of consciousness, to get my conscious mind out of the way, and to allow the 'song of my spirit' to rise, and I used it very deliberately to heal the whole.

The perspective of depersonalisation of an experience and rising to an altruistic viewpoint to work with the sensations involved is one of the most powerful pattern-interrupters I have personally worked with. I now teach this to all my clients who are on a journey with cancer or chronic illness and to my students in my esoteric courses in conscious manifestation. We are all interconnected. We are all refractions of one dazzling living mind. When we experience illness, heartbreak, loss, and pain, it is a personal refraction of a larger collective field, and it is rippling through our experience so that we may rise to heal the all. This perspective is a big shift for many, especially those living with pain or sick loved ones, yet the change in vibrational state and the reinstatement of purpose and freedom from shame and guilt can generate a wholesale shift internally, which then by extension influences outcomes within our lives. You can find a link to my version of tonglen in the appendices. Employing an attitude of service rather than taking an experience personally by viewing it as a common experience in the collective that happens to be rippling through you as you have the awareness to heal the whole is a spirited move. This altruistic perceptive removes the personal nature of the reaction and opens the heart to higher vibrations that very effectively transmute older operating beliefs and fears.

For a lot of my clients, the reactive pattern is too intense and creates a wobble and draw back into defensiveness, lockdown, and judgement. No amount of introspection or light meditation seems to work, and it's almost always when the patterns of defence and attack, folding in, and intense self-judgement originate as survival and protection strategies from childhood trauma. In these situations, I always guide them into ritual. Ritual speaks directly to the deeper aspects of mind and generates space and spiritual perspective. Ritual combines choice, intentional action, correspondent words and tools, raised energy, and lightly altered consciousness. It is the language of spirit, and it subverts well-laid reactive patterns that are too difficult to shift or even understand fully by the conscious mind. There are as many rituals as there are people on the planet, but all of them contain the same ingredients: planning, a sacred space, thought-through correspondences, energy practice, and decree. All rituals are more powerful when witnessed. The most effective and useful ritual for dissolving the hardwired patterns, stories, and perceptions that keep us small and unspirited is what's commonly referred to in magical practice (also evident in most major religions and shamanic practices) as a banishing ritual.

A banishing ritual is a ritualistic burning of the reactivity felt in regard to a situation that is carried out to allow spirit to rise and heal. I always recommend several weeks of preparation before engaging. I encourage my clients to observe and journal the patterns in action. What triggers them? What are my clients' immediate reactions? Can they describe the familiar sensations? Where do they occur in the body? What are some of the verbal responses that automatically get voiced when in situations that are perceived as threatening? This can be done with regular journaling.

There is no judgement involved in the enquiry. It's all about throwing as much light as possible on the reaction itself, not what causes it. I suggest my clients diarise the ritual ahead of time. During the waning moon, and especially on the last quarter moon, is the traditional time for this kind of ritual. I then ask them to distil their descriptive journaling down to a set of key words, circled from their ponderings, and to then transcribe them onto a piece of parchment.

When the time for the ritual arrives, it's important that a sacred space is established. The practitioner should obtain a cloth, candles, and a container that can handle fire, all with colours and numbers and items that are personally symbolic of the pattern and, moreover, the symbols for their freedom from it. It's worth spending some time to settle the system into present awareness and to raise the energy in the body. This can be done with meditation, breathwork, drumming, music, dance, or intuitive movement. The body and space should be anointed for the ritual with special oil or sacred smoke. All of these steps are hugely evocative to the deep mind, a kind of calling out to spirit to rise. At a point in the ritual that feels right, you'll know when, light the centre fire in the container and start to tear the parchment into as many small pieces as possible. As you do this, hold the awareness that you are dismantling the pattern. You are no longer governed by it, and all the energy entangled in maintaining it is being freed to return to you for conscious deployment. And then there is the decree. Use your own words, as they must be deeply felt and truthful to you. But something as simple as this does it: 'From my I Am presence, from my sovereign heart, my spirit, I dissolve this pattern of smallness; I reclaim my spiritual sovereignty over my energy and ways. I cast it into the flames to return it to its native nothingness. It no longer dwells within me. It no longer influences my life. I am free.' Then place the pieces of paper into the fire and watch them burn.

With total presence and raised energy, a banishing ritual can radically alter patterns. In the days following a powerful banishing, there's a definite feeling that something deep within your tectonic plates has shifted. Familiar places and faces seem different to you on observing them. There can be some emotional release that follows too, but always with an underlying vibration of promise. The life force invested in the old pattern rushes back to you. I have personally experienced and observed spontaneous healings and an influx of inspiration and creativity afterwards. You will notice that the very same experiences, people, and exchanges that triggered the old reaction no longer hold the voltage they once did, which makes it much easier to start to set in place more expanded responses and free yourself from the illness-inducing stress these old patterns created.

## The Unsent Letter Ritual

When the pattern was established in the past via a key relationship and at some point you have chosen to remove yourself from the influence of this person, or he or she has faded from your life or passed on, the unsent letter ritual can be hugely useful to let it all go and free up space in the heart for spirit and spirited living. Whilst this is a popular tool within psychotherapy, in my observation a lot of people can use it to rehash hurt and blame rather than as a tool for liberation. There are a couple of key features to the unsent letter which make it a very powerful ritual for release.

Firstly, approach the writing of the letter as a sacred ritual. Make time and space for it, use paper and pen, and spend time centring yourself and fully holding the intent for what it is you are about to do. Alter your state of consciousness with meditation and breathwork so that you feel settled onto stable central ground, and only then start to write the letter as if you actually intend to send it, as if you're writing to the particular person for real.

The letter should include the following aspects:

1. The letter should include a recognition that the person involved was on his or her own journey, doing what he or she knew with what he or she had. This is not at all excusing or justifying the person's behaviour towards you. It is, however, opening your heart to the

human aspect of the other's journey—the suffering and trauma that culminated in his or her behaviour towards you.

2. The letter should include a recognition of the good stuff. Even within the most traumatic of experiences, there is always good stuff: that alcoholic mother who never hugged you but also ensured you went to school and attained an education, that schoolyard bully who taught you how to intuit damaged people, that jealous mean sister who showed you the importance of raising your children with equality, and so on. Find the goodness in the relationship, even if it's miniscule, and express it.

3. The letter should include a recognition of the effect the person's behaviour has had on you and how it has affected your life and relationships, your health, and your sense of well-being.

4. The letter should include a declaration that upon writing and signing this letter, you are hereby ceasing the continued effects of this relationship on you, your power, your life, and your legacy. You are now free.

Once the letter is written, read it out loud in the ritual, and then tear it up and burn it. By casting it to the flames, you cast into dissolution the knot that has entangled your life force. That energy is returned to you.

After a powerful unsent letter ritual, you will feel the

same things as described above after a banishing ritual. You will find that people with the same personality types, or even the actual person that has governed your responses to yourself and life, have lost their grip and voltage. You will have generated the space to make different choices and expanded responses. And in time, you may even be able to bring challenging past relationships into your brahmavihara cultivation and bless them.

**A Sacrifice Ritual of Sitting in the Fire**

When high emotion is a feature of your reactive pattern, it can be difficult for the logical mind to hold it and for you to find a way to own the experience as essential to your move into a spirited life. When this is the case, I guide my clients to work solely with the vibrational element of the pattern, the sensation. It can be useful to engage with the perspective that the high sensation (however 'uncomfortable' it may feel) is raw energy, fuel for your transformation.

The sitting in the fire ritual can be an incredible pattern-interrupter because the action is intended to allow the high sensation to fill you to the very brink and then to 'sacrifice' the energy of it towards your transformation in a ritualistic action. So rather than resisting it, judging it, and trying to 'love and light' it away, you fully indulge it. To engage in sitting in the fire (a shamanic term), you need to have a well-honed witnessing capacity, as it can get intense. The spirit move is intended to create stillness—no reaction, no aversion, no resistance, and no attachment—and allow the 'fire' of the emotion to dance around you and fill you. When it hits peak voltage, then through ritualistic action, offer it to your transformation process as though it's fuel for growth (which it always is). I might, for example, use a taper candle, which represents the fire that's filling me, to light a large central candle that symbolises my spiritual process, and then extinguish the taper. Or I might use a chalice of water, breathe all the built-up energy into it, and then pour it out into a bigger bowl that represents the container of my transformation. Pick a ritualistic action that feels strongly symbolic of the energy you are working with.

Engaging in every experience with spiritual awareness is the game; this allows us to treat experiences as spiritual experiments and to change the choices we put into action according to a new operating system, one of expanded awareness. Each time we choose differently, we weaken the old contracted, defensive, or fearful patterns. They become invalid. Each time we make a spiritual choice not to be averse, not to be attached, not to be defensive or to attack, but simply to see things as vibrational grids that are rotating, shifting, recalibrating, and inviting you to engage with life in new ways, you will be able to embody a spirited state.

With presence, the ability to witness our ordinary reality, and the intent to clear the heart space of beliefs and patterned behaviours that keep us tethered from living in spirit, we bring the present mind and intuitive heart into balance. We start to heal and come back to ourselves fully. This process of expansion never stops; we just become much better at it. We start to recognise the challenges in ordinary reality for what they actually are: invitations to freedom. The more we raise our resonance and create space in the heart and an abiding presence in the mind, the more our lives take on a flow, and anything that we hold internally that stops us from moving upwards and outwards will become very evident. Any self-limiting beliefs will be revealed to us through our ordinary reality and when the flow's current is strong, the dissonance created can whip up quite a storm. And this is where regular meditation and the calm, still centre that it creates really serves us; we can redirect that raw energy into growth.

When we're not centred and observant, we can ninja-kick the triggers rather than going within to understand what it is within us that has brought the triggers into our fields of awareness. It's a bit like fighting your reflection in the mirror. Every resistant, reactive move you make will be met by the reflection, in ordinary reality, with equal force and timing. When we are triggered by life experiences, such as illness in the body, repeated situations that really rile us, circling personalities that we find hurtful, or repeated mishaps or injuries, there's nothing wrong with feeling the energy of our reactions to them. Sometimes a reaction must be strong for it to catch our attention. But it's how we respond which determines whether we can transmute the inner bond. The only solution is to go within, own it, and then apply transformative practices to release it. The release feels amazing, and afterward you know without any doubt that you have expanded. Many students describe the feeling as being similar to taking their first breath. Once the underlying energetic pattern or belief has been weakened and released, it makes it much easier to change behaviours; and after a very quick turnaround, those very same situations or personalities that caused so much upheaval within us in the past just don't affect us. Moreover, we are able to increase our vibrations further and access greater fields of spirit. We really start to surf, and this divine reality is easily recognisable. We stop feeling fear.

Being spirited does not mean that if you do all the work, then at some point you have arrived and you never experience challenges again. It's a process, not a destination, and the rotations of the ever-expanding spiral of self are infinite. We can never reach maximum expansion or height, and realising this is exquisite. We do, however, become deeply connected with the creative forces that are within us. Our ability to raise our vibration, our resonance, becomes honed and easier, and we access direction, guidance, and enablement to free ourselves further. We redefine how we engage with life from being responsive to it to expanding with it, and we become familiar with our causal aspect and the causal field that underpins everything we experience. This is when we start to create the life experience we choose; we shift from *expansive* to *creative* through consciously engaging in weaving new realities that allow spiritual living and expression. And because our expanded awareness brings with it the revelation that we are all interconnected with each other and with the earth, these new realities that we seek to create almost always involve helping others and the planet.

# CHAPTER 20

# From Expansive Living to Creative Living

We had a wonderful family that lived opposite my childhood home. They were the most industrious, hardworking family I knew. They worked together as a team and were abundant, happy, and very joyful. The father was a disciplined man, very strong and wise, and whilst they enjoyed many parties and happy times, they lived within an orderly routine and had an incredible work ethic, all of them. They were all very successful in whatever business endeavour they undertook, and there were many.

Despite their children being much older than my siblings and me, our families were good friends, and we'd often socialise. The father had a wonderful saying. Each time we caught up and he'd tell us of their latest endeavour, he'd laugh and say, 'People keep telling me I'm lucky. And my response every time is "Well, the harder I work, the luckier I get!"'

People tell me that I'm lucky a lot too: lucky that I am living my purpose and doing what I love; lucky I don't get sick; lucky not to ever have broken a bone, had a tooth filling, or been stung by a bee; lucky my projects fly; lucky to win so many raffles and door prizes at events—just so lucky. Without a doubt, I am grateful for my life and all these blessings, but I do not at all believe it is down to luck. What I know and have observed in my life is that the more spirited I live, the 'luckier' I get. It's of course not luck at all. There's no such thing. It is simply operating from broader fields of information and engaging with the underlying energy grid of situations and events to create. These broader fields of information give us not only useful guidance but also timing and motion of probabilities and possibilities, as well as an understanding of the difference between the two and how we engage with the moving feast of life. Being spirited engages us with life, its movements, its timing, and its energies.

Living creatively—that is, consciously creating our life experiences—shouldn't be confused with the pop spirituality of 'manifesting.' There is a plethora of content out there that leverages the imbalanced needs of the unaware. Titles like 'Ten Steps to Manifesting a Million Dollars' or 'Manifesting

Your Love Life in Five Easy Steps,' for example, tend to reduce spiritual living to mere superstition, mainly because they work from a paradigm of *need* or *lack*. To make the shift from *expansive* living to *creative* living, it's worth taking a closer look at the dynamic of spirit.

The very nature of spirit is a spiral, a circle in motion. It pulses. If you turn a spiral on its side and follow its movement, whether clockwise or anticlockwise, there is a motion of rise, transition, fall, transition; generation, pause, degeneration, pause. This pulsing between rise and fall, growth and dissolution, inhalation and exhalation exists in all life, from our breath to the moon cycle, the tides, the seasons, and the cycle of life itself. It is a state of constant flow, and to access it we also must shift into the realisation that we and our life experiences are one thing and are an expression of the spiral, and we must nurture a state of responsive flow. These are the elements that are missing in much of the 'manifestation' content of the New Age movement.

Flow occurs when our bodies, minds, hearts, and spirits are aligned and connected with our life fields, consciously. When we are in a state of flow, we are happy; and in my observation, people who operate in flow are well, vital, grateful, successful, and fulfilled. Being in flow doesn't mean we don't experience challenges; this is simply the nature of life. But it does mean that we move through them quite differently—with presence and grace. Flow allows a momentum which steers us into higher possibilities, because flow brings the realisation that ourselves, our life fields, our relationships, and all that we experience are inextricably linked. Flow also enables greater flow. Just as a healthy, flowing river shapes and widens it banks, flow expands our awareness and capacity and vastly changes our inner landscapes and connections with life.

People come to my meditation classes and healing sessions for all sorts of reasons. But if I were to distil those reasons down, I could say that all of them are related to a disconnection with flow. This disconnection may present as a physical illness or low vitality, or a feeling of lack in love, abundance, or sense of purpose. These seem to be the big four. And when we are out of flow, we see these aspects as separate from us: as things to be attained and held on to—as things that we lack. We sense our lives are blocked or stagnant in some way. When we are disconnected from flow, we are disconnected from life. Vitality, love, abundance, and fulfilment are by their nature flows, and giving these aspects to others unconditionally and consciously triggers their movement into and through our life experiences, and it has a multiplier effect. It generates the flow of these energies not only through us but also through those we engage with, just as rivers flow, join with other rivers, and all converge in the sea.

The perception of obstacles that stop us living creatively— feelings of frustration with life, a victim mindset of 'things being done to us', comparison to others that gives rise to jealousy or envy, and, worse, feelings of unworthiness of our dreams—are all symptomatic of living in separation from the spiral, from flow. Embodying unity consciousness is key to living creatively. It requires some conscious and deliberate 'reprogramming' from how our modern (and particularly Western) paradigm is formed when we are children.

Triggers within our lives that generate reactions are simply pointing us to a much greater invitation to nurture the perception, knowledge, and embodiment that we and everything we experience in our life fields are actually one thing; there is no separation, no duality. The same goes for our inner gifts and abilities, our life purposes, our dreams. They are not separate and outside of us, things to be attained. They are present and active within us now. When we embody this truth, we start to see and experience our wholeness, our purposes, our abilities, and our dreams because we are dwelling in that state.

It's just like a reflection in a mirror. And this is how I explain unity consciousness in my classes. Your ordinary reality—your life field, your 'world'—is one big mirror of your inner state. When you fight or resist the reflection in the mirror, it fights and resists you with equal and instant force. When you retract from the mirror, life retracts from you. But when you lean into the mirror with love, grace, and ease, your reflected life experiences lean in towards you with love, grace, and ease.

This can all sound a bit conceptual, but the reality is

that it's quite easy to move our awareness in this direction, because that is our natural state. The first step is to meditate daily and steer your state into present awareness to nurture a state of mindfulness, a state of detached observation to what is going down around you. This creates a pause point between the experience and your response, so you give yourself a choice as to how you engage rather than being swept into reaction. This is key, because when you react to the reflection in the mirror, you consolidate a state of separation. When you react, you weave the triggers into a karmic loop, which brings them and similar experiences around again and again until you transmute them. That old bumper sticker reading 'Be the change you wish to see' holds deep metaphysical truth. The challenge is to action it. We are creating our life experiences all the time. When we emanate into the field unconsciously through what we think, say, and feel; the choices we make; and our actions, which are driven by limited belief systems and fears, we draw to us experiences that reflect the limitations. When we engage consciously, we energise different patterns of potential that soon convert into possibilities, then probabilities, and then through to phenomena in our experiential realities.

Situations that create a trigger, usually an emotional response, are simply the spirit of things highlighting a perception or belief we are holding that is keeping us small. Everything is working in our favour, always. Rather than ninja-kicking the trigger, go within and contemplate the perception in you that could be expanded or shifted. When you start doing this consciously, you will start to see that the triggers dissipate. They are no longer needed, and you are not creating them from your smallness, because you are expanding your awareness. You also then shift from wading through experiences on the ground and relying on your intellect and force to progress, to flowing through them, guided by your intuition and spiritual power to progress, because you see them as signs and messages from self and spirit; you take responsibility for them, and this is when you're cooking with gas.

Maintaining the circuitry and energetic flow of our energy bodies is essential. This flow of vital life force that is felt with practice is the same flow of the spiral of life. It guides our engagement and timing. It is the engine of our intuition and tells us when we are in a generative cycle and it's time for action, a pause, a time for stillness, or a degenerative turn of the spiral (i.e., time to focus on dissolving certain denser energies, beliefs, or perspectives to prepare for the upturn in energy that is to follow).

Unity consciousness merges our realities with the spiral, and the spiral is the movement of spirit. Within the spiral lies all possibilities and potentials, including our highest possibilities as human beings, and the highest possibilities for our lives. It's in there, pulsing and waiting to be dreamed, energised and actualised into being, just like the potential for fire lies within a match. The fire needs a striking point to materialise. Spirited living enables that striking point.

Creative living cannot be rushed or systemised. It is the raw spiritual expression of spirit and engagement with spirit. And the greater the acknowledgement and beautification of this, the wider the gateway to spirit opens and the more spirited our operating modes become for modern living, for being human. Once we are engaged at this level, the entire of our life experiences, inner and outer, becomes aligned with the creative forces of the universe.

Many of us might not have a specific dream or intent other than to live happy, fulfilled lives. Some of us have a clear purpose and deep desire to live that purpose. Regardless of whether the intent is specific or thematic, a liberated state of being always includes four elements: to experience love, to be well and vital, to experience abundance, and to feel fulfilled. The amazing metaphysical writer Florence Scovel Shinn describes this foundation of a liberated life as 'the square of life.' When this foundation is in place and stabilised, it makes it much easier to expand into a fuller life purpose, and for the people I work with, the starting points for being spirited are to do just this—to secure our 'square of life.'

There is an optimum refraction into the world from each of us—a soul purpose. Clues of it are very often evident in our childhoods, and we know when we're not expressing it, because we feel a dissonance in our activities and an ache for meaning, joy, and fulfilment. In yogic philosophy, this 'soul purpose' is called our sankalpa, which means 'highest vow or oath.' It is not about our activity, what we do, although the natural consequence of distilling our sankalpa and embodying the vibration of it is expressing it in what we do. Rather, it is a state of being—an alignment with mind, body, heart, and spirit.

The life experiences we choose to create consciously, which are linked to our soul purpose, rise within us as desires at first. Life starts to introduce us to elements, aspects, and ingredients of our life purposes. Little peaks of interest, attention-capturing conversations, inspirations, and images collect around us in our fields, and if we are consciously engaged, an inner picture starts to emerge, enabling us to hone our intent for creative, purposeful living.

Sometimes, at the outset, we don't know what we want; we just feel that we want change, such as when I knew that I was to leave corporate life, but at that time where I was heading was still outside my immediate field of awareness. I knew enough about the flow of abundance to enable a move out, but I didn't know to what exactly. However, the act of creating the initial movement rotated me into an expanded turn of the spiral. My field of self-awareness and possibility expanded with it, and my life purpose came into view, and I was able then to engage consciously to embody it and then express it. You choosing this book is a step towards this. And me writing this book is also an expression of it.

Spirited living is an ongoing process. We don't arrive. We

ride our spirals within a larger current that operates both within us and far beyond our current awareness, but the difference is that we are engaged with it, we receive direct revelation and guidance from it, and we steer our movement within that current. When we expand into larger spirals, we often lose sight of where we're heading because our horizons shift. It's almost as if we need to start again, because our current perceptions are too limited in the context of the broader field of information. This is a point where many can lose trust and heart in spirit. But when you have experienced enough rotations to understand that this loop is part of the ongoing process, this juncture becomes very exciting; and with trust and practice, spirit enables us again to ride higher and wider. We just need to remain in responsive flow, align with a generative turn of a wider spiral, and get our practice on; then we create movement and change. There are many beautiful frameworks to access this enablement from the spirit, and all of them involve the same requirements: intent, raising the energy body, ritual, and present awareness.

Years ago, I started to explore shamanic journeying with my teacher in a process of deep meditative ritual to access direct revelation about myself, my life, and the expression of my purpose. Shamanic journeying is a beautiful process of opening awareness to aspects of your higher self, the part of you that exists always within spirit, and asking specific questions for guidance. When I started journeying, spirit would come to my inner awareness in the form of a huge, powerful lion and speak with me. It was an enchanting exploration. The lion mostly taught me about the principles of journeying itself, which I still use and now teach others today. Whilst I love lions, I had no particular affinity with them, and so I found it interesting that a lion appeared as my first totem guide.

After a year of connection, as readily as the lion arrived, he just stopped coming in my journeying. I fell flat. At the end of that year, I went on my annual vision quest into the wilderness to divine direction for the coming year, and I couldn't sense anything beyond the next few months. My doubts had lowered my resonance, and I couldn't tap a stream of any guidance. I had retracted into the limited boundary of current awareness, and I was reaching, grappling for signs and clues. I thought I had slipped out of the spiral, and I admonished myself for becoming far too cocky with my earlier journeying work.

Then, in February of the following year, my husband's work asked us to relocate to Singapore, which we did mid-year. This opportunity was outside my own assessments of probability, and as I had let myself retract, I couldn't see it. When it came into my field, however, I saw the beauty in the direct revelation from spirit. The earlier guidance in journeying and spiritual dynamics had come in the form of a lion to prepare me to move to Singapore, known as the Lion City, and to move fully into teaching spiritual practice. I re-established my inner practice and connected with the equatorial wild field, and the wider spiral opened again. The desire to formally teach meditation and guide people in spiritual living started to grow. Even though my initial plan was to enjoy being an expat wife for a while, do a lot of yoga and lunching with other expat women, and resume formal studies, I started investigating how I might get permission from the Singapore government to set up a teaching business, and the advice from friends and others was that it was near impossible. The government was looking to sponsor local employment, and unless an offering was unique to the market, the chances of a letter of consent being granted to operate a business as a dependant foreigner were very low. Teaching meditation and spiritual practices in Asia, where many of the original systems and practices hail from was hardly unique, or so I thought.

The desire grew and grew within me regardless, and it got to a point that one day, after yet another expat ladies' lunch, I set to work. The draw to teaching was so strong and undeniable that I knew that on a wider spiral, which I could access with wider perception, all that was required to start was waiting for me. Despite the appearance of probable failure, I engaged what I knew to covert probability into possibility. The moon was about to enter a waxing, generative cycle. I prepared my documents that afternoon, entered ritual that night on the new moon, and sent them off the next day.

Over the next few weeks, I met new people day to day who had the skills I needed to set myself up. I met an accountant, a photographer, a social media expert, and several women in Singapore who were very influential opinion formers. I traded meditation lessons for their skills. I entered practice every day to energise the rotation, to energise my intent and desire to teach, and to stay in an expanded state—a kind of detached expectation. Four weeks later, on the following new moon, to the day, the consent was granted. A month later I had collected exactly enough teaching fees to pay for a website. As soon as the setup was completed, without dipping once into any savings, I then dedicated at least 10 per cent of my earnings through teaching and spiritual guidance to worthy causes. I now donate 20 per cent each month. This creation of flow of funds and assistance to others maintains the incoming flow and expands it monetarily and through people coming to my door. I have spent nothing on advertising to date, and I am operating at capacity, joyfully.

Sometimes we energetically sense an expansion of our offering to the world before we have a cognitive perception of it. We can sense a change coming, tremors in the force, but we can't see what they mean. But the messaging is around us if we are in flow.

Two years into teaching meditative practice in Singapore, I started to receive more and more requests for one-on-one work for healing and spiritual guidance. It was an emerging theme. I didn't regard myself as a healer, and I hadn't formally trained in any coaching modality and had shamanic healing techniques which I principally used on myself. But this was what was being asked. So I started to augment my material into deeper explanations and experiences in understanding our innate ability to self-heal, through knowledge of the human system. And then, within a year of living in Singapore, my reiki master came to one of my women's circles. We had an immediate recognition and both felt a voltage of vibration. Jane encouraged me to learn reiki, which I did, and I continued through to master level in the usui reiki tradition. I found the beautiful energy of reiki complemented the shamanic healing techniques I had learnt in Australia, and the regular 'running of the reiki' honed and sharpened my intuitive senses radically.

Within a very short period, my healing sessions booked out. I opened up more days for healing work, and they filled. This is now the greatest aspect of my work. It had evolved again into mediumship, and I run a three-month waitlist for my sessions. Having worked with thousands of clients within a short period of time and having gained all the learning this experience gave, I wrote a course called Intuitive Healing. This combines usui reiki and intuitive reads in a powerful combination that facilitates both short-term alleviation of symptoms and wholesale guided healing of the underlying causes, which are always energetic in the mental, emotional, and spiritual body. It was my ordinary reality that signalled the shift. That feeling of a desire building in the heart, almost breaching its boundaries, always draws into our ordinary experiences and inner awareness revelations and clues to help us gain clarity of intent and the enablers to act upon it. Sometimes this initial expansion can feel uncomfortable, marked by a restlessness and dissatisfaction with current activities, and this discomfort makes us reach for clarity, for change.

A great example of this may be seen in one of my mentoring clients, a beautiful, intuitive woman and regular attendee of my workshops and rituals. She had been feeling a building desire to step out from the shadows and be far more explicit with her offering, which was to be a sounding board and perspective shifter for women to also expand their offering. She asked to meet with me because she was in a high state of dissonance, but she couldn't deduce why. I asked her to tell me what the most recent 'high-sensation' experiences had been for her. At a time when she had been searching for clarity on her own offering, several seemingly unrelated experiences had shaken her. She said she had been working for a woman whom she felt intimidated by because she was so confident with her own offering and drew large crowds to her talks. It made my client feel a mix of envy, competition, and admiration. At the same time, her son had finished his final exams and she was feeling the shift in her role as a mother and coming into the realisation that he would soon leave the nest. Also, in this same phase, a very good friend of hers was preparing to pass as a result of a long-held illness. In addition, the night before we met, she had a very strong dream about watching a new mother give birth.

This woman's issue was that she was seeing all these events as separate and unrelated, even though all of them carried with them high sensation, and she was looking at everything literally rather than thematically, or with 'symbolic sight.' She was reacting to the uncomfortable emotion she was feeling, and judging it as 'bad.' She couldn't see the wood for the trees. The dissonance she was feeling was signalling a limited perspective, a slip outside of oneness. She was able to sense the importance of each experience, but she couldn't see the revelation that was being presented to her. Each experience was a thread in her overall weave of sankalpa.

I proposed an alternative perspective in our session. Perhaps the woman that was unsettling her so much was inviting her to address her own belief systems of self-worth that were causing her energy body to contract. Her son, her friend, and her baby dream were giving her the ingredients of her offering—supporting people through major life transitions. After a beautiful conversation that raised her perspective, she left committed to regular inner practice. She recently launched a sublime offering that helps people move through life's major transitions with ease and grace.

In my experience, when the larger life shifts are approaching, it can feel as if the spiritual winds have left our sails. The energetic tide draws out to feed the building incoming wave. When a more complex creation is birthing, it takes its own time to gestate and gathers the threads, people, avenues, and our own inner state to be able to receive it.

Things can become very still, a bit like when a tsunami is forming far out to sea. The tidewaters draw so far out that the sand bed is exposed. There's an eerie stillness which only the animals can sense, and they start to quietly migrate to higher ground. Then is the time to engage deeply in spiritual practice, to keep the inner field strong and distil and energise our dreams, and to move to higher inner ground. When we do this, we make an inner choice and put it into action. We start to build and feed energy into that potentiality.

Choice releases a huge amount of energy into the field and generates movement. If our hearts' desires are based in limiting belief patterns, paradigms of lack or fear, they either will not demonstrate or will demonstrate in limited and dissonant ways, and this is the self-organising system of life illuminating the limiting pattern to be addressed first if we can see it and not react to it. This is where the practices and perspectives of earlier chapters really kick in. We have to be honest and dig into whatever is triggering strong emotional or physical responses within our ordinary lives and bodies, and use inner practices to enquire into their nature and what they are reflecting to our awareness. Then we can create the desire freely. I have found it much easier and far more delightful to stay out of the detail of *how* the demonstration will occur. I keep my intent thematic and highly charged with meditative ritual, and allow spirit to sort the details. Through guidance I know, desire, and intend to move from point A to point B in my life, but I am not attached to any mode of movement whatsoever. Whether I get there by foot, by airdrop, by swimming, or by bilocation makes no difference to me. The means by which life is created are limitless and far beyond my immediate awareness. If I engage with the desire and intent to move to point B, but it has to be by helicopter, I limit the field and energy movement. Usually an attachment to *how* something should be done has a root in a limiting belief pattern I am holding that needs to be uprooted.

If our desire to transform is coming from a challenging experience in ordinary reality, like a serious illness or poverty for example. Creating the intentional field and energising it can be difficult. It's hard to envisage and embody the vibration of a pain-free body when you are straddled by constant chronic pain. Cancer in children, disabilities, and tragedies raise challenging questions and cause the mind to find some reasoning to what appears to be totally unfair experiences for some. It can also require a dip into energy grids that may have been held over lifetimes or inherited from ancestral lineage. Seeking direct revelation in these situations is helpful to hone intent and open the heart to the possibility of a different reality, but we don't need a specific understanding of why we are dwelling in a certain state. The desire, intent, and determination to transmute it is enough and brings a new possibility into the frame. If we doubt it's possible, however, it requires a lot of inner work; and in these situations, seeking the help of a practitioner who has a stable and operating understanding of spirited living is enormously helpful, as is group ritual.

By now you have digested a new way to perceive the self and this game called life. You may have started to use the beautiful inspirations and practices listed in the appendices too. I hope so. Maintenance of your resonance, the energy that you are emanating, is so important. In the following chapter, I list the steps that work for me. None of it will be new to you, but the context of engagement will be. That is, the context of regarding your system as an emanator of creative patterns of vibrating energy and looking after it accordingly.

CHAPTER 21

# Raising Resonance

O ur resonant field is how we interconnect with others, the wilderness, all life—all things. We sense each other's resonance, and we emanate through resonance. When we meet someone with anxiety or depression, often we can sense depression or heaviness around him or her and within ourselves. When someone is being dishonest or not acting in his or her truth, we can sense the disharmony. When someone means us harm, we can sense it. When we meet a soul mate, soul friend, or destined lover, we can feel it.

Our resonances affect the immediate community of people we operate in, our work teams, families, and communities of friends. Our resonances particularly affect our children. Our resonances morph with broader and broader fields, both contributing to them and being affected by them. It is through mastery of our own resonant fields, our energy bodies, that we can perceive information otherwise hidden to our ordinary senses and we can impact the underlying energy patterns that hold our ordinary realities in place. I like to think of resonance as the 'carrier' of the vibration of aligned desire, intent, and choice for an experience I am seeking to create.

When our resonances are raised, our senses are sharpened and we can catch our intuitive messaging. It is through our fields of resonance that we sense intuitively. Our relationships deepen, and opportunities and the right paths become clearer. The old adage, 'Where there's a will there's a way' is describing how the energetic field is clearer when an inner choice is made. The actioning of our free will is potent, highly vibratory, and magnetises the 'way' to appear.

There is a regenerative, healing, and protective nature to a strong resonant field of a raised energy body. Raised resonance is a similar vibration to joy, bliss, gratitude, and love, and it more readily accommodates these feelings and energies. When we engage in heart-centred meditations, such as gratitude meditations, for example, our immune functions strengthen, our heart rates smooth, lower-vibe people tend to drop away from our lives, and higher-vibe people draw in. A reshuffling of relationships is very common for people who start to live spirited lives. As our vibrational rates change, lighten, and quicken, people who aren't vibing at the same rate distance themselves, and others vibing at the same rate draw in, as do experiences and opportunities. Raised resonance is contagious. It can spontaneously raise the resonance of lower fields when they come into contact with it.

Our resonances are carriers for intent, desire, and will, the ingredients of conscious creation. Our resonances are the creative tensions within our auric fields that host the creative process. When our resonances are heightened, we are better able to sense movement and incoming demonstrations of spirit.

Raising our resonances is about tending to our energy bodies. Many of us deplete our resonances unconsciously, through habit. I have learnt that some of the top ways to deplete the energy body are as follows:

- having a heavy, contracted physical system either because of diet or toxin buildup, not sweating enough, poor breathing, poor sleep, and, especially, stress
- engaging in negative thought patterns—having a dissipated non-present mind that cycles through past regrets, hurts, and future worries
- engaging in negative talk and gossip
- neglecting inner practices, such as meditation
- keeping low-frequency company and consuming low-frequency content
- engaging in unbalanced sexual expression

It is entirely within our control and our choice to maintain and raise our levels of resonance. Some simple ways to start experimenting are listed below. There are many more, but all of them are achievable micro-adjustments in a busy modern life that collectively enable a higher resonance.

## Raising the Resonance of the Physical Body

Keep the diet light. The tantras instruct us that a full belly should contain one third food, one third water, and one third air. Buddha's upturned rice bowl and staff create the Buddhist stupa that adorns ancient Buddhists sacred sites like Borobudur in Java, Indonesia. Buddha was also telling us that we should turn over our rice bowls before we feel full. Christ fasted and ate sparingly, based on what we can see in the Gospels. When our digestive system and organs are overworked, our overall field slows down. It zaps available energy, and it distorts the production and release of a whole suit of psychoactive chemicals from the digestive tract that help raise our physical resonance and mood, and improve our sleep. This is why every major religion and spiritual framework advocates regular fasting. Intermittent fasting has also re-emerged in the health and wellness arena for the proven healing effects it has on the body's cells.

Physical movement and exercise are also important in keeping the overall metabolic and energy rate active and slightly higher than when one is at rest. Sweating is good! Sweating generally gets a bad rap in modern society. Multi-billion-dollar industries based on stopping or curbing sweating keep us paranoid about body odour and looking shiny. Moving to an equatorial country at the same time as entering perimenopause years ago cured me of that brainwashing once and for all. I had no choice but to embrace sweating. But the truth is that sweating is essential to healthy body function and a clear energy body, and the sweat of a well, healthy, balanced body smells beautiful. It's musky, sweet, and sexy. Scent is one of the major ways we communicate subliminally.

A good daily sweat has an effect on the overall energy body that is similar to the effect a good cry has on the heart; it creates space and expansion and releases dense, constricted energy from the system. There's a surrender involved in allowing the body to sweat unabated, which is a useful state for release. When we sweat, we thirst, and this movement of water through the system brings with it a state of flow and healing, which, when connected with consciously, is then demonstrated in our lives. Sweat has an antibiotic effect and helps heal wounds. It releases from our systems toxins—both those naturally produced and those that are environmental, such as chemicals and pollutants. Dedicated exercise and the drinking of water flushes the system more effectively, improving organ function and preventing the onset of stagnant, solidifying illnesses, such as kidney stones.

Regular exercise produces more sweat glands, which help release from the skin grit and grime that hold in place the bacteria that produce body odour and acne. The more we sweat, the better we smell and look.

Adding kinetic energy to your inner practice amplifies it considerably. For me, running or cycling at dawn is a potent and effective way to clear stagnant, unhelpful energy and to raise my inner state to hold higher vibrations of love and service. I start and end each physical activity with an intent-setting meditation, and I dedicate the effort and the sweat to the demonstration of that intent. When I do this, the manifestation is quickened.

Physical movement promotes deeper breathing. In the main, we breathe from the top 20 per cent of the lungs. When we breathe mindfully, we shift the breath from thoracic to diaphragmatic, and this oxygenates the blood, releases toxins, synchronises our nervous systems, and sends signals to our brains to relax and be calm. When we're calm, we can perceive our resonance. The practices of pranayama, described in chapter 18 and listed in the appendices of this book, are beautiful additions to inner practice. Your workouts are actually spirited!

You can also amplify the resonance-raising effects of conscious breathing with regular use of a neti pot! A neti pot is a small pot, much like a little teapot, that is specifically designed for nasal irrigation. The solution used is purified water and salt. You can buy plastic neti pots from most chemists, but for me the more traditional ceramic pots garner a better energy in the water and the practice. (I tend to be arching against plastics generally these days.) You can buy pre-made saline satchels to add to the water, which are very handy, as well as pre-mixed neti salt that can be added to water that has been boiled and then cooled to tepid.

The actual process is very simple and, once you get used to it, feels fantastic. It requires you to lean over your basin, gently insert the pot nozzle into one nostril, tilt your head slightly forward and to the side, and allow the water to run through the nasal passage and sinus cavity and out the other nasal passage. Once half the pot is finished, swap sides. It takes a little practice to get the tilt and breathing through the mouth right, but once you have it, you can feel the benefits of the practice immediately. It flushes out irritants like pollen, dust, smoke, and so forth, and it thins out mucus. This typically leads to less congestion and easier breathing through the nose, which is also essential for entering deep states of meditation through breathwork, and this is when the body's cells and chemistry start to regenerate. A neti pot acts as a booster for your body's own natural operations.

Physically, regular use of a neti pot is proven to treat and defend against chronic sinus infections, bacterial sinus infections, rhinitis, allergic reactions, viral upper respiratory infections, irritant-based congestion, and rhinitis due to pregnancy. It's one of the very few natural remedies allowed during pregnancy.

But it's the energy amplification it creates in the breath which is what makes it a fantastic practice. It bathes the microscopic nerve endings that line the nasal cavities and sinuses, the cilia, and makes them work better. And it is the gentle, rhythmic, balanced nasal breathing of all meditative breathing practices that stimulates the cilia to send nerve impulses to the brain that calm and balance brain waves and the activity of the central nervous system. Neti pot usage cleanses the mechanism for the energy breath, and therefore your breathing not only boosts immunity and the physical system but also cleanses the energy body, releasing blocked energy and increasing the intake of vital life force through breathing. It aids in entering deeper meditative states and staying connected to broader energy fields, such as those in your healthy detox foods and the environments where you are exercising. In addition to breathing easier through their noses, many neti pot users also report a better sense of smell and taste after a neti pot session, which provides amplified sensory stimulation and enjoyment, as well as wonderful vibrations for raising the energy body and accessing natural pleasure and awe.

The skin also has a role to play in raising our resonance. Along with most of the internal organs, our skin is also an organ of elimination. It is estimated that one third of our bodies' daily impurities are excreted through the skin. Dry brushing keeps the pores clear and the skin active to assist the body in this cleansing process. Dry brushing exfoliates the buildup of dead skin cells and stimulates sweat and oil glands. This has a number of wonderful effects. The first and most obvious one is smoother, glowing, healthy skin. It helps keep younger skin free from breakouts. Dry brushing increases the skin's ability to absorb oxygen and other nutrients into the body, and it works to cleanse the whole physical system by releasing excess stress on other detoxifying internal organs. Dry brushing also increases blood circulation, which helps to contribute to healthier muscle tone and better distribution of fat deposits, reducing the appearance of cellulite (always a winner!).

On an energetic level, the increased cleansing of toxins generally lightens the system and releases more bioenergy for use in meditation and inner practice. Our skin is one of our main physical systems that signals intuitive information. We have all had the skin ripple or 'goose up' when we have become aware of a spiritual movement, coincidence, or encounter worth exploring. If the skin is free, vital, and sensitive to energy, it serves us more reliably.

It's worth finding a dry skin brush with a long handle so you can reach the much- neglected skin on your back. The basic method is to start at the extremities and work the skin in firm small circles up towards the heart. I move from fingers up arms towards the heart, focusing on fingers, palms, backs of hands, forearms, upper arms, and elbows. Then I brush from soles and tops of feet, calves, shins, and tops and backs of thighs towards the heart. I dry brush abdomen, stomach, and breasts with rotating sweeps towards the heart and towards alternate sides of the waist, buttocks, and lower, middle, and upper back. I usually do this when I return from my morning exercise and meditation, before I jump in the shower. In my experience, dry brushing brings an immediate increase in vitality and mental clarity, and it feels fantastic.

Another resonance-raising body practice is salt bathing, otherwise known as balneotherapy or, if you're old school like me, witches' baths. Soaking the body in a mineral salt bath is one of the most relaxing, restorative, and energetically potent practices you can adopt. A bath by its nature is a singular activity in a space where most distractions are reduced (e.g., a bathtub or bathroom, which are usually acoustically insulated by tiles). It is highly sensual, especially if you make the experience a sacred and beautiful act of self-care with oils, candles, and maybe some soft music. Aside from myriad physical health benefits from regular salt baths, salt is also a potent agent to use for spiritual practice. Along with the extraction of toxins, salt baths also extract dense, low-vibration energy from the system and prevent the energy body from 'picking up' low-vibration energy from others. I prescribe it regularly to students and clients who are particularly sensitive to the energy of others or who are losing energy to a situation or relationship that is out of harmony.

On a physical level, mineral salt bathing is evidenced to relax and de-stress mind and body, regulate stress hormones, and reset hectic brainwave activity. Through the process of dermal absorption, the skin also soaks up minerals from the salt that are critical for our health and vitality. Epsom and Himalayan salts are rich in calcium, copper, iodine, iron, magnesium, manganese, phosphorus, potassium, selenium, sodium, and zinc. Through a process called reverse osmosis, a salt bath will also extract toxins through the skin, greatly increasing the benefits of any dietary detox measures. Regular mineral salt bathing reduces inflammation, which in turn eases joint aches and muscle pain. Mineral salt bathing before bedtime is shown to increase length and quality of sleep. The salt also has antibacterial and antiseptic qualities that are useful in keeping skin clean, regulating body odour, and easing eczema, acne, and psoriasis. The salt creates a protective layer on the skin that reduces loss of moisture and dry skin. It also reduces bloating and water retention, eases the discomfort of bites and blisters, and increases blood circulation. Those with weak or poor heart function should always consult their physicians before engaging in regular mineral salt baths because of the extra activity of the circulatory system that the baths trigger.

My extraction bath recipe is simply a cup of Epsom or Himalayan salt, a cup of bicarb of soda and ten drops of lavender oil. It's best to soak in this water for at least twenty minutes and ensure you thoroughly rinse the skin and bathtub afterwards. We release a lot of low-vibration energy through the feet, so if you do not have access to a bathtub, a foot soak with the same extraction recipe is also very effective, as is a dry salt scrub before a shower; however, regular soaking produces the best effects and benefits, and quickly.

Adding various essential oils, crystals, and fresh herbs to the water for different effects is a beautiful way to keep the practice interesting and to observe your energy system's response to various high-energy tools.

Some basic, easily sourced, but very effective essential oil additions are as follows:

- for relaxation, stress relief, and toxin and low-vibration energy extraction: lavender, clary sage, bergamot, angelica
- for aiding sleep and promotion of dreaming: lavender, chamomile, cedar wood (my favourite), valerian
- for aches and pains and revelation: peppermint, clove, sage, rosemary, and thyme
- for circulation, opening the heart space and nurturing gratitude: orange, jasmine, grapefruit, lemon, rose, and frankincense (another favourite)

The energy of water is programmable, so the most effective ingredient to get the most out of mineral salt bathing is your intent. Use the time when preparing the bath to clarify and express the intent for the bath—whether this be to release, restore, protect, or generally treat your physical and energy bodies with love and to honour their majesty. Sounds a little woo-woo? Get into the habit and just experience the result!

Smile! Our bodies respond physiologically to a smile— not just a smile on the lips, but a smile from the heart that is projected from the eyes. Maintaining a soft secret smile can ease and open the energy body and create a sea of beautiful smiles back to you by the people that you pass. This is good medicine!

Our sexual energy is a massive localised generator for our energy bodies. This appears in all cultures and many spiritual frameworks, and it has been deliberately downplayed from the exoteric Christian model, perhaps because of its power and its dangers when it is unbalanced and driven by need. Some traditions advocate the physical release, or orgasm, and then recycling of sexual energy through the energy body with meditation techniques; others advocate celibacy to create a build in unexpressed sexual energy, to infuse into the energy body. Tantra explores the relationship between raw, delicious sexual energy and our invisible spiritual selves and techniques to transmute energetic states.

Another shared feature of modern life, whether one is married, solo, oriented in one's own wonderful way, or somewhere in between, is periods of celibacy. We are bombarded on all fronts by advertisements, millions of them, with the message, 'If you are having sex all the time, you are blazing in life. If you are not having sex at least three times a day, then you are a loser.' Okay, perhaps this is slightly exaggerated, but the message is the same. Many people come to meditation as they think something is wrong with them because they don't fancy having sex at particular times in their life. Whilst this can be a symptom of an underactive parasympathetic nervous system, which regular meditation rebalances, it is also perfectly normal. Here's the thing: it is totally normal, universal, and healthy to have periods of celibacy throughout our adult lives. All animals do this. Those periods may be a week, a month, a year, or three years. They may be the result of choosing not to hitch our wagons to others, a dissolved marriage or relationship, or a dissolved sex life within an otherwise happy union. There is nothing wrong with this. It is totally abnormal to have sex fifty times a week, every week, from the age of sixteen to eighty, as we may have been led to believe is the norm.

Periods of celibacy bring with them the opportunity for accelerated spiritual expansion. Exploring tantra with a recognised tantric teacher (beware the self-acclaimed tantric expert ... run!) can give access to many accessible meditation practices that help you raise the unexpressed energy from the lower body into the higher centres. There are also some amazing rituals that do the same thing. I had the privileged of experiencing an initiation ritual with Kamakshi a few years ago. Kamakshi is the aspect of Shakti in Hinduism that helps women transmute desire into light. It was a powerful and well-timed ritual for me at the time, and it had an immediate result.

'Balanced sexual expression' is a term that encapsulates any expression of your sexual energy that make you feel totally and unashamedly fantastic across all your aspects: body, mind, heart, energy, and spirit. It builds and swirls your entire system in spirals: spiralling thoughts, feelings, heart beat, and exchange. Balanced sexual expression has no trade-offs; that is, everyone involved is enthusiastically consenting and feels fantastic, free, and spiralling. Balanced sexual expression holds no trace of shame, guilt, or secrecy.

'Unbalanced sexual expression' is any form or thought of sexual expression that doesn't result in the above. Extracting ourselves from unbalanced sexual expression and enthusiastically welcoming the periods of celibacy in our lives is a powerful way to raise resonance and keep it humming!

And get outdoors! There's a lot circulating across media channels about the importance of walking barefoot on the earth for grounding, calming, and presence. But similarly to sweating, the modern take on walking barefoot is not so positive. It can be perceived as dirty, even risky. Obviously, where we choose to go barefoot is important, but research tells us that the wilder the place, the better, both physically and energetically for the system.

We now have scientific measurements of changes that occur in the human system when exposed barefooted to the earth, and all of those changes are amazing and very good for both body and spirit. Some, but by no means all, are a marked drop in the stress hormone cortisol in the bloodstream, and therefore reduction in feelings of anxiety and stress, as well as reduction in inflammation and pain. Regular barefoot walking in the wild has been shown to directly affect our cells. Red and white blood cell counts rebalance for greater immune function, and it increases the surface charge of red blood cells, reducing clumping in the cells and therefore heart disease. Exposure to the earth and, in particular, the earth's negative charge resets our circadian rhythms and other biological processes, thereby improving sleep and the process of getting to sleep.

But it's the impact on our energetic circuitry induced by the wilderness that makes barefoot walking, and time spent out of doors generally, essential to spiritual health. We are by nature beings of both the earth and energetic realms. Our thoughts, feelings, energy vibrations, and awareness, when aligned with the body and the earth, become powerful spiritual forces for transformation. Spending time directly exposed to the wilderness connects these aspects within us, just as the wilderness itself connects these aspects within it. A tree is both earthed to the soil and transmutes the energy of light into growth. Spiritually, we operate the same way. The wilderness brings our systems—physical, mental, emotional, energetic and spiritual—back into alignment. It brings us into presence and bathes us in beauty, the rhythm of cycles, and a constant reminder that all things move and change.

The sun always returns after the storm, the spring after

the winter, the dawn after the night. This is the human state and the nature of life. When we sit calmly with this truth and simply flow with it, we find freedom, gratitude, and joy, and these are the greatest forces to amplify our vitality and love for life.

## Raising the Resonance of the Mind

Regular meditation creates a platform for mindfulness, a pause point before reacting and speaking. It generates a viewpoint to recognise and reprogram contracting negative thought, emotion, and speech patterns. When we live mindfully, we don't dance in the drama unless we choose to. You may be able to raise your resonance through the physical aspect, but without mindfulness your field will continually be depleted. It can feel a bit like blowing up a big balloon with a small puncture, a slow leak.

Seeking inspiration in what we read and absorb via art, music, TV, and talks, for example, and mindfully assessing and choosing our online content sources, books and commentaries, helps to protect the psyche from limiting collective beliefs. The company we keep is also important to our level of resonance. A higher vibration tends to attract higher-vibrational people around you, but it can also attract the vibration-starved as well. Staying aware of our energy bodies helps us feel depletions of our energy fields by others. We need to choose when and how we expose our energy fields to long-term friends who loop through worries and indecision or who keep making the same mistakes but can't see things another way, or friends or family members we love to gossip with. Loose lips sink ships—or, more precisely, loose lips sink energy bodies. Spending time with your spirit tribe and people who really get you and love you despite any differences is worth seeking out. There's nothing like an activated spiritual conversation to raise your mental resonance. Finding opportunities to experience awe and wonder, and absorbing content that inspires and stirs, raises your resonance in unexpected ways.

### Raising the Resonance of the Spirit

Heightened states during meditation lift resonance and maintain it off the meditation stool throughout the day. Extended pranayama (breathing) techniques particularly, align and synchronise the nervous system and alter the brain enabling deeper and deeper meditations. Heart-centred meditations that nurture gratitude, awe and wonder, bliss, forgiveness, and unconditional love powerfully raise resonance. These meditations, random acts of kindness and generosity, and a mindset of helpfulness and caring create enormous expansion within the heart space as we jettison our own smallness and take the higher road.

What I have learned looking back over my own spiritual journey and learning to raise my energy body is that the clues to the most effective ways to do it often lie in our childhoods and those moments and activities when we feel connections to something bigger, something beautiful. For me it was steeping myself in nature and writing. For you it may have been daydreaming in a tree, belonging to a team you loved, or a particular beach holiday. It may have been at family lunches, Sunday prayers, or with a clean sheet of paper and colouring pencils. Remember how you felt in those moments and where you were at the time. These moments in childhood are portals into the connection and raise spiritual resonance. They may be overgrown by the inner jungle, but they're there in your memory and heart. Find what it was in your early, wild free years that enabled a touch of spirit, and start to bring these elements, these channels, back into your life. Join an art class, write, spend more time in the wilderness, return to a favourite prayer. These raise your spiritual resonance strongly because they are what you have always loved doing, and they almost always involve spiritual expression. In my observation, they also point to an aspect of your life's purpose and how you might embody it and live it.

Engaging with spirit through meditative ritual, writing, and the wilderness are my greatest ways to raise the resonance of my spirit and, therefore, my entire system. Meditative ritual is an event that takes place when attention, desire, intent, and action are combined in specific ways to create a change or 'movement' energetically. Ritual shifts our resonances or vibrational states. The energetic changes that ritual creates naturally run their course through to the physical plane if the field of intent created remains strong until the desired change presents—or 'demonstrates', in other words—if the creator's resonance remains high and engaged.

In all of my transformational courses, there is an element of simple modern ritual as a home practice or in group classes. Why? Because ritual is a powerful way to generate change. The combination of symbolic gesture, evocative meaningful objects and elements, and actioned intent sends a poetic message to our deep minds that can generate a wholesale reset in how we are engaging with ourselves, others, and life.

This is one of the reasons I love shamanic practice so much, because at its core, it utilises ritual to effect change. It's sensory, beautiful, and a lot of fun, and most importantly, it works! There are several deeper esoteric reasons why ritual is so effective: the shift in subconscious patterns, the generation of new felt and energetic patterns into the field of possibility, and the correspondences to causal energy fields, to name a few. But you don't need to understand any of that deep spiritual jazz to engage. The reason for this is that we are made for generative ritual. Our spirits ache for expression because at our cores we are essentially creative, and creativity requires expression. And you don't need antler horns, eagle feathers, sage bundles, or ancient Elysian hymns to engage; all you need is to bring your presence and spiritual awareness to whatever it is you are doing and imbue it with a clear intent to convert mundane motions into 'mythic manoeuvres.'

Work with water. In every spiritual tradition around the world, the element of water is associated with cleansing, healing, and preparation. Water is essential to all life on Earth; we form within it and are carried by it into the world, and it makes up around 85 per cent of our physical form. It nourishes and cleanses the body and ensures abundance and beauty in our homes and communities. However, we also now know that water interacts with our vibratory state in far more mysterious and wonderful ways. The groundbreaking work of Dr Masaru Emoto proved that there is a vibratory exchange between human consciousness and water molecules. His work is definitely worth exploring. In effect, through his experiments of exposing distilled water samples to various emotional states that were expressed directly to the water samples, the molecular structures of the water samples changed to reflect the vibratory fields generated. Water molecules exposed to love or gratitude have very different structures to those exposed to hate and anger, for example.

Many traditions use water as a spiritual conduit. My Intuitive Healing students learn how to infuse distilled water with reiki and moonlight to induce inner healing and lucid dreaming, for example. With practice they can develop a powerful substance that has incredible effects on the communication between the subconscious and conscious minds, and that heightens intuition. Whether we are serious spiritual seekers or are happy to explore and dwell in the mundane, we all connect with water every day. Here are some easy conversions into the mythic power of water.

You may know an aspect that you wish to diminish and expel from your habitual behaviour. This could be an addictive habit, an anger response, a habit of jealous comparison, or self-sabotage default. Anything that you identify within yourself that is a sticky habit and one that you would love to jettison for a more positive lifeward one is perfect for shower smudging. If you're like me, you might have quite a list. My tip would be to choose just one to work with so you can observe the effects of this beautiful practice. Commit for nine straight days that you will use your daily showers to dissolve this habit and run it from your system. It's important that you make time for your showers during this ritual. A rushed ritual is simply going through the motions and achieves very little spiritually. Tell whomever you might be sharing your home space with that you're checking out for a spell and you're not to be disturbed. Leave all devices out of range. Make your bathing space as evocative as possible with candles, scents, and even soothing music. Run the shower for a moment or two before you step in, and use the sounds of the flowing water as your soundtrack to set your intent. For me decree is always the most efficient and powerful way to do this. I use something like the following: 'With the power of my presence and my actioned intent, I dedicate this shower ritual to the dissolution of my anger. I acknowledge the healing life-giving power of the water element. I now cleanse myself of unhealthy anger and return this energy to the earth and the seas. I am free.'

Then step into the central flow of the shower. Stay very present and lean deeply into the physical sensations of the millions of water droplets connecting with your crown and running down over your body. As you stand there, cultivate a strong sense of knowing that something mythic is taking place, and as much as possible, hold that vibration. (I like to pop a few drops of my favourite essential oil on my crown beforehand too. The extra sensory element amplifies the ritual significantly.)

Do this for nine days in a row and observe how you are as you go about your day. Slowly but surely, you will find that the usual triggers to said anger response lose their voltage.

And just as we can use the flow of earthbound water to release, we can use the mundane action of rehydration to infuse into our systems the vibratory elements we wish to cultivate. Following Dr Emoto's lead, a very simple ritual is to bless the water you drink before you take it in. I have found that this is far more effective with clean distilled water. I use a double charcoal filter for all our drinking water at home anyway, and it creates a much more highly resonant substance. Wild fresh water is even better if it's clean. So if you're lucky enough to live somewhere where you trust the rains or streams, try using this instead or tap or town water.

The health nuts keep telling us to drink litres each day, so why not convert it from a mundane must-do to a mythic manoeuvre? Again, you need to take your time and make the ritual as evocative as possible. I use an antique crystal martini glass for my water rituals, which makes it feel sacred, ancient, and special. It's the feeling you're going for. Each morning when you wake, before you take anything else into your body, pour yourself a large glass of water. Hold the glass between both hands and settle into present awareness. Then open your awareness to the infinite possibilities within the day yet to unfold. Don't go into details of your to-do list, but rather *feel* the presence of possibilities. Somewhere within this day is the pathway to the highest of them all. Once you sense connection, allow the vibration of it to fill your heart, your mind, and your whole body. Use your breath to concentrate this feeling and visualise it streaming down your arms, through your hands, and into the glass of water. Again, you can use a decree of some kind. Stating the intent out loud is a far more powerful way to imbue the water. You can state with command something like 'With the power of my presence and actioned intent, I now claim the highest possibility of this day. It is mine, and it now vibrates within this water.'

When you sense a shift in the transferal of energy to the water, drink it very slowly. Lean all of your senses into the sensations of the water entering your system, hydrating your body and your spirit, and connecting you to the highest path. When you do this often enough, you will start to perceive a very different experience of the days started with this ritual to those that don't. Experiences that might have been seen as obstacles and hassles will become welcomed redirections. Exchanges with people that might have otherwise been annoying will be filled with compassion. Solutions to problems that have remained elusive will explode into mind in undeniable ways. Try it and see for yourself.

Healing others through the connective aspect of water is another beautiful way to create spiritual flow. I am blessed with a largely symbiotic marriage. My husband and I are polar opposites to the extreme. He's stable, grounded, mindful, non-reactive, deeply responsive, and introverted with an incredible analytical mind. He's about as un-woo-woo as you can get. I'm fluid, fiery, high vibration, emotive, expressive, wild, slightly impulsive, and about as woo-woo as you can get—and it works. One of the best examples of this is in the kitchen. I love to cook, especially as a mythic manoeuvre, and I use pretty much every pot, pan, and utensil available. I taste everything along the way, slop drips on the countertop, have music on full tilt, usually have a glass of red wine in tow, and regard preparing meals as an alchemical process. He loves to devour my meals and then restore order in the kitchen space. It gives him the same level of pleasure as the chaos creation does for me.

During the holiday season, I try to let him rest. After the meals are done, I also (not every time, but when I'm moved to) clean up to leave him rest with his full belly. Over the years with him, I have learnt the pleasure in restoring order, although it doesn't come naturally to me. I have learnt that the post-meal clean-up can be converted into a powerful mythic manoeuvre.

Each plate and utensil used in the meal holds the energetic imprint of my family or friends who used it. So when I take the clean-up turn, I choose to hand-wash everything and convert it into a ritual. The same elements apply: presence, clear actioned intent, and decree. With each utensil and plate washed in the sink, I convert it into a cleansing ritual for all those who shared my table. I draw into presence using the soundtrack of the filling sink and the lingering smells of the meal. I stack and wipe everything that needs to be washed and put away and then survey my ritual space—a hot sink of cleansing water and a stack of objects recently touched, scraped, and licked by my loved ones. I'll then quietly make my decree: 'With this action, I cleanse suffering, unhappiness, and chaos from my loving collective. With every movement of my hands, I usher in joy, laughter, and magic. I return all elements to their rightful places in gratitude. I offer this effort in unconditional love and gratitude for these beautiful people in my life.'

You will be amazed how cool the after-meal clean-up becomes when it is converted into a mythic manoeuvre. Fond memories and thoughts flood the mind as you wash, and the heart fills with gratitude for the bounty of your table and the love in your life. And with some practice, you will notice a distinct joyful vibration that permeates the post-meal space and interchange on the days you do it.

Absolutely everything has a magical energetic aspect with the right perception. I hope you get the drift from the above examples. Here are a few other ideas you can work with:

**Convert**

Convert cooking a meal into creating a potent medicine for your most important needs, deep nourishment, and healing.

Convert putting out the trash into dispensing with low-vibration energies in the home that are resulting in illness, accidents, scratchy moods, and harsh words

Convert writing your shopping list into creating a cosmic intention list for growth. After the bananas and washing liquid, add whatever it is you are seeking to cultivate—love, compassion, patience, or joy, for example. Make it a habit of adding these items each time you write out your shopping list.

Reset your passwords. Choose passwords that are symbolic of your inner work and what you are choosing to manifest. The repetitive requirement of password security means we can repeat this 'mythic key code' often, which keeps our awareness gently pegged to the possibility of it, which in turn draws it near.

# CHAPTER 22

# Developing Your Intuition

You can develop the inner aspect of your senses by focusing on your outer senses, because they're two poles of the one sense. So, for example, in your meditations, early morning sun gazing, practising the beautiful Buddhist meditation trataka, and candle gazing stimulate the optic nerve and the outer sense of eyesight and stimulate your clairvoyance. Leaning your attention into combinations of ambient sounds whilst meditating, for example, also develops your ability to raise your clairaudience, and using chanting and mantras also do the same.

You can meditate using your sense of smell and smelling evocative substances like dried herbs or fresh flowers or essential oils and steeping your awareness fully into their complexity and their beauty. And you'll find that your inner sense of clear smelling also increases.

Another beautiful example, which helps raise the inner senses of claircognizance and clairempathy, is going to highly resonant places, such as temples, sacred sites, beautiful patches of wilderness, or cemeteries. The latter sounds a bit spooky, but they're very high vibration places because there's a lot of prayer there. There's a lot of emotion that's left in the ground and in the atmosphere around them, and meditating there and feeling into the dynamics of the space, the dimensions of the space, and the elements that make up the space will also raise your ability of inner feeling and inner empathy.

Mindful eating is another beautiful practice, in which you slow down, allow the food to sit in your mouth, and allow your senses to fully appreciate your body's response in taste. Then, when you chew, you do the same, giving a deep release of the taste. And when you swallow, you lean into your body's response to the introduction of the food into the stomach.

Another one, of course, is touch. Touching different substances, holding crystals that are highly resonant, and feeling into different textures and fabrics as a meditative practice also boosts your ability for clairtangency. These beautiful meditation practices are gorgeous mindfulness practices that slow you down and bring you into present awareness, but doing them knowing that you're actually developing and heightening your inner senses makes it much more fun and useful in the game of living a spirited life. Intentionally developing your intuition opens up a deeper intuitive engagement with life. It truly is magical and deepens a sense of wonder and awe within you, which are excellent vibratory patterns to hold within yourself, mind, heart, and body.

Another very important aspect of developing your intuition is to act upon it. When an old friend comes to mind, message him or her. When you feel the flash of a prompting to follow up on an email, do it. When you dream of someone, pop them a message and tell them. When you feel something isn't right in a situation, pause and observe further. When a person makes you feel uneasy, create space. When the smell of a food type or drink makes your energy lower, don't consume it. When mainstream media fills you with fear and despair, switch the channel. Every time we act on our intuitive prompting, it strengthens the signalling to our awareness and allows space for wider, more complex intuitive information to come through.

Once the energy body is raised and there is space established in our inner terrains, our ordinary realities reveal their patterns. We call them synchronicities, miracles, or magic, and they become our modus operandi. Another archetypal experience of embodying an expanded sense of self and raising the energy body is *enablement* to go wider and deeper. We start to experience unexplained intense moments of bliss, overwhelming gratitude, and joy that spring from unseen depths and short circuit the moment in ordinary reality. They are the first of spirit's gifts of enablement. They constantly move our systems back into balance by momentarily bypassing the mind and exploding open the heart. Sometimes we get a complete reboot via extremely heightened meditative awareness or an energy healing. These gifts are intoxicating, and they signal the waking up of our inner wisdom and spiritual tools. The inner senses sharpen and have space to catch our attention. In our meditations, we start to perceive inner energies in colours and visions and lucid dreaming. We can feel danger, opportunity, and change from further afield, yet unseen. We have a palpable sense when we meet another person vibrating at the same resonance. The connection is easy, and the exchange almost always spirals to the spiritual realm quickly. We tend to meet more and more people with the same vibrations and connections with spirit.

There are lots of different definitions of these inner senses, and there is a recent resurgence in interest, research, and measurement of these abilities that enable us to work with the causal energy of life, with spirit. In ordinary reality, they appear as superpowers, and many fall into the trap of thinking they have somehow arrived or 'awakened' when they start to stir, but they are not the end game. Regardless of what you call them or how you measure them, what is archetypal is that within the dynamic of connecting with spirit comes *enablement*—in your spiritual senses, experiences, and community.

# CHAPTER 23

# My Journey to a Spirited Life

The wilderness, yogic tradition, my childhood framework of Catholicism, and my deep explorations of shamanism, Jungian psycology and usui reiki, an insatiable appetite for spiritual texts, and a daily practice are what open me to my spiritual nature and design, and these are the methods I teach. I believe this is one of the most fabulous attributes of our modern world. We can access many alternative perspectives and frameworks for connecting with spirit today that were previously inaccessible. In my observation, the important tools of inner exploration are to start with the frameworks of your childhood, find teachers that you know and trust, and use the immense pallet of spiritual wisdom now available. Different traditions offer a multitude of dance steps for the cosmic dance floor of life, and it's easier now to find teachings and teachers who can show us dance steps that we really like, but the starting point for your inner journey is to work with the framework that gave you your first direct experience of spirit—that first stirring of your heart.

I was raised in a very traditional Catholic home in Sydney, Australia. It was an abundant childhood steeped in nature. I was enamoured with nature and with the Catholic rituals of the Mass and sacraments. Back when I was a young girl, perhaps around five or six, before the formal teaching of church dogma began, when I could *feel* spirit, and not have any framework to 'think' it, I had profound and exquisite experiences of spirit. The two frameworks that informed my six-year-old consciousness when *felt* spirit and *felt* expansion were the wilderness and the Catholic faith. For me, the rituals of the Church, the fire of the Holy Spirit, the breath of God, the bread and wine of the earth, and the holy waters encapsulated a wild beauty and connection with nature. It was the white dove of the Holy Spirit, the tongues of fire at Pentecost, and the stories of the saints (especially those with advanced spiritual abilities) that had me.

At home it was my mum who was my most important spiritual teacher when I was a girl. Mum is an unusual mix. She is deeply and wildly connected to spirit as a woman, artist, and mother, as well as through her total love affair with the natural world. Yet at the same time, she is a devout Catholic with very conservative views. She is intelligent and is also a voracious reader. Whilst we disagree on certain things, such as some politics and religious moral judgements, I respect her position because I know that it is based on a lot of thinking and a rigorous pursuit of facts. We have just learnt to agree to disagree on certain things. It is the wild spirit-connected side of Mum that I love, and it is this part of me that she nurtured.

To this day, Mum has a deep and abiding devotion to Holy Mary, and she acknowledges and prays to angels. Every day, she prays the rosary, and she has continually nudged me to explore this divine, spiralling, and powerful prayer more deeply throughout my life. As a girl, I would hear her pray them in a half-whispered soft voice at high speed. My parents' faith taught me discipline and a knowing of a wider, deeper invisible world. It taught me ritual and chant. It taught me meditative states through prayer and song. I am enormously grateful for it.

As Mum was growing up in North Queensland, her childhood was alive with wild duck hunts, fruit picking, the Great Barrier Reef, floods, cyclones, electrical storms, and long, hot summers. She has a deep connection with nature. At the heart of this devout Catholic woman is a dynamic, wild relationship with nature. It was Mum that had me searching in the garden for the first white flower of the giant azalea that heralded the coming of spring. It was Mum who taught me how to sense the weather changing, to taste the sunshine within a ripe mango, and to recognise the fascinating intelligence within all creatures. It was she that had us out on the balcony under the full moons, giggling and howling before we went to bed. We watched David Attenborough throughout my childhood, and my children grew up with his documentaries too. As a painter, she expresses this relationship through light, movement, and colour on her canvasses. She knows how to weave energy in her art and, especially, in the home. To watch Mum prepare for a dinner party was to watch spell-weaving in action. The colours, flowers, candles, pretty glassware, and plates, right through to the recipes and ingredients, the music, and the timing, were all woven together in a pleasure spell for her guests. Perhaps the most precious gift Mum gave me, though, was her constant encouragement to express my spirit. She bought me new exercise books for my poetry and writings, constantly, and listened patiently to each new offering as I filled book after exercise book. The house was stocked with paints and canvasses, sketchbooks, and craft boxes, and school holidays always involved some form of creative project.

In the primary school classroom, however, I started to question the way Catholicism was being taught to me, because it didn't match my direct experience of spirit. The idea of original sin, for example, just didn't make any sense to me. How could the intelligent forces that created the natural world in all its sophistication create a human that is basically broken by some inherited disobedience from the beginning of time? (I am obviously stating this question in my adult phrasing, but it was there at the age of seven or eight.) I couldn't understand the imperfection. I couldn't understand the silence of the women of the Bible. The mother of Christ, Mary Magdalene, and nearly all the other female characters are either silenced or besmirched in the Gospels. What is that about? I didn't like the agency required to access spirit via a priest and obligatory participation, when I had freely felt spirit directly as a young girl, usually when I was up a tree of day dreaming on a wild beach. I especially, later in my life, had a serious wobble when large-scale systemic child abuse at the hands of the clergy and hidden by the Church was revealed, as it continues to be, in all its disturbing and heart-wrenching detail. As a young teenager, there were some things that just didn't make sense to me, and no one liked me asking about it.

So, in my late teens and twenties, I went underground and started to read. I read anything I could get my hands on that spoke of a reality closer to what I used to experience as a girl. I was strongly drawn to yoga and Eastern philosophy. It sat easily with my own understandings, and the practices of asana and pranayama are still my staples. I got involved with a charismatic Christian community for around two years and rediscovered spiritual expression in the beautiful mantras of Taze, a French Christian devotional community, renowned for the incredible harmonic resonances achieved in group chanting. My own devotional ritual, and pray strayed from formats and dogma and streamed from my heart. In my teens, I also explored occult practices and seances. This taught me the reality of the invisible and its realms. It taught me that consciousness prevails after physical death, and it especially taught me not to mess with energetic practices that I didn't understand and until I was spiritually stable. I also discovered boys and partying, and I took to both with great enthusiasm. My deep spiritual inner life remained hidden but vibrant and evolving. I aced school, was voted school captain for my final year, and matriculated into the degree I wanted.

My university days were fun and wild. It was as if I had saved up all my rebellion from my childhood in a pressure cooker and the minute I stepped onto the campus of NSW University and into my first lecture, that pressure cooker started to release steam—a lot of it! I still find it a miracle that I walked out of there with a degree and some remaining brain cells. I had an ache to travel and walk through the cultures and lands that the wisdom I was ingesting hailed from, and at the same time I was partying hard. I finished my undergraduate degree in commerce, majoring in commercial law and finance, and left the next day. I didn't even attend the graduation ceremony. I moved my base to Italy. It was meant to be a six-month sabbatical to learn the language and steep myself deeply into the all-time-world-leading divine way of living that the Italians excel at. I ended up staying three years and completing an arts degree in eighteenth-century Italian literature and EU capital markets. I never used the degree really, but it was a symbolic certificate of my graduation into the immense power of place, culture, and the planet itself.

During those years I walked through ruins of ancient civilisations. I mastered other languages. I fell in love with the human story of art and food in all its forms, and I felt the spirit within it all. I started a list of sacred sites around the world that I intended to walk across, and I realised that to continue this journey of discovery, I had to fund it somehow. It was time to stop studying and to start working. But soon work became the enabler to my inner plan. Within two years of living back in Sydney, Australia, at the age of twenty-eight, I was stationed in London for a wonderful Australian property company.

A very old blood memory of the early British Isles and Druidic mysticism woke up in me, and along with it, the certainty that I had lived there before. Celtic memories in my blood stirred when I walked the cobbled stones of Covent Garden on my way to the office every morning. My skin tingled when I stood in the middle of Stonehenge at dawn and when I hugged the stones at Avebury. My blood ran cold in the ruins of the convents sacked and pillaged by Vikings on Scotland's Hebridean Islands. It was the memory in the land that woke it up in me and opened me up enough to enter one of the most extraordinary periods of accelerated inner growth of my life.

By thirty I was progressing rapidly in my career. I was

stationed between London and New York, and I was good at my game and loving it. I had *the* most beautiful suits and shoes, a solid career record, and, I admit, an ego the size of the Iron Kingdom. And yet quietly in the background, I was working my way through writings on Celtic art and the Druids, and finding the same spiralling wisdom in the Bhagavad Gita, Bible, Kabbalah texts, writings on the Essenes, yogic philosophy, *The Tibetan Book of Living and Dying*, and within *Autobiography of a Yogi*. I bought a flat in Swiss Cottage, North London, in the middle of this inner renaissance. It was the ground-floor flat of a converted Victorian house. I shared ownership of the back garden with my lower ground-floor neighbours, Rich and Kalinka, and I absolutely loved living there and love them to this day. This awesome, mad, creative, spirit-fuelled couple are one of my treasured examples of spirit tribe. We connected immediately, loved each other deeply, and we were all excitedly exploring our spiritual aspects, unabated.

During those three years that we shared our pretty little garden, we tried everything—and I mean *everything!* Most nights of the week, there was a delicious prana party happening in the garden. Drummers, musicians, astrologers, numerologists, healers, artists, and crystal-keepers all came from near and far to hang out in our garden. The knowledge downloads were immense, as were the soundtracks, and I felt as though I was finally drinking from a rich fountain of wisdom that I had been thirsting for, for years. It was then that I found ashtanga yoga—intense, relentless repetitions of asana that took me to the very edge where mind meets matter. And I started to meditate regularly. I was self-taught and sort of slashed my way through the spiritual jungle of meditation books, looking for my way in. I started with transcendental techniques but soon found my practices becoming more and more ritualistic and wild. I was rebalancing my inner and outer aspects. My tectonic plates started to shift, because my inner life was emerging as an equal player in my ordinary reality.

This chapter of my life was wonderful and very fun, but it was starting to create a serious inner wobble. The further I moved in my career and got closer to the decision-making top of the company, the more disillusioned I became, because at the same time my inner life was moving me to expanded thinking and perspectives, and my career was no longer expressing or matching the inner me. I wasn't exactly sure what it was that I was supposed to be doing; I just had a growing knowing that being the head of communications for a huge global property company was not it. I also felt top-heavy in the theoretical and intellectual understanding of spiritual principles, but ungrounded in their application. I ached to apply the theory and to live fully by what I knew to be true. I ached for embodiment.

Within a year of the wobble manifesting, I lost all interest and loyalty to the company. I had low energy and started to resent the all-night conference calls across time zones that I used to love. I kept getting a sore throat as I swallowed the wobble each day and went into work. I had a large mortgage on my Swiss Cottage flat in London, and the repayments were in pounds sterling. How on earth could I meet them if I left my career? The probability was that I would have to return to Australia—but to do what? To kind of follow what I thought was a spiritual scent trail to my fulfilment? It was a jump that would confuse many of my friends and family who couldn't quite grasp that I'd actually pull the plug on my career when I was peaking. I have since come to understand that such 'jumps' are necessary and archetypal. My story is a common one. When spirit starts to stir, so does the realisation that identity and many relationships are built on only one small aspect of the self. You start to question what you stand for. But my other side—my wild, spiritual side—was rising and seeking expression. The dance was on. I had to make a choice. And while on the beach in Sydney two days before returning to work in London, I decided to resign.

By this stage I had moved my ravenous inner reading monster onto the immense library of theosophy and, in particular, Madame Blavastsky's *The Secret Doctrine* and Manly P Hall's books. This led me into the world of metaphysical writings, and Florence Scovel Shinn remains one of my favourite writers of the early nineteenth century on this. She also activates her Christian framework, and in particular the stories of the Old Testament and words of Jesus, by looking at them as explanations of energy. I was also catching up on thirty years of New Age writing, especially Neale Donald Walsch, Eckhart Tolle, Thích Nhất Hạnh, and anything I could get my hands on regarding eco-mysticism. This enabled me to look at my own childhood framework with new eyes. Being spirited didn't negate my Catholic or natural frameworks; it made them come alive and reveal their archetypal secrets that ripple through all other organised religions in the world and through the wilderness. Moreover, it handed the process back to me and tapped me into direct revelation. Metaphysics taught me that the act of choosing something with all of one's being releases an enormous amount of energy to spiral the outcome into being. And I chose it, even though I only had a felt sense of what 'it' was and had no clue at that stage where it would lead. It was a cosmic bungee jump that I felt compelled to make. I knew it carried some kind of spiritual weight. I had to leave my job and allow space in my life to find my spiritual purpose and start to live it.

I started focussing my inner practices on my relationship with abundance. It was the main source of fear that was stopping me from making the jump. I started to see the way I was clutching to a source of money because I held a false underlying belief of finite supply and lack. I used my meditations to shift that perspective. I started to view abundance as a flow rather than something to be captured and stored. I started to see everything in terms of flow. I also realised that I didn't necessarily want any particular amount in my bank account either. What I really wanted underneath all of the practical numbers of living was to not spend any more time thinking about it. I wanted a flow through my life that enabled my spiritual development, paid my mortgage, and created the widest spectrum of choice I could manage. I wanted it to simply flow easily through my life so I could release all anxiety, worry, or fear about it completely. I was tired of thinking about security and fuelling the beliefs of lack and fears that kept me from moving forward.

I walked into my boss's office the first week back into the new working year, resignation letter in hand, and we both said at the same time, 'I have something to talk about'. He said, 'ladies before gents,' and I said, 'age before beauty'. He then told me of the board's decision to restructure the company back into regional hubs and that I could stay and run the UK hub or take redundancy. I'm pretty sure he didn't finish articulating the word 'redundancy' before I said, perhaps a bit too quickly, 'Option two! I'll take option two!'

Within a week of making the choice, my ability to do so materialised. This started a magic-filled chapter of rapid learning and experimentation. Synchronicities, coincidences, profound chance meetings, insights, and revelations abounded. I became highly creative at this time, writing poetry, music, reams and reams of journals, and a manuscript for a teen novel. Deeper and deeper I dived into this inner playground. My library expanded to include the stories of the Cathars and Templars, and the Holy Grail, as well as *The*

*Magdalene Mysteries.* I revisited the divine Egyptian writings of Christian Jacq and jumped feet first into David Hawkins's books on consciousness. I also discovered writings on DMT and the pineal gland, in particular Dr Rick Strassman's work, and I poured over (and still do) Alex Grey's incredible art. My inner attention was turning to how our human energy fields connect with spirit, within the world. I started to ache for spiritual expression.

By the time I was ready to leave London and return to Australia, I knew that for spirit to express through me, I had to start to express spirit myself. I knew I had to give back to the community to create flow, and I knew that to find a teacher, I needed to teach. Aside from an absolute certainty that my life had flipped inside out, I didn't know much else. I was having wild forays into other dimensions in my meditations and experiencing visions, lucid dreams, and kundalini activations in my yoga practice. It was exciting, but without the support and technique, it was unsettling and potentially derailing.

When I returned to Sydney, I returned to the basics. I restarted basic instruction in the Satyananda yoga tradition, and I completed three years of formal studies in meditation mastery and teaching. I started structuring and ordering my wild wisdom. I became disciplined and observed my inner practice much more closely. And under the guidance of my divine teacher Louise Gilmore and her continued mentorship, I learnt how to raise my energy body and move my awareness into wider circles of life, information, and energy at will, and in reliable ways. It was Louise who first formally introduced me to shamanic practices and the realisation that shamanism is an archetypal human expression of spirit. It is ancient, existing well before any organised religion. It is a primal system that directly works with our primary design as humans and that of the wilderness.

During this beautiful chapter, I became a mother and started a community project called GIFT that redistributes stored abundance from families with more than they need and want to families within the same local community who greatly need it. GIFT continues today with community goods drives and cook-offs that practically and joyfully support the neighbouring families who are doing it tough. I trained and enrolled in a mentoring programme called Big Brothers Big Sisters, run by the YWCA, and was immediately matched with a then seven-year-old girl, Stephanie. We saw each other weekly and became very close friends and 'sisters' for years. Steph is now in her twenties and living her life, happy and real. I love her very much, as she taught me about how to impart female wisdom and the importance of gentle guidance. She showed me how hard life can be for many. She showed me how real resilience works.

I also volunteered at local state schools to teach scripture classes, and I continued this in Sydney, and then in Singapore, for over fifteen years. My journey through comparative religions and inner practices made me want to teach Christianity in the way that I understood it, rather than how it was taught to me. I replaced the lessons that were meant to cover the different types of sin with discussions on the conscience and how the energy of a mistruth makes the heart space actually feel. We stepped up lessons that involved connecting with spirit, noticing how this felt in the heart and expressing this feeling, this vibration, through voice and art. By the end of each first term, word would spread in the playground about the Catholic scripture class that did meditation, mandala, soul symbol craft, and freestyle prayer. Then the defectors would come. New little faces arrived at the door each week, from their own religious classes. My class sizes swelled through the year as long as the parents of the children gave permission for their children to try my class. I found that most parents of defectors were happy that their children felt drawn to explore something, anything.

This beautiful activity generated movement, a flow, a turning of my life spiral. It was then that I started to feel spirited all the time and learned the practices that are in this book. It was a general shift to raising my resonance, mainly through practising meditation that synthesised everything I had learnt to this point and made it useful.

In 2014, we moved to Singapore for my husband's work. I formalised my offering, registered a business, and started to teach meditation full-time. I also embarked on annual pilgrimages to the world's most ancient and sacred sites and began to learn directly from lineage shamanic teachers.

Since then I have studied usui reiki and incorporated it into my teaching and mentoring offering. My largest course communities are people engaged in transformative inner healing and practice through spiritual perspectives and tools from Shamanism, Western Magical traditions, Jung and classical meditation. I have a beautiful local and global community of clients and students, and now, thanks to the pandemic, I have a growing and well-received online offering too. I moved into the flow of my purpose, and like all healthy rivers, what started as a small trickle has transformed into an ocean. I absolutely love what I do.

Being spirited is not necessarily about identifying with a particular framework, and there can be a danger in this. When we associate our processes and identities with particular frameworks, we run the risk of attachment to the frameworks rather than what they offer us. In my observation, within the spiritual community, this can be a subtle trick of the ego too. Declarations like 'I am a shaman', 'I am a healer', or 'I am a seer' are often used to set the practitioner apart; to claim some unique power and by inference to somehow be further awakened or have a proprietary connection with spirit. When our spiritual senses are uploaded, perhaps the truest declaration of the spiritual self is 'I am human', and inherent in that is acknowledgement that you have connected with the spiritual nature of life through the unique and dazzling design of your human system. I try to avoid selecting any one of the frameworks I have encountered or use in my spiritual practice as a statement of my truth (which can make articulating an offering tricky), because I have found that as I move more deeply into my life process, spirit is constantly introducing me to beautiful new frameworks that achieve specific things.

# CHAPTER 24

# Navigating the 'Spiritual Industry'

There are some amazing and light-filled modern spiritual guides doing their best work right now in the world. There are also works and teachings that were before their time that are finally hitting a more receptive and evolved mark, and very ancient practices that are now being received beyond the boundaries of their traditions. There's enough of a choice for spirit to speak to millions of hearts, and I believe this is what is happening in the world today. The diversity of message and medium is important, as we are all on our own trajectory and have our own filters.

The psychic abilities that naturally kick in when we start to live in spirit can become the end game for some. The flush of the new power and the admiration it attracts is a well-documented and known trap for the ego. Many traditions call it a test, and for the authentic spirit-seeker, discernment is required if you are seeking guidance.

Trends also seem to ripple through the spiritual industry. For example, currently in Singapore, everyone seems to be a channel. I can't tell you how many people I meet who are either seeking activation for channelling or setting themselves up to sell channelled messages for people. Thoth seems to be the ascended master of choice, although he's competing for airspace with quite a number of galactic councils, stargate keepers, twelfth-dimensional beings from Sirius, dragons, Metatron, the archangel Michael, and what seems to be a cast of thousands of goddesses and gods and mythical beasts from across the aeons who are bursting through the human minds of the self-appointed channels. They usually start with 'Greetings, my beloveds' or 'Dear ones, we come to you in peace.' I do wonder why an ascended master who is channelling his or her consciousness through a human mind to help ascend humankind beyond sure destruction wouldn't choose more engaging language. And why do all these interdimensional beings from vastly different traditions all speak in this same quite awkward and condescending way? It's just a bit off. It feels engineered.

I have been to spiritual meetings with the expectation of group meditation and realised I was actually in the middle of what I call a 'cosmic channel-off.' 'I will see your Thoth and raise you Isis, Kali, Quan Yin, Babaji ... oh, and Jesus just showed up too!' Pleeaaasseee!

Another one to watch for is anyone who claims to have channelled an exclusive process for enlightenment. There are plenty of these going around too. And for a tiny 'energy exchange' of thousands of dollars, you can clear past lives and change your DNA into quartz. Walk away! This type of cosmic BS makes me mad because when the disappointment sets in, along with the realisation that the victim may have fallen for a ruse, he or she may turn away and dismiss his or her true spiritual nature, never to return. I have a lot of people come to my classes having been disillusioned by some self-appointed 'master' or 'high priestess' or some other fancily-titled person they have given their power to and become reliant upon and then just been dropped cold, usually when their 'master' has sensed that his or her understudy is starting to suspect something isn't right. This type of behaviour is also very damaging for the physiologically vulnerable.

It's also very 'in' to be a reincarnated superpower currently. It is often plonked into an introduction, much like how you might introduce yourself at a corporate party. Instead of 'Hi, lovely to meet you. I head up the marketing team', it can sound like 'Hi, nice to reconnect with you after lifetimes. I am originally Paeladian and can see that you have negative imprints in your DNA.' Oh yes, it happens. I have met people who have bought and believed the idea that they have lived a human life from the Greek, Roman, or

Egyptian pantheon—lots of women who have lived as Isis, for example. Or they have been a ruler of the ancient world (lots of Cleopatras), a high initiate of some secret all-knowing cult, or an Atlantean. I have met others who believe they are Elohim, aliens who are the original seeders of human consciousness.

Now these many cases of reincarnating cosmic superstars of the supernatural world may well be what's happening. Neither I nor they will ever really know in measurable logical terms. But when it is touted as a reason for superiority or, worse, a licence to manipulate others, then I'm not so open to the possibilities. It has to be asked, How does knowing this affect the person you are today and the life you are living now? The way I see it is that we are the culmination of the entire journey of the soul—right here and right now. The experiences that have carried and that influence my transformation today are relevant; the titles and airs and graces are not. And for me, at least, it is private knowledge. I love the wisdom about archetypes, and the experiences described above show our universal attraction to archetypal energies and traits within us. It just doesn't ring true that the lesser lives lived that are the reason we might still be circling around the material plane are never claimed. I'm sure that for every life lived as a queen, many more have been lived as thieves. For every life lived as a persecuted witch, many more have been lived as the ones who lit the pyre.

There's an interesting rehashing of terminology and

ideas across the Internet too. You can see the same articles and authors being rehashed, represented, and regurgitated; and then somehow, after it has echoed around several times through forums and groups, it becomes truth, and a lot of it is totally indecipherable or so motherhood that it's useless. If the language is exclusive, makes you feel stupid, or is not translatable into modern life, don't listen to it.

Following are some of my top tips for navigating the spiritual industry (and it's a huge industry):

- Nothing is new under the sun. Nothing. If you are being promised an exclusive patented method to enlightenment that is accessible through only one source and can only be drip-fed to you for higher and higher fees, look closely, question everything, and follow your heart.
- Do the 'I/me' count. When you hear someone speak about spirit, notice how many times he or she refers to himself or herself, that subtle self-stroking of ego. If he or she presents himself or herself as being the source of his or her power and abilities, go carefully.
- Trust only a spiritual guide who has earned that title through personal mastery, preferably in a known system. Check out his or her followers and students. You'll get an immediate gauge. Is the guide empowered and free, or is he or she being manipulated? I once went to a talk with a 'master' that did an online

metaphysical course that allowed him to choose his title. He chose 'master.' His students looked as if they were in a group trance when they gathered. He didn't seem too shiny to me, and he was decidedly sleazy. I obeyed my heart and walked.

- Be very alert to predictions of accidents, death, injury, bad luck, or illness if you don't engage the provider. Believe me; it happens. I once met a shamanic teacher who emailed me urgently t saying she had a warning dream that I was going to be hit by a car and I needed her protection—for a fee, of course. I followed my heart and walked. I am alive and well.

- Be very wary of anyone who attributes all his or her words and behaviours to his or her 'guides.' This is a real red light. I once met a woman who sent me an unsolicited email for some past-life regression treatment that only she could offer for a huge 'energy exchange' (a term I can't stand). When I sent it back saying no thanks and that I felt neither need nor compulsion for it, she replied saying that her guides were playing with us and they had sent the email. BS!

- Be aware of unsolicited divinations and readings. You are in control and should always decide what support you need. I received an urgent message once from a woman in Australia who had seen my Facebook profile picture and was very concerned about my blocked upper chakras. Ironically, this was during a time when I was studying the most sublime heart-expanding practices, and I felt the best I had ever felt. I politely replied, thanked her for her concern, pointed out that the profile picture was actually two years old, and told her 'No thank you.' She was very persistent, and if I were a more vulnerable person, I might have listened to her. I explained that I was not in need of, or want of, her help. She then changed the direction and thought she may have been picking up on someone close to me, maybe a family member. Again I politely said 'No thanks' and wished her well. She then came back with 'Well, I can't help what I see or for whom I see it ... all I know is that you need help', to which I replied, 'Well, if you don't know what you're seeing or whom you're seeing it for, then you haven't quite mastered your art, have you? Leave me alone!'

- Exorbitant 'energy exchanges' can show that your provider is conflicted materially. In my experience, those who are truly connected to spirit are not focused on material gain. They're looked after materially when they are in true service, and most give a lot of what they earn to the needy. This is not to say that spiritual teachers should give their services for free either. This life, if chosen, is an investment of time, intention, studies, and practice. It should be charged for, but realistically.

- Just because someone exhibits some psychic ability or has dedicated his or her life to spiritual service does not mean he or she is a good person or aligned with spirit. We have seen this in all too stark detail with the systematic child abuse in the Church (amongst other institutions). I have seen this with spiritual practitioners—especially those offering tantric services. If it feels hinky, despite how amazing it might seem or what promises are made, just walk. Walking away doesn't mean you are spiritually blind or 'unable to accept higher truth'—yes, that one has been used on me too! It means you are discerning; you are listening to your heart, and you hold the power of free will and choice.

I acknowledge that what may ring true to me may not for others, and vice versa. It also has to be said that channelling and other psychic skills and the possibilities for DNA alteration, as evidenced in the fascinating field of neurobiology and epigenetics, are all possible; they happen, and they are described in this book. They are also not privy just to an elite 'spiritually advanced' few. I see this false spirituality, and its obvious trends described above as a part of the entranced material world. It's just disguised in spiritual terminology. These are the traits of addiction—addiction to separateness, competitive edge, and the needs of ego. My sense is that the people swept into these false beliefs (many of them well meaning) have gone there in their heads because they are based in a belief system of lack and low self-worth. They haven't yet learnt how to listen to their hearts.

So then—how do you know when it's the real deal? When should you prick up your ears, buy that book, enrol in that course, or pursue that friendship? This is not exclusive, but I have listed some of the main ways it flashes into one's awareness here:

- The arrival of content, a teacher, or a lesson sometimes comes when you aren't reaching for it, often when you least expect it. You may have called for it in your heart, but its arrival will catch your attention. Spirit uses the element of surprise a lot.
- When you draw close to it, you feel a true sense of expectation, gentle excitement, delight, and joy in your heart. These feelings are spontaneous, and they can start as a little tinkle or a flutter and then grow the more you consider the idea, thing, or person.
- You may also feel it in your body, as the heart's truth is communicated in several different ways into every part of your body; truth is visceral.
- Sometimes the seed content is laid in your life but its season comes later. Often I have been given a book or item that has sat in my bedside drawer for weeks or

even months, and then—without much thought, but with a strong heart compulsion—I will pick it up one day and it will be perfect for the current themes and perspectives I am focusing on at that time. Spirit plays in and out of time.

If there is a practitioner you are drawn to, take a look at his or her other students and clients and his or her life generally, and don't rely solely on written testimonials. Testimonials are sometimes engineered by the unscrupulous, and sometimes the vulnerable are forced to write them as a sign of loyalty. This sounds medieval, I know, but I have experienced attempted cajoling for testimonials. I walked. If a spiritual teacher has a history of broken relationships, chaos, conflict, and persistent illness, I usually take this as a sign that there is inner chaos and conflict. As within, so without.

Look at the flow of the practitioner's service and offering. When a spiritual practitioner is aligned with spirit and in flow, his or her offering and reputation grows swiftly. He or she is loved, and there seems to be a lack of chaos, obstacles, and setbacks. This is true of all of us when walking in spirit.

There's a joy and vitality about spirited people. Sure, they have their bad days, but they don't see them as bad days, because their hearts are reading a bigger pattern. There is a glow, a light, and a lightness about them. You know that you can trust them and that they will honour you, and very often they feel quite familiar, but you may not be able to explain why logically.

You have everything you need within you, within your design. You are spirit manifesting through a human nervous system and form. If you feel you need some guidance or a new perspective as you move along, look around, keep searching, and don't rush things. Ask spirit to send you the right teacher and content for this time. In my observation, the soul-calls that are made for spiritual truth and enablement are answered swiftly and delightfully, and they make your heart sing. When you make it a priority to build awareness of your spirited self, your intuition is undeniable. Go for it!

CHAPTER 25

# Be Spirited!

The words in this book are only the beginning of what could be the most incredible journey of your life: a move into spirited living. If you are inspired by the perspectives and ideas presented here, then use that momentum to start an inner practice, or revive the one that modern life almost snuffed out. We are so fortunate to live in this age of technology where we can access so much content and guidance to do this, and it is important that you find the content, sound, and resonance that feels right for you.

To this end, I have listed links to most practices mentioned in *Spirited* in the appendices. The gold is in putting that inspired feeling into action to unleash your own spiritual expression. Start to make some tiny changes in your life. For a few minutes a day after you wake up, bring intention into your day-to-day actions, lean into your other senses for guidance, and breathe.

Everything mentioned in this book is inherent in your dazzling human design. This essentially is a book to help you remember who and what you really are, to help you live in collusion with life and your system rather than in conflict with them, to help you operate creatively and intuitively in a state of flow, and to help you heal and be whole. You are designed to be spirited in this game called life.

Be spirited!

Love,

Dani

# Appendix A

## Meditations

The following meditations are referenced in the book. You can access them for free at www.insighttimer.com/ daniellevandevelde. Download the app for free and you can stream from there. Or find them on Spotify under 'Danielle Van de Velde.'

### Sensory Meditations to Develop Intuition:

- trataka
- wild sounds
- AUM mantra
- om mani padme hum mantra

### Body Awareness Meditations

- yoga nidra
- progressive muscle release

## Meditations for Mastering the Breath

- mindful breathing
- ujjayi breath
- nadi shodhana
- counting breath

## Heart-Centred Meditations

- brahmavihara cultivation
- gratitude cultivation
- ksepana mudra
- tonglen

If you are interested in a deeper understanding and instruction on these and other meditation practices, go to www.daniellevandevelde.com/meditation

If you're interested in a deeper understanding and story share on Shamanism, the Energy Arts and many more upcoming spirited topics, go to my podcast The Modern Crone.

Links to all major podcast platforms can be found at: www.daniellevandevelde.com/listen

# Appendix B

**Energetic Correspondences**

**Muladhara**

| Traditional Symbology | Colour | Bija Mantra | Yantra | Element | Sense & Organ of Action | Tonal Note | Trigger Point | Asana | Bandha & Mudra |
|---|---|---|---|---|---|---|---|---|---|
| Muladhara is symbolised by a four-petalled lotus that is deep red in colour. At the centre of the square is a lingam called the 'swayambhu linga', which represents consciousness. A red serpent representing kundalini shakti is coiled three and a half times around the linga. In some depictions, an elephant with seven trunks, symbolising the solidarity and stability of the earth, also supports the yellow square.<br><br>• Lotus flower—a four-petalled lotus | Deep red | Lam—pronounced 'Lum' | In the middle of the lotus is a yellow square (although in this illustration there is only the outline of the yellow square). The yellow square is the yantra of the earth element. | Earth | Smell and the anus | C | No trigger point | Padahastasana (hand-to-foot pose)<br><br>Tadasana (palm tree pose)<br><br>Bhadrasana (gracious pose)<br><br>Hanumanasana (Hanuman's pose)<br><br>Brahmacharyasana (celibate's pose)<br><br>Moolabandhasana (perineal contraction pose)<br><br>Gorakshasana (Yogi Gorakhnath's pose) | Moola bandha (perineum contraction)<br><br>Ashwini mudra (horse gesture—contraction of the anal sphincter)<br><br>Nasikagra drishti (nose-tip gazing) |

| Herbs | Foods | Gland | Mineral | Herbs for Incense | Metal | Planets |
|-------|-------|-------|---------|-------------------|-------|---------|
| Dandelion root tea | Root vegetables: potatoes, beets, parsnips, radishes, red onion, garlic, and turnips.<br><br>Red fruits, veggies, and spices: apples, tomatoes, red peppers, cherries, watermelon, pomegranates, red beans, hot paprika, cayenne pepper, cranberries, pink grapefruit, kidney beans, red raspberries | Adrenals | Lodestone, ruby, garnet, bloodstone | Cedar | Lead | Saturn, Earth |

**Swathisthana**

| Traditional Symbology | Colour | Bija Mantra | Yantra | Element | Sense & Organ of Action | Tonal Note | Trigger Point | Asana | Bandha & Mudra |
|---|---|---|---|---|---|---|---|---|---|
| Swathisthana is traditionally depicted as an orange-red lotus with six petals. The element of Swathisthana is water, and in this illustration it is represented by an image of the ocean. The white crescent moon in the centre of the lotus is also related to water. The outward-turned petals represent the conscious dimension of existence. On the inside the image, the ocean at night represents the formless dimension and the store of formless karma. Traditionally there is also a white crocodile symbolising the subterranean movement of the karmas, and it is the vehicle which carries the phantom of the unconscious life.

Lotus flower—a six-petalled lotus | Orange | Vam— pronounced 'Vum' | Two circles which make the shape of a crescent moon | Water | Taste and the sexual organs, kidneys, and urinary system | D | The pubic bone | Shakti bandha series (a series of poses to remove energy blockages in the body, particularly the pelvis)

Bhujangasana (cobra pose)

Shashankasana (child pose)

Dhanurasana (bow pose)
Shashank-bhujangasana (striking cobra pose)

Pascimottanasana (back stretch pose) | Vajroli/ Sahajoli |

| Herbs | Foods | Gland | Mineral | Herbs for Incense | Metal | Planets |
|---|---|---|---|---|---|---|
| Calendula, gardenia, coriander, fennel, licorice, cinnamon, vanilla, carob, sweet paprika, sesame seeds, caraway seeds | Cantaloupe, oranges, mangoes, peaches, pumpkin, butternut squash, almonds, yams, honey, cinnamon, ginger, carrots, apricots, nectarines, tangerines | Ovaries, testicles | Carnelian, moonstone, coral | Orris root, gardenia, damiana | Tin | Moon |

Maniupura

| Traditional Symbology | Colour | Bija Mantra | Yantra | Element | Sense & Organ of Action | Tonal Note | Trigger Point | Asana | Bandha & Mudra |
|---|---|---|---|---|---|---|---|---|---|
| Manipura is symbolised by a ten-petalled bright yellow lotus. In the centre of the lotus is a blazing sun representing the heat and energy of Manipura. Around the sun is an inverted red triangle, and written in the apex is the mantra ram. In some depictions, a ram is also pictured.

**Lotus flower**—a ten-petalled lotus | Bright yellow | Ram— pronounced 'rum' (with slightly rolled r) | Inverted red triangle | Fire | Sight & the feet | E | The navel centre | Pawanmuktasana Series 2 and 3 (a series of postures which work specifically with the abdominal/ digestive region)

Mayurasana (peacock pose)

Chakrasana (wheel pose)

Poorna dhanurasana (full bow pose)

Ashtanga namaskara (eight-point pose)

Setu asana (bridge pose) | Uddiyana bandha (abdominal contraction)

Tadagi mudra (barrelled abdomen technique) |

| Herbs | Foods | Gland | Mineral | Herbs for Incense | Metal | Planets |
|---|---|---|---|---|---|---|
| To balance the energy flow, one can use lavender, bergamot or rosemary oil. Marshmallow also relaxes the third chakra and softens our efforts to control life. Other useful herbs and spices are aniseed, celery, cinnamon, lily of the valley, ginger, mints (peppermint, spearmint), melissa, turmeric, cumin, and fennel. | Maize, butternut squash, lemon, sunflower seeds, chamomile, chickpeas, mustard, pears, cumin, turmeric, pineapple, bananas | Pineal | Amber, topaz, yellow citrine, rutilated quartz | Dragon's blood, sandalwood, saffron, musk, cinnamon, ginger | Iron | Mars and the sun |

**Anahata**

| Traditional Symbology | Colour | Bija Mantra | Yantra | Element | Sense & Organ of Action | Tonal Note | Trigger Point | Asana | Bandha & Mudra |
|---|---|---|---|---|---|---|---|---|---|
| A twelve-petalled blue lotus symbolises the Anahata chakra. In the centre of the lotus are two interlacing triangles which form a hexagon; this is the yantra of the air element. At the centre of the diagram is a candle flame, which symbolises the consciousness and the individual soul. Traditionally there is often an image of a black antelope, representing alertness. At the bottom is written the mantra yam.<br><br>**Lotus flower**—a twelve-petalled lotus | Traditionally green (however, in some texts blue) | Lam (pronounced 'lum') | Hexagon | Air | Touch or feeling; hands; the giving and taking | F | The level of the heart behind the sternum | Supta vajrasana (sleeping thunderbolt pose)<br><br>Matsyasana (fish pose)<br><br>Ushtrasana (camel pose)<br><br>Kandharasana (shoulder or bridge pose)<br><br>Gomukhasana (cow face pose) | Hridaya mudra (heart hand mudra) |

| Herbs | Foods | Gland | Mineral | Herbs for Incense | Metal | Planets |
|---|---|---|---|---|---|---|
| Many issues of love, grief, hatred, anger, jealousy, and fears of betrayal and loneliness, as well as the ability to heal others and ourselves, are centred in the fourth chakra. A tea or tincture of hawthorne berries increases trust in the process of life and encourages you to feel safe following your heart. It also helps to strengthen the heart and blood vessels. You can also use Cayenne, jasmine, lavender, marjoram, rose, basil, sage, thyme, cilantro, and parsley for a healthy heart. | Broccoli, kale, spinach, swiss chard, dandelion, greens, parsley, peas, cilantro, asparagus, artichokes, courgettes, cabbage, celery, limes, green tea, basil, sage, thyme, Brussels sprouts | Thymus | Emerald, tourmaline, jade, rose quartz | Lavender, jasmine, orris root, yarrow, marjoram, meadowsweet | Copper | Venus |

**Vishhuddhi**

| Traditional Symbology | Colour | Bija Mantra | Yantra | Element | Sense & Organ of Action | Tonal Note | Trigger Point | Asana | Bandha & Mudra |
|---|---|---|---|---|---|---|---|---|---|
| The symbol for the Vishhuddhi chakra is a purple lotus with sixteen petals representing the number of nadis, or energy channels, associated with this chakra. Traditionally on each petal, one of the sixteen Sanskrit vowels is inscribed in red.<br><br>In the centre of the lotus is a white circle representing the element of ether, or akasha, space. Many traditional diagrams also portray a snow-white elephant as a vehicle of consciousness. The ethereal region of the Vishhuddhi chakra is the gateway to liberation for one whose senses are pure and controlled.<br><br>**Lotus flower**—a sixteen-petalled lotus | Traditionally sky blue (however, in some texts, purple) | Ham (pronounced 'Hum') | Circle | Ether (in some texts, sound) | Hearing and vocal chords | G | The front of the neck, at the throat pit or thyroid gland | Parvatasana (mountain pose)<br><br>Matsyasana (fish pose)<br><br>Supta vajrasana (sleeping thunderbolt)<br><br>Sarvangasana (shoulder stand)<br><br>Yipareeta karani asana (inverted pose),<br><br>Balasana (plough pose) | Ujjayi breath (ocean Bbeath)<br><br>Jalandhara bandha (chin lock)<br><br>Pasinee mudra (folded psychic attitude)<br><br>Vipareet karani mudra (inverted psychic attitude) |

| Herbs | Foods | Gland | Mineral | Herbs for Incense | Metal | Planets |
|-------|-------|-------|---------|-------------------|-------|---------|
| Red clover blossoms assist in allowing a free flow of communication and self-expression. A cup of red clover tea can unlock the emotions and thoughts that are waiting to be spoken. Lemon balm is capable of healing several ailments, including thyroid dysfunction. Eucalyptus oil is a beneficial oil for decongestion: simply rubbing a few drops of oil on the throat will help. Other herbs and spices that can help with the throat chakra are coltsfoot, peppermint, sage, salt, and lemongrass. | Liquids in general (e.g., water, juices, broths, teas), sea vegetables (e.g., seaweed, kelp, kombu, and dulse), fruits | Thyroid, parathyroid | Turquoise, aquamarine, celestite | Frankincense, benzoin, mace | Mercury | Mercury |

**Ajna**

| Traditional Symbology | Colour | Bija Mantra | Yantra | Element | Sense & Organ of Action | Tonal Note | Trigger Point | Asana | Bandha & Mudra |
|---|---|---|---|---|---|---|---|---|---|
| The Ajna chakra is symbolised by a two-petalled lotus in a silvery-white moonlike colour. Traditionally on the left petal is Ham and on the right petal is Ksham. Ham and Ksham are the bija mantras for Shiva (consciousness) and Shakti (creativity). However, in this visual there is an image of the moon on the left petal, representing the Ida nadi, and the sun on the right, representing the Pingala nadi. Within the lotus is a circle symbolising the void. Within that circle is an inverted triangle, which represents Shakti. Within the triangle is a black shivalingam representing Shiva. Over the shivalingam is the symbol of om. Lotus flower—a two-petalled lotus | Silvery white, also depicted as indigo blue | Aum | A circle, symbolic of the void | Light | The mind, specifically the sixth sense of intuition | A | The eyebrow centre, known as bhrumadhya | All balancing poses Ananda madirasana (intoxicating bliss pose) Padadhirasana (breath balancing pose) Veerasana (the philosopher's pose) | Shambhavi mudra (eyebrow centre gazing) Shanmukhi mudra (closing the seven gates) |

| Herbs | Foods | Gland | Mineral | Herbs for Incense | Metal | Planets |
|---|---|---|---|---|---|---|
| Mint, jasmine, and eyebright are herbs used to open the sixth chakra. Eyebright helps to see both the light and dark sides as part of the whole, and is also used to cure eye problems. Mint has been found useful in curing depression, migraines, and memory loss. It also increases connectedness between mind and body. These are the herbs and spices that can energise and heal any imbalances in the third eye chakra: juniper, mugwort, poppy, rosemary, lavender, and poppy seed. | Blueberries, purple grapes, plums, purple cabbage, lavender, grape juice, wine, purple onions, aubergines | Pineal | Lapis lazuli, quartz, star sapphire | Mugwort, star aniseed, acacia, saffron | silver | Jupiter, Neptune |

**Sahasrara**

| Traditional Symbology | Colour | Bija Mantra | Yantra | Element | Sense & Organ of Action | Tonal Note | Trigger Point | Asana | Bandha & Mudra |
|---|---|---|---|---|---|---|---|---|---|
| Within Sahasara is the clear full moon. Inside it is a triangle of light, and inside the triangle is the Great Void—pure potentiality; all possibilities are represented here by the Sanskrit word 'om.' Lotus flower—a thousand-petalled lotus | Violet to white | None (However, through connection with Sahasara in deep meditation one can access the music of the spheres and one's own soul sound.) | Triangle | Thought | Cerebral cortex and central nervous system | B | The crown of the head | Meditation | Meditation |

| Herbs | Foods | Gland | Mineral | Herbs for Incense | Metal | Planets |
|---|---|---|---|---|---|---|
| Lavender flowers and lotus assist in opening your seventh chakra. Lavender brings you into alignment with divine wisdom on a daily basis and is a popular herb for enhancing meditation. While lotus leaves and stems are widely used in Japanese and Chinese cuisine, and each part has its own set of benefits, lavender is your best bet because it works well on all the chakras. | None—fasting | Pituitary | Amethyst, diamond | Lotus, gota kola | Gold | Uranus |